External Auditing
Tutorial

John Taylor
Jo Osborne

© John Taylor, Jo Osborne, 2016.

All rights reserved. No part of this publication may be reproduced, stored in a retrieval system, or transmitted in any form or by any means, electronic, mechanical, photo-copying, recording or otherwise, without the prior consent of the copyright owners, or in accordance with the provisions of the Copyright, Designs and Patents Act 1988, or under the terms of any licence permitting limited copying issued by the Copyright Licensing Agency, Saffron House, 6-10 Kirby Street, London EC1N 8TS.

Published by Osborne Books Limited
Tel 01905 748071
Email books@osbornebooks.co.uk
Website www.osbornebooks.co.uk

Design by Laura Ingham

Printed by CPI Group (UK) Limited, Croydon, CR0 4YY, on environmentally friendly, acid-free paper from managed forests.

British Library Cataloguing in Publication Data
A catalogue record for this book is available from the British Library

ISBN 978 1909173 965

Contents

Also available from Osborne Books...

Workbooks
Practice questions and assessments
with answers

Student Zone
Login to access your free ebooks and
interactive revision crosswords

Download **Osborne Books App** free from the App Store or Google Play Store
to view your ebooks online or offline on your mobile or tablet.

www.osbornebooks.co.uk

Introduction

Qualifications covered

This book has been written specifically to cover the Unit 'External Auditing' which is a mandatory Unit for the following qualifications:

AAT Professional Diploma in Accounting – Level 4

AAT Professional Diploma in Accounting at SCQF – Level 8

The book contains a clear text with worked examples and case studies, chapter summaries and key terms to help with revision. Each chapter concludes with a wide range of activities, many in the style of AAT computer based assessments.

Osborne Study and Revision Materials

The materials featured on the previous page are tailored to the needs of students studying this unit and revising for the assessment. They include:

- **Workbooks:** paperback books with practice activities and exams
- **Student Zone:** access to Osborne Books online resources
- **Osborne Books App:** Osborne Books ebooks for mobiles and tablets

Visit www.osbornebooks.co.uk for details of study and revision resources and access to online material.

1 Introduction to auditing

this chapter covers...

The aim of this chapter is to give you an introduction to auditing. We will cover the detailed aspects of auditing later, but in this introductory chapter we explain what an audit is, why auditors are needed, who they report to, and the difference between what people think they do and what they actually do.

This chapter covers:

- *what an audit is*
- *why we need audits*
- *who needs to be audited*
- *who can do an audit*
- *appointment of auditors*
- *the auditor's report*
- *the expectation gap – what people think auditors do and what they actually do*

AUDITING IN CONTEXT

It is quite likely that, if you work in an accounts environment, you will have come into contact with auditors. You may even be involved in audit work if you work for a firm of Chartered or Chartered Certified accountants.

Auditors seem to arrive once or twice a year, ask a lot of questions, look at accounting records and go away again. What are they doing, what purpose does it serve and why is it important?

The role of the auditor is often misunderstood. Quite often people who come into contact with auditors, or even staff actually involved in auditing, only see part of the process. They are quizzed by auditors or they carry out audit tests but rarely see the whole process through from beginning to end.

This book explains the whole audit process from start to finish so that you will better understand why auditors are there, the job they have to do and the reasons why they have to ask so many questions.

WHAT IS AN AUDIT?

First we need a description of what an audit is.

In **International Standard on Auditing (ISA) 200 'Overall objectives of the independent auditor and the conduct of an audit in accordance with international standards on auditing',** the overall audit objectives for the auditors are to express an opinion as to:

- whether the financial statements present a **true and fair** view of the financial position of the company, and
- whether or not they comply with International Accounting Standards and the disclosure requirements of the Companies Act 2006

This means that the financial statements of a company are reviewed by an independent, qualified accountant who signs a report to say that they properly reflect the financial position of the company and have been properly prepared.

The users of financial statements will, primarily, be the shareholders of the company but could also include lenders or other investors.

The purpose of an audit is to give the users of financial statements confidence that they do not contain serious errors or misstatements. The audit process is designed to reassure users of a set of financial statements that the content has been examined by an independent third party. The auditors will examine the financial statements objectively and come to a conclusion as to their truth and fairness.

The audit process involves testing designed to gather all the evidence the auditors need to support their opinion on the financial statements.

As we will see in Chapter 2 the conduct of the audit is governed by legislation, mainly the Companies Act 2006, and by a set of guidelines and principles called International Standards on Auditing (ISAs). These aim to ensure that all audits are carried out with the same thoroughness and to a common standard.

responsibilities of management

One important thing to understand is that preparation of the financial statements is the responsibility of the management. The auditors carry out their audit on the understanding that the management:

- has prepared the financial statements in accordance with the requirements of **Generally Accepted Accounting Practice** ('GAAP')

- acknowledges their responsibility for maintaining an effective system of **internal control** within the organisation (internal control is covered in Chapter 4)

- will give the auditors access to all the information and explanations they need to carry out their audit

reasonable assurance

ISA 200 requires the auditor to gather sufficient, reliable evidence to give them **reasonable assurance** that the financial statements are true and fair, in other words that they do not contain any significant (material) errors or misstatements.

The concept of **'reasonable assurance'** is that the auditors gather enough evidence to be able to conclude that there are no material misstatements in the financial statements as a whole. We look at this in more detail in Chapter 7.

As you will know from your accounting studies, the preparation of a set of accounts includes accounting estimates and judgements about the value of certain items, such as trade receivables or inventories. Because of this it is impossible for the auditors to give complete assurance that the financial statements do not contain any **material**, or significant, errors or misstatements. We will look at the concept of materiality in Chapter 3, but for now the word 'significant' will do as a substitute.

audit approach

Later in the book we will look in detail at how auditors gather audit evidence and come to their conclusions. Briefly, the auditor must:

- assess the risks of a significant error or misstatement going undetected in the financial statements that the directors have prepared. This includes the risk of fraud, as well as the risk of errors. It requires the auditors, among other things, to assess the strength of the internal controls which act as the checks and balances in the accounting system

- gather sufficient reliable evidence to support their audit opinion on the financial statements

- form an opinion on the financial statements and report to the shareholders on the truth and fairness of the accounts. They may also report to management on weaknesses in accounting controls or other matters they have encountered during the course of their audit

Throughout this process the auditors will need to exercise their professional judgement in deciding whether or not their evidence is sufficient, reliable and relevant and also whether or not any errors they have uncovered are significant to the accuracy of the financial statements.

professional scepticism

ISA 200 states that throughout the audit process the auditors should adopt an attitude of **'professional scepticism'**. This means that the auditors should keep an open-minded attitude that presumes that in preparing the financial statements the management are neither totally honest nor totally dishonest. They should not accept anything at face value but should always attempt to find additional evidence which supports what they have been told by the management.

WHY DO WE NEED AUDITS?

Why do most companies have to be audited when, for example, a business, which is run as a partnership, does not?

Consider the situation of a company and the way in which it operates.

You will be aware from your studies that a company is a legal entity, separate from its owners and managers. Once this principle was established in law it became necessary for the interests of the owners of the business to be safeguarded. In all but the smallest businesses, the shareholders were simply investors who were not normally involved in the day-to-day running of the business.

Consequently, they needed reassurance that the professional managers (the directors) whom they employed to run the business had been doing so properly. Who better to give the shareholders that reassurance than professionally qualified accountants who were independent of the business and who had their own code of ethics and professional competence? The shareholders employed accountants to provide them with a report on the accuracy of the financial statements, and so the auditing profession came into being.

It is important for you to understand the distinction between shareholders (sometimes referred to as '**members**') who own a company and directors who manage the business on behalf of the shareholders.

In small companies these may be the same individuals, but in larger companies shareholders and directors are more likely to be completely different people. Study the diagram below.

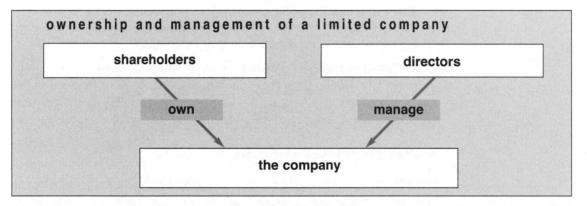

In Chapter 2 we will examine in detail the legal framework within which auditors and directors must operate. This is based on the **Companies Act 2006.** It is this Act that forms the basis of the legal relationship between the auditors, the shareholders, the directors and the company itself.

WHO NEEDS TO BE AUDITED?

All limited companies, except small companies, are required by the Companies Act 2006 to have an audit. In this respect the law makes no distinction between a private family run limited company and a large company such as Tesco plc. Both are equally required by law to have their financial statements audited and auditors must make a report to the owners of the business.

Sole traders and partnerships do not require an audit and small companies satisfying certain criteria are also exempt.

how is a small company defined?

The official definitions, which you need to remember, are:

■ **small companies** – private limited companies, which are not part of a larger group, and are not banking or insurance companies. To qualify for an audit exemption the company must meet at least two of the following three criteria:

- turnover must be £10.2m or less
- Statement of Financial Position total must be £5.1m or less
- average number of employees must be 50 or fewer

■ **small charities that are companies** – these are charities which are companies with a gross annual income of £1,000,000 or less unless its statement of financial position total exceeds £3.26m and its income exceeds £250,000 per annum

■ **dormant companies** (ie companies which have not carried out any transactions in the financial period)

WHO CAN DO AN AUDIT?

Because of the role they play in the financial community, auditors should have specific qualities. They must be technically proficient accountants with a strong code of ethics. They must also be independent of both the company they are auditing and the shareholders they are reporting to.

There are, therefore, some strict rules concerning who is, or is not, eligible to be an auditor.

One point it is important to make clear is that the person who signs the auditor's report must be qualified to do so.

When we refer to an 'auditor' therefore, we are referring to a person who is qualified to sign an audit report. The staff who work for the auditor, despite the fact they will carry out most of the detailed checking work, may not have the necessary qualification, although, of course, they may be studying for it.

eligibility to be an auditor

The Companies Act states that auditors must be a member of a **Recognised Supervisory Body (RSB)**.

recognised supervisory bodies (RSBs)

RSBs are organisations which have the responsibility of overseeing the regulation of the auditing profession in the UK and the maintenance of professional standards.

Their rules say that persons eligible for appointment must either hold an appropriate qualification or be firms controlled by suitably qualified individuals.

These are the Recognised Supervisory Bodies:

■ Institute of Chartered Accountants in England & Wales (ICAEW)
■ Institute of Chartered Accountants of Scotland (ICAS)

■ Chartered Accountants Ireland (CAI)

■ Association of Chartered Certified Accountants (ACCA)

■ Association of Authorised Public Accountants (AAPA)

The AAT is not an RSB, so members of the AAT cannot act as auditors unless they are also a member of one of these qualifying bodies. However, AAT members often form part of an audit team.

An individual who holds a similar overseas qualification may be eligible to practice as an auditor in the UK but his/her status would have to be confirmed prior to them commencing work.

The RSB's role is to monitor and inspect their members on a regular basis to ensure that professional standards are being maintained.

who may and may not be an auditor

The Companies Act 2006 (Section 1214) states that a person may **not** be an auditor if he/she is:

■ an officer or employee of the company being audited

■ any person in business partnership with an officer or employee of the company being audited

This is clearly to ensure that the auditor remains independent. It also implies that the following **may** be appointed as an auditor of a company:

■ a shareholder of the client company

■ a payable or receivable of the client company

The Recognised Supervisory Bodies have stricter policies on independence than the law. In practice, an individual who is, for example, the wife of a director of a business, will not be able to accept the appointment as auditor to that business, even though the law does not specifically prohibit it.

APPOINTMENT OF AUDITORS

When a company first requires an audit the directors appoint the auditors. Their appointment lasts until the end of the first Annual General Meeting (AGM) of the company. If the shareholders wish to they can re-elect the auditors to serve for another year until the end of the next AGM, and again at the AGM of each subsequent year, if they are happy with the auditors.

If the shareholders do not re-elect the auditors, another firm can be appointed to act as auditors in their place.

Before accepting an appointment an auditor should carry out a certain amount of preliminary investigative work to ensure that:

■ there are no legal or ethical issues which might prevent them from being appointed

■ they have sufficient resources to carry out the audit assignment; this will include practical issues such as staff availability as well as issues such as technical competence if the client operates in a highly specialised industry

■ there are no problems with any outgoing auditors

■ the client is suitable to be an audit client particularly in relation to the competence and integrity of its management and the nature of its operations

We will now use a Case Study to show how the relationship between the auditors and shareholders works.

Case Study

TASHA: THE ROLE OF THE AUDITOR

situation

Tasha has shares in a company that operates a small chain of restaurants and shops in the South of England.

Henry, who is Tasha's brother, and his assistant Hugo, are the directors and manage the business on a daily basis. Tasha is not a director as she initially only invested in the company to help her brother get started.

The company is growing quickly because Henry has worked hard to expand the business.

Tasha is concerned that, as the business grows, she will lose touch with it and that Henry and Hugo could, together, do what they want without telling her.

She is also concerned that if it goes wrong her investment may be lost.

required

You are the auditor to the company. Explain to Tasha the role of the auditor in this situation.

solution

The main points that would help reassure Tasha would be as follows:

- the company must prepare accounts that have to be audited and sent to the shareholders

- the auditor has to be professionally qualified and independent of the company and the directors

- the role of the auditors is to express an opinion as to the truth and fairness of the accounts sent to the shareholders

- a company has to comply with the requirements of the Companies Act 2006 which has quite specific requirements about how the company must be managed and what books and records it must keep

- Tasha has the right, as a shareholder, not only to receive an audited set of accounts but also to come to the Annual General Meeting where they would be formally presented

THE AUDITOR'S REPORT

We will deal with the precise wording of auditors' reports in Chapter 7. At this stage you need only be aware that it is the job of the auditor to report on the company's financial statements for an accounting period.

The important thing to remember is that the auditors are appointed by the shareholders, not the directors, and consequently report to the shareholders.

What auditors have to decide, based on the evidence they have collected during their audit work, is whether the accounts show a true and fair view of the Income Statement (statement of profit or loss) and the statement of financial position for the financial period.

They also have to confirm that the company has maintained proper books and records. We will examine what this means in practice in Chapter 7.

After it has been signed, copies of the auditor's report must be sent to:

- the shareholders
- the Registrar of Companies

What happens in practice is that the report is included with the statutory accounts when these are sent out to the shareholders and when the accounts are sent to Companies House to be filed on the public record.

THE EXPECTATION GAP

The **expectation gap** is the name given to the difference between what the public thinks auditors do and what they actually do.

When large organisations are seen to fail, whether through poor management or fraud, auditors are often criticised in the press or at shareholder meetings for failing to meet the expectations of the public. These are often unrealistic demands and do not form part of auditors' duties.

The result is often criticism of the auditing profession, loss of confidence in the audit function and legal action taken against individual audit firms.

Research has discovered that the general public thinks that auditors:

- check every single transaction
- prepare the financial statements
- guarantee that the financial statements are correct
- are responsible for finding and reporting frauds, however small
- are responsible for detecting illegal acts by directors

The truth in the real world is, of course, very different.

Chapter Summary

- An audit is a process in which a suitably qualified third party expresses an opinion as to whether a set of accounts prepared for shareholders represents a true and fair view of the company's financial position at the period end.

- Shareholders are not always involved in the day-to-day running of the business, so it is the duty of auditors to report to them on the financial position of the company in which they have an ownership stake.

- All companies need to be audited except small charities, dormant companies, and companies with a turnover of £10.2m or less.

- Auditors have to be members of a Recognised Supervisory Body. They should not be closely connected with the audit client and must be able to demonstrate that they are independent of the company they are auditing.

- The audit process is a series of steps the auditor will go through from investigations prior to accepting an appointment to reporting on control weaknesses.

- Reasonable assurance is a high but not absolute level of assurance that the auditors require in order to sign their Auditors' Report.

- The directors appoint the first auditors who hold office until the end of the first Annual General Meeting.

- Auditors are re-appointed at the Annual General Meeting, or if they are not re-appointed, a new audit firm is appointed until the end of the next Annual General Meeting.

■   Firms should institute quality control procedures to ensure that audits are all carried out properly.

■   The form of the audit report is laid down in the Companies Act 2006. It requires the auditors to report whether, in their opinion, the financial statements present a true and fair view of the company's financial position.

■   There is a gap, called the expectation gap, between what the public thinks auditors do and what their role actually is.

Key Terms

audit	a process by which a suitably qualified third party expresses an opinion as to whether a set of accounts prepared for shareholders represents a true and fair view of the company's financial position at the period end
true and fair	the opinion required by the Companies Act 2006 to be given by the auditors on the company's financial statements
financial reporting period	the period for which accounts are prepared, normally one year
members	an alternative word for shareholders – the people who own the company
internal controls	the policies, procedures, attitudes and internal checks within an organisation which together combine to ensure that the likelihood of significant error or material misstatement is minimised
annual general meeting	the meeting at which the directors account to the shareholders for their running of the company during the accounting period – the accounts are presented at this meeting and the auditors can attend to present their report

Companies Act 2006   the statute which sets out the responsibilities of directors and auditors and governs the conduct of company affairs

Recognised Supervisory Body (RSB)   one of the main accountancy bodies recognised for the regulation and supervision of auditors – all auditors must be a member or work for a firm controlled by members of such bodies

Registrar of Companies   the Government official with whom annual accounts and other statutory documents must be filed – documents kept by the Registrar are available to the general public

reasonable assurance   a less than absolute level of assurance, for which the auditors will gather evidence, in order to satisfy themselves that the financial statements are true and fair

professional scepticism   an open-minded attitude that presumes that in preparing the financial statements the management are neither totally honest nor totally dishonest

Activities

1.1 The following statements have been made by a trainee auditor. Decide whether you think that they are true or false and write down your reasons for your decision.

(a) If there is a fraud within a company the auditor will be in trouble if he/she has not found it.

(b) The main legislation which relates to auditing is the Companies Act 2006 and associated regulations.

(c) Auditors are responsible to the directors who appoint them.

(d) All companies have to have auditors but partnerships and sole traders do not.

(e) It is primarily the responsibility of the auditors to prepare the accounts and ensure that they comply with the legislation.

(f) You can be an auditor if you have a professional accounting qualification.

(g) The directors run the business on behalf of the shareholders and the auditor is there to comment on the company's accounts.

1.2 Complete the statement below on the definition of an audit by filling in the gaps with terms from the selection below

- independent
- opinion
- fair and accurate
- International Auditing Standards
- International Accounting Standards

- reasonably
- view
- financial statements
- true and fair

An audit is a process by which an [_____] , qualified third party expresses an [_____] as to whether a set of [_____] of a company represent a [_____] view of its financial affairs for a reporting period and comply with the Companies Act 2006 and [_____] .

1.3 Which of the following statements are true? Tick the appropriate box.

	True	False
Auditors are responsible for preparation and validation of financial statements		
Auditors should gather sufficient reliable evidence to give them reasonable assurance		
Auditors should adopt an attitude of 'professional scepticism'. This means they should actively search for frauds and errors		
AAT members can carry out audit work but cannot sign the Auditor's Report		
Auditors should not accept a new appointment without some preliminary investigation into their proposed client		

1.4 Complete the following from the list of terms below

- Absolute
- £5.6m
- Reliable
- 25
- Credible
- Charitable
- Institutes of Chartered Accountants

- AAT
- 50
- Expectation
- Reasonable
- ACCA
- Evidence

- £5.1m
- Sufficient
- Dormant
- £2.8m
- £10.2m
- Enough

All companies must have a statutory audit except those that satisfy two of the following three criteria: a turnover less than [   ] ; a statement of financial position value less than [   ] ; employs fewer than [   ] people. [   ] companies are exempt.

The [   ] Gap is the difference between what the auditors actually do and what the public think they do.

Only members of the [   ] and the [   ] are eligible to be auditors. [   ] members cannot be registered.

The role of the auditor is to gather [   ] and [   ] evidence so as to give them [   ] assurance that the financial statements represent a true and fair view.

2 Auditing – the legal framework

this chapter covers...

This chapter describes the legal framework which governs the work of auditors and directors of a company. It explains the duty of care owed by auditors to shareholders and the responsibility they have to third parties. It describes the principles which govern the professional behaviour and personal qualities that are expected of an auditor when dealing with client information and client staff.

The chapter covers:

- *the responsibility of directors for maintaining financial records and preparing financial accounts*
- *the responsibility of auditors to shareholders and third parties*
- *limiting auditors' liability*
- *the legal framework governing the work of auditors*

    - *in statute law (particularly the Companies Act 2006)*

    - *International Standards on Auditing (ISAs)*

    - *Case law (court decisions relating to auditing)*

- *quality control procedures*
- *the issue of professional ethics – the responsible way in which auditors deal with clients and keep confidentiality*
- *the auditors and fraud*
- *dealing with clients*

OVERVIEW OF THE LEGAL FRAMEWORK

Companies are required by the Companies Act 2006 to prepare annual financial statements and to have these statements audited. The directors and auditors have separate responsibilities in the process. The fact that directors and auditors have an ultimate responsibility to the shareholders of the company means that these responsibilities will inevitably be linked.

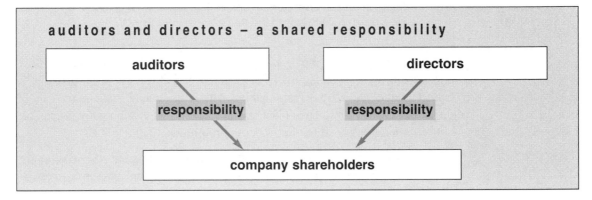

a shared responsibility

Directors have a primary responsibility to prepare the financial statements and report to the shareholders, who own the business, telling them how well the company has performed financially in the accounting period.

The **auditors**' responsibility follows on: they must check these financial statements and report to the same shareholders whether or not the directors have accounted fairly and truthfully.

RESPONSIBILITIES OF DIRECTORS

The Companies Act 2006 states that the directors of the company are responsible for:

- maintaining proper financial records
- preparing financial statements in the prescribed format

We are now going to look at each of these responsibilities in turn.

maintaining proper financial records

An extract from the Companies Act 2006 is set out below. Whilst it is useful for you to read this, you don't have to remember it word for word and will not be required to refer to the section number.

Section 386 of the Companies Act 2006

(1) Every company must keep adequate accounting records.

(2) Adequate accounting records means records that are sufficient:

    (a) to show and explain the company's transactions

    (b) to disclose with reasonable accuracy, at any time, the financial position of the company at that time, and

    (c) to enable the directors to ensure that any accounts required to be prepared comply with the requirements of this Act.

To put this more simply, the directors of the company have a legal responsibility to keep the books of account of the business up-to-date and in sufficient detail so that reasonably accurate financial statements can be produced at any time. They must also make sure that the company keeps hold of all related information that was used to produce them.

In practice, this means that documentation relating to the day-to-day financial transactions of the business such as sales and purchase invoices, credit notes, bank statements etc, must be kept by the company even when they have been recorded in the accounts.

In addition, directors must ensure that they keep financial information in such a way that the requirements for disclosure of information in accounts as required by the Companies Act, can be met.

The Companies Act specifies the minimum requirement for accounting records that it expects a business to keep. Set out on below is an interpretation of what this means in real terms for a company.

Companies Act requirement	Books and records required
A record of payments and receipts:	Cashbook Petty cash book
A record of assets and liabilities:	Asset register Sales ledger Purchase ledger
If the company deals in goods:	A record of inventory Inventory lists at the period end All statements of inventory counts from which the inventory listings have been prepared, ie the inventory count sheets

Note that where the company is not engaged in a normal retail trade it must also keep records of goods sold and purchased in enough detail so that sellers and buyers can be identified.

The records must be kept at the office registered with the Registrar of Companies, known as the Registered Office, or at some other location the directors consider to be suitable. Smaller businesses often choose to have their accountant's office as their Registered Office but keep all the accounting records at their business premises.

These regulations must be complied with – if the directors of a company are found to have failed to keep records in sufficient detail they are guilty of an offence under the Companies Act and can be imprisoned or fined.

preparing financial statements

We will now examine the legal requirement to prepare financial statements. This may touch on some of the points you cover in Financial Statements, which deals with the formats for preparing annual accounts. You should be aware from your studies that these formats are now increasingly regulated by International Accounting Standards (IAS).

So what do we mean by the term 'financial statements'? The Companies Act specifically refers to the preparation of:

- the statement of financial position
- the income statement
- a directors' report
- a directors' remuneration report
- the notes to these statements and notes of the accounting policies adopted
- the auditors' report

The Companies Act also sets out some specific duties for the directors when preparing the financial statements. These should be familiar to you from your financial accounting studies. The directors must:

- prepare the financial statements on a going concern basis, unless they consider that the business will not be able to continue for the foreseeable future
- select suitable accounting policies and apply them consistently
- make judgements and estimates that are reasonable and prudent where revenue and potential costs or losses are not known with certainty
- state whether the relevant accounting standards have been followed
- explain any reasons why accounting standards have not been followed

As you can see from the points above, the legal requirements of the directors regarding the maintenance of financial records and the preparation of financial statements are both strict and detailed.

In addition to all of this the directors have a responsibility to allow the auditors access at all times to the books and records of the business. This leads us into the next section on the rights and responsibilities of the auditors.

REGULATORY FRAMEWORK OF AUDITING

Over the years the rights and responsibilities of auditors have been established in three different ways:

■ **statute law** – particularly the Companies Act 2006

■ **International Standards on Auditing** (ISAs)

■ **case law** – where decisions relating to auditing have been decided in court

These three regulatory influences have created a framework of rights and responsibilities within which auditors operate. They work broadly along the lines of the flowchart shown below.

Statute law: the legal rights of auditors and their basic responsibilities are defined in the Companies Act.

The auditors' rights and responsibilities are then further defined in the **International Standards on Auditing** (ISAs), which are issued by the Financial Reporting Council Codes & Standards Committee (www.frc.org.uk).

The two main functions of ISAs are:

1 they expand on the wording of auditing legislation and set out in detail what is expected of auditors and what rights and duties they have

2 they tell auditors how to deal with specific sets of circumstances and give examples and guidance on how audit work should be carried out

Case law gives auditors guidance as to how the court decisions have interpreted the law and the ISAs under certain circumstances. It also helps to define the extent of auditors' responsibilities.

auditors' responsibilities

The auditors' primary responsibilities, set out by the Companies Act, can be summarised as:

■ to give an opinion to the shareholders as to the truth and fairness of the financial statements

■ to give an opinion as to whether the financial statements have been properly prepared in accordance with the Companies Act

They must also include in their report reference to:

■ whether proper books and records have been kept

■ whether proper information has been supplied to them from any branches of the business they have not visited

■ whether the financial statements agree to the underlying financial records and supporting information

■ whether the contents of the Directors' Report is consistent with the financial statements

■ a statement of the separate responsibilities of auditors and directors

There is obviously a comprehensive list of requirements regarding the content of the audit report. We will look in more detail at the form and content of these reports in Chapter 7.

Fundamentally, the auditors' role is to report to the shareholders, who are the owners of the business, on the truth and fairness of the financial statements prepared by the directors and to confirm that proper records have been kept and full explanations received where necessary. It is important to appreciate that the auditors act for the shareholders collectively – as one body. They are not responsible to any one individual shareholder.

The auditor's responsibility is not simply a statutory responsibility. When the auditors are appointed they sign a contract, known as a Letter of Engagement, with the client. This sets out the respective roles and responsibilities of the auditors and the directors. Should there be an issue with the work carried out by the auditors, this document will form the basis of any legal action taken by the client.

auditors and fraud

ISA 240 The auditor's responsibilities relating to fraud in an audit of financial statements states:

> 'The objectives of the auditor are:
>
> (a)   To identify and assess the risks of material misstatement of the financial statements due to fraud;

(b) To obtain sufficient appropriate audit evidence regarding the assessed risks of material misstatement due to fraud, through designing and implementing appropriate responses; and

(c) To respond appropriately to fraud or suspected fraud identified during the audit.'

Management are responsible for the preparation of the financial statements and it is part of this responsibility to ensure that the financial statements do not contain misstatements due to fraud. ISA 240 takes the view that the auditors should approach their work with an attitude of 'professional scepticism', in other words they should always be alert to the possibility of misstatements arising due to fraud.

The auditors' responsibility for detecting fraud was decided in 1896 in the Kingston Cotton Mill case. The judge in that case established that the auditors' role was that of a '**watchdog not a bloodhound**'. What he meant by this was that, whilst auditors should be alert to the possibility of fraud, they are not required to search for it.

Auditors are required to use 'reasonable skill and judgement' when carrying out their audit work. Their role is to express an opinion on the financial statements presented to them by the directors, not to search for what has **not** been included.

ISA 240 requires that the auditors consider the possibility of fraud as part of their planning process and should identify any risk factors which might make the presence of fraud more likely. The auditors should also consider management's evaluation of the risk of fraud and the steps they have taken to minimise the risk of fraudulent activity.

The ISA also recognises that the management have the authority to override controls and to hide fraudulent transactions from the auditors if they wish to. Auditors should therefore pay particular attention to:

- journal entries and adjustments made at the time the financial statements are being prepared, particularly those at the end of the reporting period

- accounting estimates made by management, for possible bias or distortion. This should also include a retrospective review of accounting estimates made in prior years

- any transactions made outside the normal course of business or that appear unusual given the auditors' knowledge of the company

What this process does is increase the emphasis on the auditor's approach to fraud during the risk assessment and planning stages of the audit.

Auditors need to separate deliberate fraud from accidental error. If something has been misstated in the financial records, or omitted completely, this is not necessarily fraud. A good auditor must bear in mind the possibility that it might be.

auditors' responsibilities to third parties

As we have seen, the primary responsibility of the auditors is to report to the shareholders. But what about other readers of the accounts?

The auditors are appointed by the shareholders and this creates a contract between the parties. The law says that auditors owe a duty of care to shareholders, as a body not individually, to carry out their work in a professional and thorough way.

This duty of care means that, if auditors fail to do their work properly, the shareholders have the right to take them to court to recover any losses that the auditors' negligence has caused them.

Is this same duty of care extended to other users of the accounts? In short, can the auditors be held liable to any one at all if they get it wrong?

If any person decided to sue the auditors in court because they had suffered some loss, they would have to show that the auditors:

- owed a duty of care to the person who suffered the loss and
- failed to carry out their audit work using reasonable skill and care

Once this had been established, the person bringing the court action against the auditors would have to prove:

- the auditors were negligent in the way they carried out their work (ie they failed in their duty of care)
- the person bringing the action suffered a loss
- the loss arose as a result of the auditors' negligence

If all of this can be proved then the auditors are likely to be found guilty by the court of negligence and ordered to pay damages and compensation.

This could amount to a considerable sum – in the past, such claims have resulted in audit partners being made bankrupt and the audit firms ceasing to exist. It is no surprise that the partners in audit firms are naturally very interested in the law on responsibility to third parties!

One court case that has become very important in clarifying the extent of the duty of care of auditors is the Caparo decision, which is explained below. You do not have to remember all the facts of this case for your studies, but it is important that you understand how the principle it established affects the auditing profession.

---

the Caparo case

the facts . . .

In 1990 Caparo Industries sued audit firm Touche Ross for negligence in their audit of Fidelity plc, a company that Caparo had subsequently purchased.

Caparo stated that they had relied on the audited accounts to value Fidelity plc. It emerged that the asset value of Fidelity was substantially less than the audited accounts had shown. Caparo said that had they known the true position they would not have bought Fidelity.

The key point was that, at the time Touche Ross signed the audit report on Fidelity's financial statements, they were not aware of Caparo's intention to buy Fidelity nor that Caparo would be relying on the accounts.

the decision . . .

The judge in this case decided:

- that the auditors did not have a duty of care to third parties, unless
- they knew that these accounts were going to be relied upon for the purposes of making an investment.

Much to the relief of the auditors, Touche Ross, this was not found to be the case here.

In addition to the financial implications of being found guilty of negligence, there is also the damage it will have on an audit firm's reputation, which could result in a loss of client business.

The audit firm may also face an investigation by their own professional body.

limited liability partnerships (LLPs)

Audit firms have traditionally been set up as partnerships, with a number of partners sharing the profits and losses.

However, since 2000 firms have been allowed to set up as limited liability partnerships (LLPs). These are partnerships which have been turned into limited liability companies. This has some significant advantages for audit firms but also some disadvantages.

The advantages are:

- an LLP is a company so its members, normally the partners, have limited liability. This means they are only liable to the extent that they have invested in the business. In the event of the LLP crashing the members will not lose all their personal assets as they would if a traditional partnership failed.

- as the LLP is a legal entity in its own right, it can own the business assets. Also the staff are employed by the LLP and not by a group of partners. This makes things much simpler when the partnership changes through partners retiring or new partners joining.

- an LLP has a flexible structure; there are no partners, but neither are there directors or shareholders, instead it has what the law calls 'members'. The main difference is that the process for members joining and leaving the LLP is much simpler than under the complex partnership rules.

- an LLP is not required to have annual general meetings or even members' meetings, although, in practice, LLPs will have members' meetings to make decisions or discuss important matters.

However there is one significant disadvantage of forming an LLP which does not apply to partnerships.

Because the members of an LLP have limited liability, in order to protect those who deal with the LLP (typically its clients), they must maintain accounting records, prepare and deliver audited annual accounts to the Registrar of Companies and submit an annual return in a similar manner to limited companies.

This means that the financial affairs of accountancy firms which were previously confidential are now available to anyone who wishes to see them.

LIMITING AUDITORS' LIABILITY

There are three ways of limiting the effect of a successful claim:

- by operating as a limited liability partnership (LLP), which we looked at in the section above

- by taking out **professional indemnity insurance** to cover the auditors' liabilities in the event of a claim

- by coming to an agreement, known as a **limited liability agreement (LLA)** with the client which will set a maximum amount of any possible claim they could make against the auditors

The Companies Act 2006 allows auditors to come to an agreement with their clients as to the maximum amount of any claim. The intention of the LLA is for the client to receive sufficient compensation for any failures by the auditors rather than the total of any loss the client suffered.

The maximum amount of any claim may be set as a multiple of the audit fee, or a percentage of profits or asset values.

An LLA must be agreed by the shareholders of the client, as the auditors work for the shareholders, not the management.

WHAT GOVERNS THE AUDIT?

So far we have covered the responsibilities of the directors and the responsibilities of the auditors. We will now examine the legal rights that the auditors have which allow them to carry out their audit work effectively.

As we have seen, the work of the auditors is regulated in three ways:

- through the Companies Act 2006
- through International Standards on Auditing (ISAs)
- through legal decisions made in individual cases in the courts

We will now look at these three areas in turn.

auditors' rights under the Companies Act 2006

Just as the Companies Act establishes the responsibilities of the directors, it also sets out the legal framework within which auditors function. In order to help the auditors carry out their audit work the Companies Act gives them certain specific rights, which are set out in the table below.

Auditors have the right to . . .	
the records	Auditors have a right of access at all times to the company's books, accounting records and vouchers.
information and explanations	The auditors have the right to all explanations and information from the company's officers that they consider necessary for their audit.
attend meetings	The auditors have the right to receive notice of all meetings which a shareholder can attend, and the right to attend those meetings.
speak at general meetings	The auditors have a right to speak at any general meeting of the company on any part of it which concerns them as auditors.

written resolutions	The auditors must be sent copies of any written resolution proposed.
require presentation of accounts	Auditors have the right to give notice in writing requiring that the company holds a general meeting for the purpose of laying the accounts before the shareholders.

In conclusion, the auditors basically have the right to access all the company's books and records and to ask any questions of the directors (and their staff) that they feel necessary to complete the audit. In addition to this they are entitled to attend company meetings and to speak to the shareholders at these meetings on any points that relate to their position as auditors.

It should be pointed out that in most cases the audit client is happy to provide the auditor with the information that is needed and will not obstruct them from addressing company meetings.

International Standards on Auditing

Accounting and auditing in the UK is regulated by the Financial Reporting Council (FRC). The FRC is responsible for:

■ developing and maintaining auditing and assurance standards

■ providing guidance to auditors

■ maintaining audit quality and promoting improvement to the auditing process through a programme of monitoring audit performance

■ the disciplinary function for auditors as the FRC operates the disciplinary scheme for accountants and is responsible for the enforcement of professional standards of ethics

■ maintaining links with the IAASB (see below) and making representations to it relevant to the UK

One part of the FRC is its Codes & Standards Committee which is responsible for issuing International Standards on Auditing (ISAs). ISAs detail:

■ the role of the external auditor

■ what auditors must do in certain circumstances

■ how they should approach their work

■ how they should carry out their work – ie what work they must do, as a minimum, to achieve their audit objectives

These ISAs are the UK version of the international standards which have been produced by the International Auditing and Assurance Standards Board (IAASB). The IAASB is part of the International Federation of Accountants (IFAC), the global organisation for the accounting profession which is responsible for developing international standards on ethics, accounting and auditing.

The IAASB is responsible for promoting audit quality on a global scale and encourages global convergence of auditing standards by encouraging countries to adopt the International Standards on Auditing.

The FRC does not have to adopt all the standards the IAASB has produced, as some do not readily apply to the UK. However, they have adopted most of them, with suitable modifications. Details of these ISAs can be found on the FRC website, www.frc.org.uk.

ISAs exist to support, advise and regulate auditors and their work and to provide guidance and instruction in specific situations. This is similar to the International Accounting Standards (IASs) that you will look at in your financial accounting studies which govern the preparation of financial statements.

As part of your auditing studies you need to be aware of the fundamental ISAs which influence the way audits are carried out. The AAT have set out a list of ISAs which they consider to be essential reading. This is quite a comprehensive list but remember that you do not have to remember numbers nor do you have to be able to quote from any of the text.

The ISAs considered to be essential are:

ISA 200	Overall Objectives of the Independent Auditor and the Conduct of an Audit in Accordance with International Standards on Auditing
ISA 220	Quality control for an audit of financial statements
ISA 230	Audit documentation
ISA 240	The Auditor's Responsibilities Relating to Fraud in an Audit of Financial Statements
ISA 250	Considerations of Laws and Regulations in an Audit of Financial Statements
ISA 265	Communicating Deficiencies in Internal Control to those Charged with Governance and Management
ISA 315	Identifying and Assessing the Risks of Material Misstatement through Understanding the Entity and its Environment
ISA 320	Materiality in planning and performing an audit

ISA 450	Evaluation of Misstatements Identified during the Audit
ISA 500	Audit Evidence
ISA 530	Audit Sampling
ISA 700	Forming an Opinion and Reporting on Financial Statements
ISA 705	Modifications to the Opinion in the Independent Auditor's Report
ISA 706	Emphasis of Matter paragraphs and Other Matter paragraphs in the Independent Auditor's Report

Throughout this book we will refer to relevant ISAs as we cover the different topics. Although we may quote some of the relevant paragraphs so that you can be aware of the precise wording of the key ISA, you are not expected to remember either the precise wording or the ISA number.

case law

A ruling in a previous decision made in the courts forms an important element of the legal framework affecting the work of auditors. The outcome of these cases and the comments of the judges have provided valuable guidance for auditors as to how to carry out their work (or in some cases how not to!). An example relating to auditors' responsibility to third parties has already been given on page 24. Over the years many firms of auditors have been sued for negligence – ie where a 'duty of care' has been neglected.

You are not expected to remember the names of cases or the exact words used by judges. They are quoted in this text to help to give you an impression of what is expected of auditors and how they should approach their work and dealing with clients.

QUALITY CONTROL PROCEDURES

ISA 220 'Quality control for an audit of financial statements' says that all audit firms must have a system of quality control. This is to ensure that the firm and its staff comply with all the relevant professional auditing standards and legal requirements when carrying out assignments for the firm.

Quality control procedures are there to make sure that all ethical and legal requirements have been complied with and all the necessary audit work has been completed to the appropriate standard, before the financial statements are signed by the audit partner. The audit partner is responsible for ensuring that the firm's quality control procedures have been applied to each audit.

In particular the quality control procedures for each audit should include:

- confirmation that all the appropriate ethical standards have been maintained throughout the audit. This includes ensuring that the audit staff are objective and competent and that they are honest and truthful

- confirmation that the audit firm's independence from the client has not been compromised during the course of the audit

- ongoing procedures to ensure that it continues to be acceptable for the audit firm to audit the client and that nothing has happened since the start of the audit to change this

- a system in place to review all audit work so work carried out at each level is reviewed by a more senior member of the audit team

Where individual audits are complex, or are particularly large or significant to the audit firm, the work of the audit partner should be reviewed by another partner to ensure that nothing has been missed or is incorrectly recorded. These reviews are known as '**hot reviews**' as they are carried out whilst the audit is still ongoing and before the auditors' report is signed. A hot review should consider the independence, ethics and client suitability and should also review any contentious issues or judgements made by the audit team during the course of the audit.

Audit firms should also carry out '**cold reviews**'. This is where audit assignments which have been completed and signed off are reviewed by an independent partner or senior manager from within the audit firm to ensure that the firm's quality control procedures were followed throughout the audit.

In addition to ISA 220, referred to above, there is also an International Standard on Quality Control (ISQC 1) **'Quality control for firms that perform audits and reviews of historical financial information and other assurance and related service engagements'.**

Under ISQC 1 responsibility for the audit firm's system of quality control is placed on the firm's chief executive officer, managing partner or management committee (as appropriate). The reason for this is the increasing emphasis on what is known as '**tone at the top**'. This refers to the quality of the leadership shown by the senior staff in a business.

Consistent messages from senior management about the importance of quality control are a vital part of internal communications, meetings, training events and staff appraisals. The very senior individuals in a business must set a good example and must never give the impression that the firm's quality procedures do not apply to them.

PROFESSIONAL ETHICS

As we have seen, the rights and responsibilities of auditors are set out in several ways – by statute law, through ISAs and by case law. In addition to adopting the ISAs, the Financial Reporting Council (FRC) also sets the standards expected of auditors with regard to their professional behaviour. This is known as the **ethical framework**.

Rather than setting out a large number of detailed rules on the behaviour of the auditors, the professional bodies have decided that it would be simpler to list the fundamental ethical principles that they expect a professional auditor to comply with. These are set out in ISA 200 **'Overall objectives of the independent auditor and the conduct of an audit in accordance with International Standards on Auditing'**.

ethical standards

The AAT has its own Code of Professional Ethics, which you will have already studied. Student members are required to comply with this code. The AAT requires its members to accept responsibility to not only act in the best interests of their client, but also to have a responsibility to act in the public interest as well.

Clearly not every situation in which an auditor finds him/herself in can be anticipated by an ethical code so the AAT have set out a conceptual framework approach to ethical behaviour which they expect all members, including student members, to comply with.

There are five fundamental principles that are set out in the AAT Code of Professional Ethics. These are detailed below with specific reference to auditors:

- **integrity** – this means honesty, truthfulness and openness in dealing with clients' affairs

- **objectivity** – this means that auditors must not get too involved with their client

- **professional competence and due care** – auditors must know what they are doing, so they must keep up with all the latest standards and guidelines. They must act with reasonable skill and care in dealing with the affairs of their clients

- **confidentiality** – to respect the confidentiality of information acquired as a result of professional and business relationships and not disclose any such information to third parties without proper and specific authority, unless there is a legal or professional right or duty to disclose. Confidential information acquired as a result of professional and business relationships must not be used for personal gain

- **adopt professional behaviour** – auditors must themselves comply with relevant laws and behave with courtesy and consideration to anyone they come into contact with in the course of their professional duties

We will look at some of these points in more detail.

integrity and objectivity

ISA 200 states that the two most important personal qualities of an auditor are integrity and objectivity. These both contribute to the auditor's independence. An auditor's integrity will mean he/she is always honest with a client, explaining any audit issues clearly and fully, no matter how difficult that task may be.

The role of the auditor is such that they must take great care to ensure that their independence is not compromised in any way. They must be independent and must be 'seen to be independent'. At no point must their opinion on the truth and fairness of the client's financial statements be influenced either by their client or by anyone else.

An auditor's objectivity in dealings with the client ensures that he/she does not allow personal feelings or beliefs to influence his/her decisions. By maintaining his/her objectivity and by being straightforward in dealing with clients an auditor not only maintains their independence but is seen to have maintained it.

If an ethical issue arises during the course of an assignment, this should be discussed with the directors and senior management so that it can be overcome. If that is not possible, the auditor must withdraw from the assignment.

Guidelines have been issued by the Recognised Supervisory Bodies (RSBs) as to what might compromise an auditor's independence. A summary of these guidelines is detailed here.

Auditors are not permitted to:

- have one single client that represents a high proportion of an auditor's total business – this is usually defined as having one client whose fee is more than 15% of the auditor's total fee income
- have family or close relatives working in the senior management of the client – for example, it would be unacceptable for the audit manager to be married to the financial controller of one of his/her clients
- hold shares in the client, either directly or indirectly
- accept loans from clients or lend clients' money
- accept gifts or corporate hospitality – unless this is quite minimal
- provide bookkeeping or accountancy services other than audit services to the client

Professional judgement must be exercised in all of these cases. If the audit is being performed on a major UK bank, for example, it is acceptable for members of the audit team to have mortgages with this bank. It is not, however, acceptable for the audit partner to have a substantial personal loan from the bank at a preferential rate. On the other hand no one would be very concerned if the audit client provided all the audit team with a free diary. However, it would be inappropriate for members of the audit team to be taken by the client on an all expenses paid trip to Aintree for the Grand National weekend.

professional competence and due care

We have now established that the auditors must maintain independence at all times. We will now discuss the area of professional competence. It sounds obvious, but the auditors need to know what they are doing. This means that auditors should:

- be familiar with the principles of auditing which we have described in this book

- be aware of what the Companies Act 2006 says about how financial statements should be prepared and the disclosure requirements

You will already be familiar with this from your financial accounting studies. The fact that auditors must be members of Recognised Supervisory Bodies (RSBs) should ensure that they are also fully aware of these requirements.

In the area of professional competence case law goes some way to giving us a definition. Specifically, the judge in the **Kingston Cotton Mill** case defined what 'professional competence' actually means. The judge said:

'It is the duty of an auditor to bring to bear on the work he has to perform that skill, care and caution which a reasonably competent, careful and cautious auditor would use. What is reasonable skill, care and caution must depend on the particular circumstances of each case.'

What the judge meant in this case was that the auditors had to use 'reasonable skill and care' in carrying out their audit work and that, as long as they did this, their duty to their client was fulfilled.

To summarise:

- the auditors owe a duty of care to the shareholders who appoint them

- as professionals, auditors are expected to carry out the work they have to do in a professionally competent way; but they are not expected to be all seeing and all knowing

During the course of their audit work the auditors have a professional duty to:

- make reasonable enquiries
- carry out sufficient work to support the audit opinion they are signing as to the truth and fairness of the accounts

confidentiality

During the course of their audit work the auditors discover a great deal of information about their client, some of which might be commercially sensitive and much of which will be **confidential**.

Confidentiality is, therefore, seen as being a very important aspect of auditors' responsibilities.

The fundamental rule is that auditors must not reveal any information that they have learned about a client to unauthorised third parties except in the most exceptional circumstances.

confidentiality – the exceptions

The Recognised Supervisory Bodies (RSBs) have established certain circumstances in which auditors are permitted to reveal information about their client to a third party.

These circumstances are:

- when the **client gives permission**
- when **required to by law** – for example, under money laundering regulations, if the auditor suspects the client's involvement in this kind of activity they have a duty to disclose this; similarly if they suspect the client is involved in treason, bribery or terrorist activities this should be reported to the relevant authorities
- when there is a **professional duty to disclose** – for example if the auditor is giving evidence at a trial
- when it is **in the public interest** – for example, if the client is guilty of serious environmental pollution or is selling a product which might prove to be a danger to the general public, the auditor is permitted to give relevant information to third parties

In all instances the auditors must think carefully before revealing any information about their clients' affairs to a third party. If in doubt they should obtain legal advice or the advice of their professional body.

confidentiality – security of information

A final practical issue regarding client confidentiality is in relation to security of information. The auditor will hold a substantial amount of client information in their audit files. Auditors must ensure the security of this information at all times:

■ audit files should be kept locked away whenever they are left unattended

■ audit files should never be left in vulnerable locations, for example in the boot of your car

■ audit working papers should not be taken away from the auditor's office or the client premises unless absolutely necessary

■ auditors should not discuss confidential client details in public places or with any unrelated third party even if it is a 'trustworthy family member'!

conflicts of interest

Auditors must avoid conflicts of interest. This happens when:

■ they find themselves acting for both sides in a dispute

■ they take on a new client and find that it has a substantial interest in an existing client's shares or business

■ they supply non-audit services to a client such as tax or financial advice to such an extent that it might compromise their independence as an auditor

When a conflict of interest is identified which cannot be resolved the auditor should resign from appointment.

threats to ethical behaviour

Threats to ethical behaviour arise through a combination of circumstances and relationships with clients. Auditors must be alert to the possibility of these threats and know how to deal with them by putting safeguards in place to eliminate these threats or reduce them to an acceptable level.

Threats can be categorised as follows:

■ **self-interest threats** – which may occur where the auditor has a financial or other interest in a particular outcome

■ **self-review threats** – this arises when the auditor is, effectively reviewing his/her own work, or where an auditor finds themselves reviewing a judgement that they were responsible for when it was first made. The auditor cannot act independently if this is the case

■ **advocacy threats** – these arise when auditors effectively speak for their client. This could imply that they have 'taken sides' which can be seen to impair objectivity. It is important to note that this is not the same as the auditor being asked to give a professional opinion or make a professional judgement, the advocacy threat arises when the auditor promotes the client's opinion or position

■ **familiarity threats** – when the auditor has acted for a client for a long time, he/she may develop personal friendships with clients or become so familiar with the client's activities that the auditor loses his/her objectivity and his/her independence may be compromised

■ **intimidation threats** – if a client wishes to influence the decisions or the work of the auditor the client could do so by means of threats, either actual or perceived. This can include threatening to stop using the auditor or in extreme cases threats of violence

Auditors must be alert to the possibility of these threats and put safeguards in place to eliminate them or reduce them to an acceptable level.

As we have seen in the case of conflicts of interest, the auditor may simply resign and remove themselves from the situation. Other situations may require the auditor to consult with the AAT for advice and assistance in dealing with the threats to his/her ethical principles.

The AAT Code of Ethics provides details of safeguards that can be put in place. These include:

■ education, training and experience – this will aid the auditor in spotting ethical threats before an issue arises

■ statutory protections such as those within the Companies Act 2006 and the **Corporate Governance Code** gives auditors some legal authority

■ professional standards and disciplinary procedures exist to support the standard of behaviour required as does the assistance provided by the AAT to its members and trainees

■ auditors' own internal procedures

internal procedures

Audit firms are required to establish procedures to ensure that professional ethical standards are adhered to. These should include:

■ a requirement that, should the firm be asked to carry out a non-audit assignment for an audit client, such as an investigation or provision of professional advice, then different partners and staff other than the audit team should be used. This should remove any possibility of a self-review threat.

■ rotation of partners and staff on an audit on a regular basis to minimise a familiarity threat

■ requires confirmation from all staff and partners that they do not hold any shares in a client

- an annual review of all clients to ensure that the fee income received from them does not exceed the recommended 15% (10% in the case of listed clients) threshold for the firm. This helps minimise the intimidation threat that could arise if one client is so large that to lose it would have a significant impact on the audit firm

- regular reviews of all clients to ensure that they continue to behave ethically in their business dealings. This involves things like monitoring and reviewing publicity about the client

Audit firms should have disciplinary processes in place should a member of staff breach the ethical code. These may range from a simple reprimand where there has been a comparatively minor breach, to dismissal for gross misconduct where there has been a serious breach of the code. An example of this might be insider trading where there has been a breach of confidentiality for personal gain.

Auditors who do not act ethically may also be disciplined by the AAT, Recognised Supervisory Bodies, or, in extreme cases, the Financial Reporting Council's Conduct Committee. This can result in adverse publicity, fines or even termination of membership. It is, therefore, important that all members and trainees are aware of the ethical standards and observe them in all their professional behaviour.

DEALING WITH CLIENTS STAFF

Client staff may not have a clear understanding of the role of the auditors – they may believe, for example, that the auditors are working for senior management and are there to find out if the staff are doing their jobs properly.

The AAT Code of Professional Ethics require that trainees and members should maintain 'professional behaviour'. Consequently, audit staff should be polite, courteous and professional at all times and, when asking for information, explain why it is needed.

Consequently, when dealing with client staff the auditors should:

- avoid making unreasonable requests for information

- deal with several queries at one meeting rather than pestering staff with a continuous stream of questions when they are trying to work

- be aware of client deadlines – for example, month-end routines should not be disrupted by demands made by auditors

Although auditors have a significant level of legal authority, where possible, insisting on exercising this authority should be avoided. Auditors should only resort to this in exceptional circumstances when they feel that they are being deliberately prevented from accessing information.

The auditors must be aware that it is in their interest to maintain a good working relationship at all times with client staff at every level to allow for the smooth running of the audit and ensure minimal disruption to the client's day-to-day operations.

professional scepticism

ISA 200 'Overall objectives of the independent auditor and the conduct of an audit in accordance with International Standards on Auditing' defines professional scepticism as 'An attitude that includes a questioning mind, being alert to conditions which may indicate possible misstatement due to error or fraud, and a critical assessment of audit evidence'.

The element of professional scepticism is the need for a 'questioning mind'. What this means is that auditors must not accept anything they are told at 'face value' – they must find evidence to prove that statements made to them are true and must validate the assertions (pages 132-133) which underlie the financial statements. This is not to say that auditors should assume in all cases that they are being lied to or that matters are being deliberately falsified, it is simply that uncorroborated statements made by management, however senior, are not sufficiently robust to accept as audit evidence.

interview and listening skills

Listening to what is said involves far more than simply hearing the words. It is important that, during a meeting with client staff auditors pay attention to how things are said and whether particular words are emphasised or repeated.

For example, a statement like, 'we don't usually treat it like that' indicates that there are times when the same type of transaction is dealt with in different ways.

Body language is important but should not be over analysed – people adopt different positions and postures for many reasons. Auditors should pay attention to facial expressions and to whether or not the interviewee appears anxious or worried about a particular financial topic or area being discussed.

Meetings with client's staff should be conducted in a quiet office where the meeting is not likely to be interrupted. Auditors should make sure that enough time is allocated to the meeting so it does not have to be cut short suddenly.

Audit staff who discuss matters with the members of client staff should prepare for the meeting and have a list of questions and topics to discuss. They should all advise the client in advance of the key areas for discussion so that the client can prepare their answers. The meeting is not intended to be combative – the intention is not to interrogate the client but to establish the facts and to gather audit evidence. Auditors must remember to adopt an attitude of professional scepticism when listening to the client's responses to questions and to challenge unclear or vague answers.

effective questioning

The ability to ask the right questions will determine the success or failure of the meeting between the auditor and client staff. It is easy to get the wrong impression or be given the wrong information if questioning is poor.

There are several different forms of questions which can be used – and one which should not be used.

open questions

It is generally sensible to start a meeting with open questions. These often start with words like 'what?', 'where?', 'how?' and are designed to encourage the client staff to talk and transfer information.

Examples of open questions are:

- 'What made you decide to capitalise this expenditure?'
- 'Why did you carry those costs forward to next year?'

The auditor will need to follow up the answers they are given to open questions with secondary questions designed to find out specific facts and specific information that they will need as audit evidence. Examples of clarifying questions are:

- 'Can you give me more details?'
- 'Who actually authorised this?'

reflective questions

Reflective questions involve the auditor repeating what someone has said back to him/her. This is another technique the auditor can use to obtain accurate information.

Examples of reflective questions are:

- 'You said you'd been told to do this?'
- 'You said that you hadn't got the information so you made an assumption?'
- 'You said you weren't sure that what you were doing was correct..?'

closed questions

Closed questions generally require a yes/no answer and are intended to confirm something specific. They tend to discourage explanation and should be used primarily for checking facts.

Examples of closed questions are:

- 'Can you confirm the rate of depreciation on computers is 20%'
- 'Did you carry out a full period end inventory count?'

Auditors should use a variety of questioning techniques when dealing with client staff.

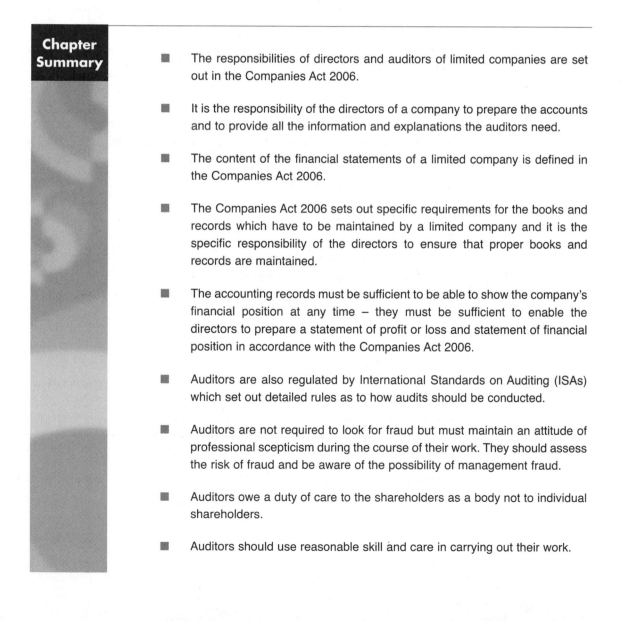

Chapter Summary

- The responsibilities of directors and auditors of limited companies are set out in the Companies Act 2006.

- It is the responsibility of the directors of a company to prepare the accounts and to provide all the information and explanations the auditors need.

- The content of the financial statements of a limited company is defined in the Companies Act 2006.

- The Companies Act 2006 sets out specific requirements for the books and records which have to be maintained by a limited company and it is the specific responsibility of the directors to ensure that proper books and records are maintained.

- The accounting records must be sufficient to be able to show the company's financial position at any time – they must be sufficient to enable the directors to prepare a statement of profit or loss and statement of financial position in accordance with the Companies Act 2006.

- Auditors are also regulated by International Standards on Auditing (ISAs) which set out detailed rules as to how audits should be conducted.

- Auditors are not required to look for fraud but must maintain an attitude of professional scepticism during the course of their work. They should assess the risk of fraud and be aware of the possibility of management fraud.

- Auditors owe a duty of care to the shareholders as a body not to individual shareholders.

- Auditors should use reasonable skill and care in carrying out their work.

■ The Caparo case decided that auditors are not liable to third parties (outsiders) unless the auditors were aware of their interest in the client (eg buying the client) at the time of the audit.

■ Auditing firms may operate as Limited Liability Partnerships (LLPs) which limit the financial liability of partners in the event of a claim by the client.

■ Auditors can limit their liability for negligence by operating as an LLP, through insurance or by making a limitation agreement with the company. Good quality control procedures are seen as the best way to minimise the risk of negligent auditing.

■ Auditors must comply with International Standards on Auditing (ISAs).

■ It is the responsibility of the audit partner to ensure that the audit firm's quality control procedures are being followed.

■ Auditors must ensure that they maintain independence from their client and avoid conflicts of interest.

■ Auditors must treat all the information they discover about their client as confidential except in certain specific circumstances.

■ Auditors should behave in a professional manner at all times and treat clients' staff with courtesy and consideration.

■ Auditors should be alert to the potential threats to their ethical principles and audit firms should have safeguards and procedures to eliminate these threats or reduce them to an acceptable level.

■ When interviewing client staff auditors should use a variety of questioning techniques to obtain information. Statements made by a client's management and staff must be corroborated by other forms of audit evidence.

Key Terms	**Companies Act 2006**	the statute which sets out the responsibilities of directors and auditors and governs the conduct of company affairs
	Registrar of Companies	the Government official with whom annual accounts and other statutory documents must be filed – documents kept by the Registrar (at Companies House) are available to the general public
	International Standards on Auditing (ISAs)	internationally accepted auditing standards which influence the conduct of auditors and audits within the UK; they are issued by the Financial Reporting Council (FRC)
	auditing case law	court decisions and judgements relating to auditing which establish rulings for the conduct of auditors and audits
	duty of care	an obligation on auditors to act with reasonable skill and judgement in all circumstances; where there is a direct relationship the auditors owe more than a general duty and must act specifically in the best interest of their client
	ethical framework	a set of principles, set out in Auditing Standards, which define the skills an auditor should have and the standard of behaviour expected of them in dealing with clients and their financial affairs
	confidentiality	the principle that auditors must not reveal any information that they have learned about a client to unauthorised third parties except in exceptional circumstances
	integrity	honesty, truthfulness and fair dealing with every party involved in an assignment
	Financial Reporting Council (FRC)	the body which regulates accounting and auditing in the UK and is responsible for issuing International Standards on Auditing through its Codes & Standards Committee
	Limited Liability Partnership (LLP)	a partnership that is set up to limit the liability of the partners

Limited Liability Agreement (LLA) — an agreement between the auditors and the client that sets a maximum amount of compensation the client can claim for negligence

Quality Control Procedures — procedures that are put in place to ensure that the audit firm and its staff comply with the auditing standards and legal requirements

'hot reviews' — reviews of audit work carried out by an audit partner not connected with the audit whilst the audit is in progress

'cold reviews' — reviews of completed audits to ensure firm's quality control procedures have been followed

'tone at the top' — the attitude and approach of senior management towards ethical issues in the organisation

corporate governance — the systems and procedures which control the actions and composition of boards of directors and their sub-committees. In the UK this is embodied in the UK Corporate Governance Code which is mandatory for all listed companies

Activities

2.1   Which of the following statements are not correct, and why?

(a)   Auditors can be sued by a client if the client has suffered a loss.

(b)   Auditors owe a duty of care to all the shareholders collectively.

(c)   The Caparo decision means that auditors cannot be sued by third parties.

(d)   Directors have to ensure that their company keeps proper books and records.

(e)   If auditors work for a client who has been money laundering they must tell the authorities.

(f)   Auditors can own shares in client companies.

(g)   If a firm of auditors receives a bottle of whisky from a client during the festive season, they must return it.

2.2   Decide which is the most appropriate response in connection with auditors' liability to third parties

Bloater plc has made a bid to take over Tiddler Limited. During the investigation into Tiddler the Financial Director of Bloater had a meeting with the auditors of Tiddler who are called Tickett & Run. During that meeting the audit partner confirmed that Tickett & Run stood by their Auditors' Report and that, as far as he was aware, the financial statements of Tiddler were free of any material error or misstatement.

After the takeover of Tiddler by Bloater, Bloater's accountants discovered that the actual value of work in progress was significantly different from that shown by the accounts so Bloater appears to have overpaid by quite a considerable amount.

The Financial Director of Bloater wants to be compensated for having overpaid for the assets of Tiddler and contacts the company's lawyers with a view to suing Tickett & Run for negligence.

What advice do they give him?

(a)	Takeovers are risky and it is a case of caveat emptor – buyer beware – Bloater must find out everything and if they missed something it's their own fault	
(b)	Tickett & Run owe a duty of care to Bloater even though Bloater wasn't their client because of the statements made by the audit partner at the meeting	
(c)	Tickett & Run don't owe a duty of care to Bloater because of the Caparo decision and Bloater would stand no chance in court	
(d)	Tickett & Run don't owe a duty of care to Bloater plc because Bloater is not their client and Tickett & Run are only accountable to the shareholders of Tiddler Ltd	

2.3 To which of the following stakeholders do the auditors of Tesco plc have a legal responsibility?

(a) The bank	
(b) The employees	
(c) HM Revenue & Customs	
(d) People intending to buy shares in the company	
(e) A supplier of goods to Tesco plc	
(f) The shareholders	
(g) The government of the United Kingdom	
(h) The council of the Stock Exchange	

2.4 State whether the following are true or false in relation to the regulation of auditors.

	True	False
(a) One of the objectives of the Financial Reporting Council is to monitor the standard of an auditor's work in the UK		
(b) One of the roles of the IAASB is to improve public confidence in the auditing process		

2.5 Which of the following statements are true? If they are false, give reasons for your decision.

	True	False
Auditors perform their work objectively and with integrity. Integrity means truthfulness and openness		
The fact that the senior partner of Tickett & Wrunne's brother in law is the sales director of Floggit Ltd would not prevent them being appointed auditors		
The audit manager on the audit of Megablast Ltd has been left some shares by his auntie. He must sell them as soon as possible		
Auditors have a duty of confidentiality to their client which can only be breached with the client's permission		

3 Planning the audit assignment

this chapter covers...

In this chapter we look at the way that audits are planned, how auditors assess audit risk and how they set materiality levels. We explain how auditors document their client's financial systems, and how internal controls are identified. Finally we explain how the audit plan is put together.

The chapter covers:

- knowledge of the business
- planning the audit
- the audit process
- assessing audit risk
- materiality
- the Permanent File
- documenting the systems
- internal control
- control activities and procedures
- internal control questionnaires

KNOWLEDGE OF THE BUSINESS

Before beginning the planning process, the auditors should find out as much detailed information as they can about their new client, its management and staff, and the business environment in which it operates.

ISA 315 'Identifying and assessing the risks of material misstatement through understanding the entity and its environment', states:

> *'Obtaining an understanding of the entity and its environment, including the entity's internal control (referred to hereafter as an 'understanding of the entity'), is a continuous, dynamic process of gathering, updating and analysing information throughout the audit. The understanding establishes a frame of reference within which the auditor plans the audit and exercises professional judgment throughout the audit.'*

the business environment

During the course of the relationship with the client, the auditor should constantly gather information about the business environment in which the client operates. This will include:

- information about the client's position and reputation within its industry sector
- the general economic conditions within the industry sector, including the level of competitiveness and political or economic factors
- the possible effect of technological change or environmental factors
- any cyclical or seasonal aspects of the business or any vulnerability to factors such as changes in fashion
- any major legislative or regulatory impacts which might affect the client
- economic conditions such as interest rates or inflation

Information can be gathered from a variety of sources including:

- industry specific publications, trade journals and websites
- previous experience of other clients in the same industry
- discussions with previous auditors
- government publications, statistics, surveys
- financial journals

the business, its management and staff

Auditors cannot begin to carry out any work on verifying the financial statements unless they have a complete understanding of the following:

- the structure of the organisation – its divisions, departments or subsidiaries
- the management structure
- the products and processes
- the financial systems

This type of information can only be successfully obtained by direct contact with the client's management and staff. They are the only real source of the detailed information that will allow the auditors to fully understand the 'who', 'what', 'why', 'where' and 'when' of the client's day-to-day activities.

The auditors should have a clear understanding of:

- the client
- the client's business activities
- the internal and external environments in which the client operates

The auditors will then be in a position to decide what audit work is required to ensure that the correct audit opinion is reached.

PLANNING THE AUDIT ASSIGNMENT

It is very important for auditors to properly plan the audit work to be carried out. Without proper planning the objectives of the audit will not be achieved and the auditor runs the risk of failing to detect a material misstatement. In addition to this, a lack of evidence of proper planning could lend support to a case for professional negligence, which we looked at in Chapter 2.

Poor audit work often arises because:

- there was no planning
- the audit started before the planning process was complete
- the audit was based on a plan which had not been updated for several years
- the auditors did not fully understand the business and how it operated

The key to proper planning is setting planning objectives. The planning objectives for an audit are:

- deciding audit priorities and establishing the most cost-effective means of achieving audit objectives

- ensuring audit work generates sufficient evidence to support the audit opinion

- ensuring that there is clear direction and control of the day-to-day audit work

- ensuring sufficient attention is devoted to critical aspects of audit work where systems are complex or the audit risk is considered to be high

- ensuring audit work is completed within predetermined time and cost budgets

THE AUDIT PROCESS

We will now examine the way in which an audit process works.

The steps which an auditor will go through, from being asked to take up an appointment to signing the auditor's report, are normally as follows:

find out as much as possible about the potential client before accepting the assignment

↓

carry out detailed investigations and document the client's structure, management, systems and accounting processes

↓

draft a programme of audit work

↓

carry out investigations and receive explanations necessary to support the audit opinion

↓

sign the auditor's report

The separate elements of this process will be dealt with in more detail, step by step, in subsequent chapters in this book.

There is another important factor to consider and that is the **timescale** of this process.

There are deadlines for companies to file accounts with the Registrar of Companies, and there is also a deadline for sending accounts to shareholders.

Shareholders must receive a copy of the final audited accounts not less than 21 days before the date of any Annual General Meeting, so once a date for that has been set, the timescale for the work has to be based on that deadline.

In reality, most companies will want to finalise their accounts within a few months of the year end, so in most cases final audits are carried out then. The Case Study that follows illustrates the way in which these timescales work.

Case Study

TIMPANI LTD: TIMESCALE OF THE AUDIT

situation

Auditors Crash & Co have been approached to be the first auditors of Timpani Ltd and have accepted. The financial year end is 31 December and they have been told that the AGM will be held on 21 April.

It is now early September and the audit has to be completed in time to send the accounts to the shareholders.

required

You are the audit manager and have been told to draw up an outline plan of how the audit assignment will be arranged. This will form the basis of detailed planning later.

solution

Your approach is to identify the key tasks and decide how much time will be needed to carry out each one.

You know that the accounts have to be sent to the shareholders 21 days before the date of the AGM and so your real deadline is 31 March.

The duration of each task is based on your estimate of how much work there is to be done and how long you think it will take based on your experience.

As this is the first audit Timpani Ltd has had, the tasks may take more or less time and the plan should allow for this.

You draw up a basic plan which is shown on the next page.

This plan depends upon Timpani's accounts staff having the accounts and supporting schedules ready on time. This is why preliminary discussions with their staff are important so that everybody knows what they have to do, and by what date.

Task	Duration	Date
Visit Timpani for an introductory meeting to explain the role of the auditor and the auditing process. Also to discuss what will be expected of Timpani in terms of preparing accounts and making information available to the auditors	1 day	Immediate
Planning visit by audit team to document Timpani's accounting system	1 week	late September
Plan a programme of audit work and meet with Timpani's staff to agree timings	1 day	by early October
First audit visit	1 week	early November
Year end work – eg inventory count etc	1 day	31 December
Final audit visit	2 weeks	late February
Review financial statements by auditors and discussion with management	1 day	mid March
Sign auditor's report	1 day	by 31 March

We have already identified that during the planning process the auditors must gain a good understanding of the client's business and must consider the following factors:

- the environment in which the company operates, ie its market, its competitors, the way it is financed, the quality of its management, its current financial position etc and

- the company's internal processes together with the internal controls in its accounting systems.

These factors will directly affect the possibility of a misstatement or fraud in the financial statements. For example, weak or ineffective controls could allow errors to slip through undetected.

The auditors must evaluate the company and its systems and decide whether there is a possibility that a serious misstatement could go undetected. This will directly affect the auditors' decision as to the level of audit risk which we will now consider in the next section.

ASSESSING AUDIT RISK

The correct assessment of audit risk is vital, and is probably one of the most important aspects of audit that you have to study.

The whole approach that the auditors take to their audit work is based on how they assess the level of risk that their audit client represents. Basically, if the auditors think that the client represents a high level of risk they will need to carry out much more detailed audit work than if they assess it as being low risk.

We will now look at what we mean by risk in the context of auditing.

what is audit risk?

Audit risk is the risk that after carrying out all the audit work the auditors give an incorrect opinion of the client's financial statements.

The auditors may certify that the financial statements give a true and fair view when they do not. In other words the financial statements contain a significant error or misstatement which the auditors have failed to detect.

audit risk and fraud

One thing that must be stressed is that audit risk has nothing directly to do with fraud. It is not the auditors' job to set out to detect fraud. As we have seen, they are not 'bloodhounds' but 'watchdogs'. Therefore, when auditors are assessing risk they are not assessing the risk that they might fail to detect a fraud.

Note, however, that **ISA 240 'The Auditors' responsibilities relating to fraud in an audit of financial statements'** requires auditors to approach any audit assignment with a degree of professional scepticism and says that they must bear the possibility of fraud in mind when planning audit work. This means that auditors should identify areas where the company's assets are at greatest risk or where its controls are weakest.

risk assessment

ISA 315 'Identifying and assessing risks of material misstatement through understanding the entity and its environment' requires auditors to identify and document areas of significant audit risk where they consider there could be a material misstatement, for example:

■ in the financial statements as a whole

■ for individual disclosures within the financial statements

Auditors have to understand and identify risk arising both out of the company's operations and from its systems of internal control by carrying out a **risk assessment**.

This is done by a combination of:

■ analytical review procedures, ie identifying inconsistencies in the figures being audited (see Chapter 4)

■ discussions with management and other relevant people in the company

■ observation and inspection of the company's procedures and controls

A quick planning meeting with the financial director is not sufficient!

When the risks have been identified, the auditors have to design audit procedures so that these risks are reduced to an acceptable level. Auditors also have to identify whether there are risks which are so great that they deserve special audit consideration, ie so significant that normal audit testing processes will not be sufficient to validate the disclosures in the financial statements.

Auditors must fully document all the steps in their risk assessment.

One important point which ISA 315 stresses is that the risk assessment must be communicated and discussed with the whole audit team so that everyone on the assignment is aware of potential areas of risk.

categories of risk

Auditors will **measure** the levels of audit risk so that they can estimate how likely it is that they will give a wrong audit opinion.

Audit risk is defined in **ISA 200 'Overall objectives of the independent auditor and the conduct of an audit in accordance with International Standards on Auditing'** and comprises two things:

■ the risks of a material misstatement in the financial statements as a whole or in the disclosure of individual transactions and balances

■ detection risk – the risk that the auditor's own procedures will fail to detect a material error or misstatement

We will look at materiality later. For the moment the word 'significant' is a good substitute. Therefore audit risk is concerned with the risk of a significant error or mistake not being detected.

Auditors assess audit risk using their professional judgement; this assessment is a key part of the planning process.

There are two components to the risk of material misstatement:

■ Inherent risk

■ Control risk

We will now look at each of these in turn, and then at detection risk.

inherent risk

Inherent risk is the risk that an item or items in the accounts will contain a material error or misstatement, simply because of the characteristics of the company or the characteristics of the particular item.

The following tables show the key signs of inherent risk that the auditors will look out for and the effect those factors may have.

INHERENT RISK

management & ownership of the business

potential risk areas	the effect
domineering owner or director	may influence the attitude of other directors and senior management towards disclosure in the financial statements or in the operation of the business
relationships between managers	direct relationships (eg in family companies) between managers or directors could reduce the effectiveness of the internal controls
level of management expertise	inexperienced or unqualified management may not appreciate the likelihood of error
expectations of stakeholders	expected levels of dividends by shareholders
	guarantees about profit levels given to lenders when applying for credit

the accounts of the business	
potential risk areas	the effect
complex accounts	complex financial structures involving subsidiary or associated businesses
	companies engaged in complex trade eg foreign currency or share trading, freight forwarding, high tech businesses
items relying on judgement the	this requires objectivity on the part of the client staff making judgements (eg high levels of provisions at the year end)
cash transactions	tracing cash transactions is always more difficult than tracing credit transactions

the business	
potential risk areas	**the effect**
nature of the business	over-dependence on a single customer, product or supplier
	business operating a trade which involves cash or goods which are easy to steal
	products which are out of fashion or obsolete (this can give problems with finished goods inventory valuations)
industry factors	a highly competitive trading environment
	regulatory requirements which result in substantial cost to the business
theft of assets	inventory or other assets which could be easily stolen and converted into cash, eg computers, alcohol and cigarettes
	large amounts of cash held in the business
information technology	lack of computer systems documentation
	reliance on a few key experts
	security issues
staffing	constant staff changes
	low staff morale
	little or no training

There are, of course, many more inherent risks unique to specific companies. As auditors it is important to remember that if some aspect of the business appears unusual or poses a significant inherent risk, then it must be considered when assessing the level of audit risk.

If a company has several areas of inherent risk, the auditor is likely to grade the level of inherent risk as high. Read the Case Study that follows.

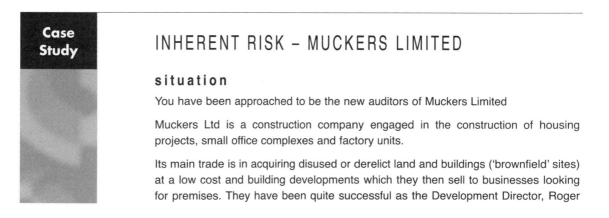

Case Study

INHERENT RISK – MUCKERS LIMITED

situation

You have been approached to be the new auditors of Muckers Limited

Muckers Ltd is a construction company engaged in the construction of housing projects, small office complexes and factory units.

Its main trade is in acquiring disused or derelict land and buildings ('brownfield' sites) at a low cost and building developments which they then sell to businesses looking for premises. They have been quite successful as the Development Director, Roger

Random, has been able to find attractive sites which the company can acquire quite cheaply. They also build new housing developments, mostly on 'greenfield' sites in development areas on the edge of town.

The Development Director, Roger Random, has recently handed in his notice as he is leaving to join a larger construction firm.

Muckers is owned and run by the Mucker family. Cyril Mucker, Chairman and Chief Executive, owns 60% of the shares. The only other director, apart from Roger Random, is Cyril's brother, Hugo Mucker, who is responsible for overseeing the building contracts.

The financial accounting section is run by Paula Poppett (who is not a qualified accountant) and produces a set of management accounts quarterly. There are no budgets or management accounts as Cyril Mucker believes that watching the bank balance is the way to run the business.

The company has recently had some difficulty with two of its sites. On the 'brownfield' site inspectors have discovered contamination from an old asbestos factory and have forbidden any further development until it is decontaminated by specialist contractors. Muckers will have to pay for this. On a 'greenfield' housing project Muckers built twelve houses but have only sold two, as there are rumours that the local authority have decided to put in plans to central government for a dual carriageway bypass next to the new development.

The company employs a large number of temporary casual staff who are paid weekly in cash.

required

Before you take on this client what would be your assessment of inherent risk?

solution

The inherent risk involved in this client is high for a number of reasons, including:

- The company is under the control of a very small group of shareholders all of whom are related. One of them, Cyril Mucker, is a major shareholder.

- Cyril is also the chairman and chief executive, so this makes him a dominant force in the company.

- There is a very weak finance function, with no representative at director level. It seems unlikely that Paula Poppett could stand up to Cyril Mucker if there was any dispute about the figures.

- There is no proper management accounting system or budgeting.

- They have recently lost a key employee, Roger Random, who was responsible for much of the company's success in the past.

- They have problems with two of their building developments. It is not known what the financial effect might be, but it is likely to be substantial. The business might then come under financial pressure.

- The business trades in a highly-regulated environment, particularly with regard to planning constraints, Health & Safety and environmental rules about disposal of materials. This requires constant monitoring to ensure that the company complies with all the appropriate statutory regulations.
- A large number of staff are paid in cash, which results in a higher risk of theft.

control risk

Control risk – the second element of audit risk – is the risk that the internal controls of the company being audited are not operating properly and so do not prevent or detect material errors or misstatements. This could mean:

- a significant error may pass through the system undetected
- transactions may be missed out completely
- transactions may be wrongly recorded

Internal controls are the safeguards that the client has built into the systems and processes to minimise risk or error. This will include procedures such as matching invoices to orders and delivery notes before the invoice is processed and authorising the invoice before it is paid.

A key part of the auditors' preliminary work is to evaluate these internal controls. Later in this chapter we will see how auditors go about doing this.

If the auditors are satisfied that the internal controls are working well, then they may be able to assess the control risk as low.

Significant weaknesses in the internal controls will lead to the auditors assessing the control risk as high. If internal controls are assessed as being weak this will limit the reliance the auditors can place on the accounting systems.

detection risk

Detection risk is the risk that the auditors' own tests will fail to detect material errors or misstatements in the financial statements.

If we think about inherent and control risk, neither of these can be influenced by the auditors. Detection risk is different in that it is the only element of audit risk which is within the auditors' control.

Suppose that, after carrying out their assessment of the inherent risk and control risks, the auditors assess the risk of a material misstatement as high. Because audit risk is a combination of the risk of material misstatement and detection risk, in order to make the level of audit risk acceptable, the auditors will have to do a large amount of audit testing in order to make the detection risk low.

On the other hand, if, after carrying out their risk assessment, the auditors judge inherent and control risk to be low, and hence the risk of material misstatement as low, they will be able to reduce their audit work to a more reasonable level, making the detection risk higher, but still acceptable.

numerical scoring of risk

As accountants you are used to attaching numerical values to things, so you may well look at this system of risk assessment and think it is a bit vague. Auditors sometimes use a **numerical scoring system** for each of the categories of risk in order to arrive at an overall estimate. Remember that in every case the evaluation of risk ultimately requires skill and judgement on the part of the auditor which is gained through training, qualification and experience.

Lastly, it is very important to remember that risk must be constantly reviewed during the course of the audit. Factors may come to light during audit testing that will change the level of risk, and this will have an immediate impact on the amount and focus of audit work.

MATERIALITY

The concept of **materiality** is closely linked to the auditor's consideration of the level of audit risk. Remember that part of the process of establishing the level of audit risk requires the auditor to review the risk of a **material** misstatement not being detected either by his/her own procedures or by the client's internal controls.

what do we mean by materiality?

ISA 320 'Materiality in planning and performing an audit' states:

> *'Misstatements, including omissions, are considered to be material if they, individually or in the aggregate, could reasonably be expected to influence the economic decisions of users taken on the basis of the financial statements'*

and

> *'The auditor's determination of materiality is a matter of professional judgment, and is affected by the auditor's perception of the financial information needs of users of the financial statements.'*

Materiality is effectively a measurement of how important something is within the financial statements. ISA 320 states that something will be considered to be material if leaving it out of the financial statements or getting it wrong would give the reader/user a misleading view of the state of the company's affairs.

There are three key points to understand about materiality before we look at it in detail:

■ the auditors will use their professional judgement to decide what is material

■ it cannot be defined as one specific value

■ the auditors' decision about whether an error is material depends on how it fits in the context of the financial statements as a whole

misstatements

Before we look at materiality in detail there is another auditing standard which we must consider when reviewing materiality, and that is **ISA 450 'Evaluation of misstatements identified during the audit'**.

ISA 450 defines misstatement as:

> *'the difference between the amount, classification, presentation, or disclosure of a reported financial statement item and the amount, classification, presentation, or disclosure that is required for the item to be in accordance with the applicable financial reporting framework. Misstatements can arise from error or fraud.'*

In other words a misstatement is the difference between:

■ the size of a figure as shown in the financial statements or how it has been disclosed or presented

and

■ the size it should be if it had been properly calculated, or what its correct disclosure or presentation should be if the relevant accounting standards had been applied correctly

Misstatements can include:

■ amounts incorrectly taken from the accounting records and included in the financial statements, for example calculation error or simple mistakes in posting figures

■ amounts or statutory disclosures omitted, for example failing to fully disclose directors' emoluments

■ incorrect estimates arising from misinterpreting facts or overlooking something which is relevant to the calculation of the estimate, for example understating an allowance for doubtful debts by ignoring some overdue amounts

■ estimates based on judgements which are clearly excessive or unreasonable in the circumstances. This includes the use of accounting policies which are unreasonable or inappropriate, for example depreciating computer equipment over 10 years where its useful life is considerably less

The auditors must consider all the misstatements, or errors, they detect during the course of their audit work and make a judgement about how they could affect the financial statements. This will involve discussion with the management about amending the financial statements where individual misstatements are material. If the misstatements are individually small this will involve deciding whether, collectively, they are significant enough to affect the presentation of the accounts; lots of small errors can add up to a large one!

performance materiality

During the planning process the auditors will review the information they have obtained about the client's financial results for the period and make a preliminary estimate of materiality for the financial statements as a whole.

They will also look at particular classes of transactions, for example inventories, where these are important figures in the accounts, and make an estimate of what they would consider to be a material misstatement for that class of transaction.

However, during the actual audit work the auditors will set **performance materiality** at a lower level of materiality than they had during the planning stage, ie smaller items now become material.

ISA 320 defines performance materiality as:

> *'the amount or amounts set by the auditor at less than materiality for the financial statements as a whole to reduce to an appropriately low level the probability that the aggregate of uncorrected and undetected misstatements exceeds materiality for the financial statements as a whole. If applicable, performance materiality also refers to the amount or amounts set by the auditor at less than the materiality level or levels for particular classes of transactions, account balances or disclosures.'*

The intention behind setting this lower level of materiality when the audit work is carried out is to minimise the risk that the sum of amounts that are individually immaterial plus any possible undetected misstatements exceeds the planned materiality limit set before the audit began.

The discovery of a huge error which is obviously significant will result in the auditors asking the management to amend the financial statements. Performance materiality aims to ensure that smaller errors, which on their own would not require the financial statements to be altered, added to an allowance for any misstatements the auditors have not detected, do not collectively add up to something which would also require the financial statements to be altered.

The levels of planned materiality and performance materiality should be constantly reviewed during the audit and revised as appropriate.

Something can be material to the financial statements for **qualitative** or **quantitative** reasons.

qualitative aspects

Qualitative means that an error or omission that the auditors have discovered is material because of the nature of the item, regardless of its financial value. In this case the error or omission is unacceptable and the auditor must highlight this to the client management for adjustment.

Examples of items that are measured for qualitative reasons include:

- a disclosure required by the Companies Act or Accounting Standards which has been omitted completely or partially from the accounts, eg director's emoluments

- an item which is misstated, eg a short-term loan shown as a long-term loan

- an item which might affect the accounts but which has not been included because it cannot be quantified with a reasonable degree of certainty, eg the outcome of a significant court case

It is the responsibility of the auditors to remind the directors of their duty to comply with legislation and with relevant Accounting Standards and to rectify errors and omissions.

quantitative aspects

Whereas 'qualitative' refers to the nature of errors and omissions, **quantitative** refers to quantity, ie to the size (value in £) of any errors found during the audit.

The auditors must take a view as to whether the value of errors found, individually, or taken all together, is sufficiently significant (material) for the auditors to request the management to adjust the financial statements. Remember that, as we saw above, for the purposes of the audit work the level of performance materiality will be lower than the level set at the planning stage.

In order to determine a numerical value for materiality, the auditors will often use percentages of some of the key numbers in the draft financial statements, for example:

- 5% - 10% of pre-tax profits
- 1% of turnover
- 5% of net asset value

Alternatively, they may decide to calculate these figures and then to use a combination of all three. The figures on which the auditors will base their calculation of materiality will depend on the nature of the client being audited.

It is important to understand that these figures are given as examples only and that you should not see them as a definitive guide to setting materiality.

It is also important for materiality levels to be constantly reviewed during the course of the audit where the level of inherent or control risk changes or where errors are found in audit testing.

When, during the audit, the auditors find errors in the accounts, these should be noted on a schedule of errors and misstatements. At the end of the audit all errors and misstatements that have been found should be aggregated and considered together.

The auditors must then assess whether they have a material impact on the financial statements and also whether they affect the truth and fairness of the financial statements.

In most cases the directors will be happy to adjust the financial statements for errors found by the auditors because they are keen for the accounts to be as accurate as possible. However, if the directors refuse to amend the accounts, the auditors will have to consider whether the error or mistake is serious enough that they should highlight it in their final audit report. This issue will be covered in detail in Chapter 7.

Case Study

MATERIALITY: LEMON LTD

situation

You are the audit manager covering the year-end audit of Lemon Ltd. You are reviewing the audit files before sending them to the audit partner for final review. Two specific points have been drawn to your attention by the audit staff.

(a) The draft financial statements currently do not include any reference to the fact that the client's Sales Director owns 15% of Tonic Ltd, a major supplier to Lemon Ltd.

(b) One of the company's major customers has gone into liquidation, owing them £40,000 which is unlikely to be recovered. Profits for the year are £200,000 and receivables are shown in the statement of financial position at £650,000.

Audit materiality on the audit has been set at 10% of the pre-tax profit. However, the client's management say they have not provided for this, as it is not material and if necessary they will write it off next year.

required

What recommendations will you make to the audit partner regarding these two issues?

solution

(a) This is automatically material (for qualitative reasons) and must be disclosed. The director has an interest in a major supplier to the business and the Companies Act requires that this type of information is disclosed in the Financial Statements.

(b) This is not automatically material as there is no requirement on the company to disclose this item simply due to its nature. The auditor must look at the issue in the context of the accounts as a whole. Would failure to amend the accounts for this item mean that the financial statements were misleading to the reader?

In this case the profits would be reduced by 20% to £160,000 and receivables by about 6% to £610,000. Whilst the effect on the statement of financial position may not be considered material the reduction in profit is large. The materiality here is clearly quantitative. The audit partner should therefore encourage the directors of Lemon Ltd to provide for this debt in the Financial Statements for the current year.

THE AUDITORS' PERMANENT FILE

Before the auditors can decide on the nature and volume of audit work they have to carry out, they need to gain a clear understanding of the way in which the client operates. This will include an understanding of the client's business, its management and its financial systems. Much of this information will remain unchanged from one year to the next, and once recorded by the auditor, will require only minimal updating each year.

Information that remains 'permanent' for the business is recorded in the **Permanent Audit File**.

the permanent file

As its name suggests, the permanent file is used to document those aspects of the client's business which are expected to remain more or less unchanged from year to year.

The permanent file should contain sufficient information so that any member of the audit team who has no previous knowledge of the client can pick it up and gain a clear picture of the client company, its ownership, management, activities, and very importantly, its financial systems.

The information included in the permanent file will be obtained largely from the client's management and staff. Before recording any information in the permanent file, the auditors must satisfy themselves that all information to be included is accurate. Consequently, at the planning stage of each annual audit visit, the permanent file must be reviewed to ensure that it continues to be relevant, up-to-date and accurate.

gathering information for the permanent file

Auditors can obtain information about their client by:

■ touring the client's premises and asking questions about what is going on

■ talking to the employees

■ interviewing directors, managers and other key personnel

■ reviewing original documentation such as minutes of meetings, internal reports and management accounts

■ approaching banks and other lenders for details of finance arrangements – always with permission from the client

It is important that, wherever possible, the auditors obtain information from as wide a range of sources as possible and obtain independent evidence to support the information included on the permanent file. Any copies of documents to be included in the file should be taken directly **by the auditors** from the original documents. These copies should then be initialled and dated to evidence that the original of the document has been inspected.

contents of the permanent file

The permanent file should include:

■ a description of the client's business activities

■ details of ownership, including lists of shareholders, if relevant

■ details of group structure, divisions or branches where appropriate

■ management structure including relationships between the client's owners/directors and other senior executives

■ financial structure, including details of loan and overdraft arrangements

■ significant stakeholders other than owners and lenders who might influence business activities, eg a major customer or supplier

■ the auditors' view of the business approach adopted, eg risk-taking and unplanned, or conservative and planned

■ relationships with other auditors or specialists involved in the audit

■ an overall risk assessment

■ an assessment of the control environment

■ the signed engagement letter

■ detailed descriptions of the financial systems

A typical index to a permanent file is shown in the Appendix on page 280.

DOCUMENTING THE CLIENT'S FINANCIAL SYSTEMS

The final point on the list of items included in the permanent file is probably the most important. In order for the auditors to plan their audit work they must have a thorough understanding of the client's financial systems. To that end the auditors must prepare detailed descriptions of these systems.

The main client systems that need to be documented are:
- revenue
- purchases
- wages and salaries
- non-current assets
- inventory
- investments

Documentation of the systems should include as much information as possible relating to:
- all documents involved including where they are kept
- the way in which transactions are verified
- the personnel involved in the various systems and their roles
- levels of responsibility of staff
- reporting schedules
- the books of accounts maintained and where they are located

There are two main methods of documenting the client's systems:
- narrative notes
- standardised checklists
- flowcharts

narrative notes

Compiling a series of narrative notes is the simplest way of recording the client's systems. It is best to record the final version on computer file, as it makes them easier to update. A set of handwritten notes prepared on previous audit visits can be time-consuming to revise and is not recommended.

Auditors must ensure that the notes that they produce describing the client systems contain sufficient detail for the user to gain a good understanding of how the system operates.

standardised checklists

As the name suggests **standardised checklists** are standard documents that can be of use for all clients. These are generally Internal Control Questionnaires (ICQs) and Internal Control Evaluation Questionnaires (ICEQs). We will look at these two types of questionnaires in more detail later in this chapter.

flowcharting

The danger of using complex narrative notes to document a financial system is that they can become extremely detailed and ultimately may become confusing to the reader, who gets 'lost in the detail'.

It is much easier for the reader to have a diagram showing how the financial system operates. With this in mind, auditors will often use flowcharts, together with brief narrative notes, where necessary, to describe and explain the system.

Flowcharts show the systems in picture form with common symbols used to represent particular documents, and their physical movement. Flowcharts can be used to show the flow of information as well as documents.

As with narrative notes, the auditors will review these charts each year and update for changes and developments in the systems.

The basic flowcharting symbols commonly used are shown below.

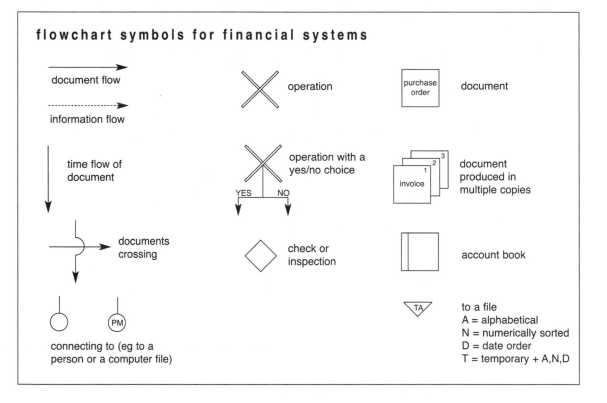

flowchart symbols for financial systems

document flow

information flow

time flow of document

documents crossing

connecting to (eg to a person or a computer file)

operation

operation with a yes/no choice

YES   NO

check or inspection

purchase order — document

invoice — document produced in multiple copies

account book

to a file
A = alphabetical
N = numerically sorted
D = date order
T = temporary + A,N,D

flowcharting rules

There are some key rules for flowcharting:

▓ use standard flowcharting symbols wherever possible

- keep the charts simple – unless the system is very simple do not try to get it all on one sheet; break the chart up into a series of sub-systems and link them together

- document flows should start at the top left of the sheet and finish at the bottom right

- chart all documents from 'cradle to grave' – ie from their origination to their final filing, and do not leave any loose ends

- connecting lines should not cross unless this is unavoidable

A simple flowchart of a goods received and invoice processing system is shown below.

flowchart for receipt of documentation from supplier

narrative	no.	Goods Inward	Purchase ledger
Goods received note (GRN) raised by Goods Inwards Department	1		
Copy filed in Goods Inwards Department	2		
Supplier's invoice given sequential number and checked for arithmetical accuracy.	3		
Invoice matched and attached to GRN	4		
If not all goods received, file in temporary file	5		
Documents checked to see that all items have been checked and initialled.	6		
Passed to purchasing manager for authorisation	7		

You should notice three things when you look at this flowchart:

■ each operation within the flowchart is separately numbered with a brief narrative where required

■ the chart is divided by functional departments, making it easier to see which department is responsible for which function, and where responsibility for checking transactions lies

■ the chart does not attempt to describe the whole system at once, for example it does not deal with payments which would be included in a different chart; this simplifies reporting and makes identification of internal controls easier

advantages and disadvantages of flow charts

The **advantages** of flowcharts are:

■ they can be prepared relatively quickly

■ by linking flowcharts even quite complex systems can be described relatively clearly

■ as standard symbols are used they can be easily followed by anyone familiar with flowcharting procedures

■ flowcharts make any weaknesses or gaps in the system or sub-system being described relatively easy to spot

■ there are a number of computerised flowcharting software packages available

The **disadvantages** of flowcharts are:

■ they have to be redrawn if systems change, even to a limited extent

■ they are fine for standard systems but for non-standard transactions they may become unwieldy and require too many narrative notes

■ they are fine for describing accounting processes where documents are moving through the system, but once the documents stop moving they cannot describe controls – for example, flowcharts can describe procedures for controlling goods inward and goods outward but not the controls over inventory in the stores

walk through tests

When the flowcharts and accompanying narrative descriptions have been drafted, the auditors should test out the systems to ensure that they work as documented. These tests are known as **walk through tests**. To carry out a walk through test you should:

■ choose a small sample of transactions, two or three, from the part of the system being verified

- follow them through the system, using the flowcharts as a guide

- ensure that the flowchart and any notes accurately record the system as it operates in practice

A walk through test should be performed each year before any audit testing begins to ensure that there have been no changes since the preceding audit.

Auditors must document their walk through tests, recording details of the transactions they have chosen to follow through the system, and keep the details on their permanent file.

As soon as the auditors consider that they have a sufficient understanding of the client's systems they can create a programme of audit work to test the internal controls within the system.

The way in which the auditors produce the audit programme will be covered in detail in Chapter 4 but at this point we must ensure that you have clear understanding of what is meant by internal control.

INTERNAL CONTROL

ISA 315 – 'Identifying and assessing the risks of material misstatement through understanding the entity and its environment' defines internal control as:

> '*The process designed, implemented and maintained by those charged with governance, management and other personnel to provide reasonable assurance about the achievement of an entity's objectives with regard to reliability of financial reporting, effectiveness and efficiency of operations, and compliance with applicable laws and regulations. The term 'controls' refers to any aspects of one or more of the components of internal control'.*

The ISA goes on to separate the elements of internal control into five parts:

(a) the control environment

(b) the risk assessment process

(c) the information systems and related procedures relevant to financial reporting

(d) control activities

(e) monitoring of controls.'

We will look at each of these components separately.

As you will appreciate, at some time or another, everybody makes mistakes. A good financial system has within it a series of checks and procedures designed to prevent, detect and correct mistakes or errors that could occur during the processing of transactions. The prime aim of these checks is to ensure that as many errors as possible are picked up so that there are no material errors in the financial statements.

In all but the very smallest companies there will be a number of layers of management, each with their own role in supervising and directing areas of the business and its workforce. The managers will therefore be the key to the effective operation of these controls within the company's systems. They will be the individuals responsible for the checks, authorisations and approvals that will make up the internal controls of the business.

It is important for you to understand that internal controls are not there primarily to detect fraud.

The purpose of internal control is to provide assurance to managers that:

■ the risk of serious error or misstatement in the financial records is minimised

■ the assets of the business are safeguarded

■ all liabilities are identified and properly recorded

■ financial records are kept up-to-date and as accurately as possible

Internal control is made up of two elements:

■ the control environment

■ control activities and procedures

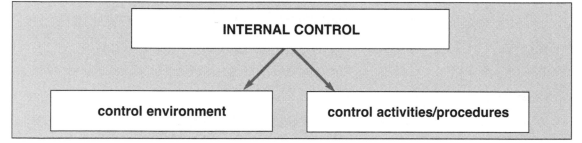

the control environment

ISA 315 – 'Identifying and assessing the risks of material misstatement through understanding the entity and its environment' states:

'The control environment includes the governance and management functions and the attitudes, awareness, and actions of those charged with governance and management concerning the entity's internal control and its importance in the entity. The control environment sets the tone of an organisation, influencing the control consciousness of its people.'

The **control environment** is, fundamentally, the philosophy and operating style of the organisation as set by its directors and senior management, ie the managerial attitude to, and awareness of, internal controls.

In order to assess the internal controls, auditors must to able to understand the culture of an organisation and the way it is reflected in:

■ the attitude of its management and staff, and

■ the effect this attitude has on the organisation's procedures

What makes a good internal control environment?

It should have the following characteristics:

■ clear communication to staff of the ethical values of the organisation reinforcing a commitment to integrity in business dealings. This commitment is seen as an essential element in influencing the effectiveness of the design, administration and monitoring of controls

■ competent, reliable staff who demonstrate a high level of integrity and commitment in their attitude to work

■ a clear, well-understood management structure with defined authority limits

■ involvement by the management in the day-to-day activities of the business

■ operating procedures which are understood and accepted by the employees who have to implement them

It is important that you understand key aspects of evaluating a control environment.

The following Case Study will illustrate these main points.

Case Study

COUNTIT & CO: THE CONTROL ENVIRONMENT

situation

You are an audit manager for Countit & Co, a firm that has recently gained two new audit clients of a similar size.

Your audit staff have completed their preliminary investigations of the two clients. You are reviewing their notes which can be summarised as follows:

Client 1 - Floggers Ltd

Floggers Ltd is an old-fashioned family company which has been in business for over a hundred years and trades as wholesalers of fruit and vegetables.

Its management structure is divided into five layers ranging from supervisor, deputy manager, manager, senior manager and director. The senior managers and directors have been with the company for many years.

Each level of management has clear authority limits set down in the company manual, which also sets out detailed written procedures for every job.

Management at all levels generally has an unforgiving attitude to errors and inefficiencies.

Most of the systems are paper-based, although the accounting ledgers are maintained on a computer and there are rigid systems of authorisation before transactions can be processed.

Staff turnover in clerical posts and at supervisor and deputy manager level is high.

Client 2 - Creatit Ltd

Creatit Ltd is a new company set up six months ago. It trades as a website design business and as an advertising agency.

Creatit Ltd is run by two brothers who manage the business jointly.

Creatit Ltd mostly employs creative people but it does have a small clerical staff to deal with billing and time recording.

The approach to work is casual, spontaneous and rather uncontrolled.

Error detection is not seen as a priority. The management's view is that they will deal with errors and problems when they arise.

Staff are happy and so staff turnover is low.

required

In your review of the control environment for each of these clients, what conclusions would you draw about the risk of error arising in the accounts?

solution

Floggers Ltd

The key points are as follows:

- Floggers has very rigid systems with a high level of internal control where error detection is seen as a priority and mistakes are not tolerated
- the senior management of Floggers is separated from the day-to-day activities of the business by several layers of administrative hierarchy
- Floggers has a high level of staff turnover which may indicate that staff have a low level of commitment to the company
- following on from the point above – there is a higher risk that frequent mistakes could be made by new, untrained staff
- there may be a temptation for staff to hide mistakes because of the attitude of the management
- Floggers management may take a negative approach to the audit and see it as an intrusion into their business

Creatit Ltd

The key points are as follows:

- Creatit has a much more 'hands on' approach to management and a more forgiving attitude to errors; their priority is the product rather than the accounts

- Creatit's financial systems will contain little in the way of formal internal control checks, but managers are much more aware of what is happening on a day-to-day basis as they are actively involved in the company

- the low level of staff turnover indicates that the employees are loyal to the business and have a strong commitment to the company

Your conclusions from an audit point of view are:

1. Providing the systems at Floggers are working correctly there would be very little likelihood of mistakes being made when recording transactions in the financial systems. The risk is more likely to be transactions which are not being recorded at all. Consequently the audit approach would focus on omissions rather than errors.

2. The business that Floggers operates involves processing large numbers of transactions of easily identifiable goods. Their systems have been in existence for years which means that the risk of posting errors can be assessed as low.

3. As far as Creatit is concerned, the financial statements may well contain errors or omissions and the lack of formal procedures might give cause for concern. However, the close involvement of the management and the commitment of the staff to the organisation would indicate that they will take a positive approach to the audit rather than see it as an intrusion.

4. The trade of Creatit is project work which carries a higher level of audit risk.

Your estimate is that the control environment in both companies is generally good, although the focus of your audit work in each business will differ.

CONTROL ACTIVITIES AND PROCEDURES

ISA 315 'Identifying and assessing the risks of material misstatement through understanding the entity and its environment' states:

'Control activities are the policies and procedures that help to ensure management directives are carried out. Control activities, whether within IT or manual systems, have various objectives and are applied at various organisational and functional levels'.

These are the detailed policies and procedures which are designed to:

- minimise the possibility of mistakes or fraud

- detect errors within the accounting system

When documenting the systems of internal control, the auditors will need to highlight these control activities as they become apparent. It is important to remember that, in order for these control activities to operate effectively, there must also be a good internal control environment.

In practice, if the management and staff of the client company do not have a positive attitude towards the control environment, they will not be carrying out the relevant internal checks effectively, even if good control procedures are in place. This will lead to an increased risk of error or fraud.

forms of internal control

The internal controls that are present in the client's systems will take a number of different forms.

Examples are shown in the table below.

FORMS OF INTERNAL CONTROL	what they involve
Organisational controls	Defined management structure Clear responsibilities for supervision Authority limits for expenditure Written procedures
Segregation of duties	The involvement of a number of different people or departments in recording a transaction to minimise the risk of error or fraud
Physical controls	Restricting access to information or assets
Authorisation and approval of documents	Fixed levels of authority to authorise specific transactions or sign cheques to specified levels Documented procedures Evidence of authorisation
Competency and reliability of staff	Staff training based on identified training need Clear Human Resources policies about recruitment and retention of staff
Arithmetical and accounting checks	Month-end routines to balance and reconcile accounts Checks of calculations on documents generated and received

Internal controls can be described as being:

1 **Preventative:** most internal controls are preventative (ie they are designed to prevent an error from occurring or fraud taking place). Thus all the controls in the table shown above are preventative **except** the arithmetical and accounting checks which are

2 **Detective:** detective control activities identify unusual occurrences or events after they have taken place, ie they are designed to detect errors. The most obvious detective control activities are reconciliations, balancing of accounts and ratio analysis.

examples of control activities and procedures

Examples of specific control activities and procedures that relate to the forms of internal control listed above are set out in the table below.

INTERNAL CONTROL	CONTROL ACTIVITIES AND PROCEDURES
Organisational controls	Company Procedures Manual Company registered under a quality standard eg ISO 9001 with documented procedures Internal auditors operating as part of the internal control environment
Segregation of duties	Staff responsible for sales invoices are not responsible for recording cash received Staff responsible for purchase ordering are not responsible for checking delivery notes or purchase invoice processing
Physical controls	Limiting access to computer applications and processes Menus on computers limiting areas to which operators have access Password controls Regular physical verification of non-current assets by managers Restricted access to ownership documents eg title deeds, vehicle log books
Authorisation & approval of documents	Authorisation of orders Approval of invoices for payment Matching invoices to delivery notes and original orders Two signatures on cheques
Competency and reliability of staff	Regular staff training Encouraging staff to achieve professional qualifications Clear guidelines for recruitment of staff Staff appraisal and review systems
Arithmetical and accounting checks	Checking calculations on invoices Bank reconciliations Reconciliation of suppliers' statements with purchase ledger Maintaining control accounts Monthly trial balance Comparison of financial records with actual counts of inventory and cash

monitoring of controls

ISA 315 'Identifying and assessing the risks of material misstatement through understanding the entity and its environment' states:

'The auditor shall obtain an understanding of the major activities that the entity uses to monitor internal control over financial reporting, including those related to those control activities relevant to the audit, and how the entity initiates remedial actions to deficiencies in its controls.'

Organisations are required, as part of good internal control systems, to monitor the effectiveness of their systems on an ongoing basis. Auditors are required to review the effectiveness of these monitoring procedures. Examples of monitoring procedures which organisations can use are:

■ Internal audit procedures – testing of the systems by auditors employed by the organisation

■ Computer programs built into IT systems that continuously monitor the systems – we look at these further in Chapter 5

■ Period end reconciliations and supervision of control activities

■ Analytical procedures to identify areas of unusual activity or inconsistencies – see Chapter 4

■ Self-assessment by management of the effectiveness of the organisation's oversight and of the control environment

INTERNAL CONTROL QUESTIONNAIRES

As we have seen, auditors have to identify the internal checks operating within the financial system and test them to ensure that they are operating effectively. One technique is to use an **Internal Control Questionnaire (ICQ)**. This consists of a series of questions drawn up by the auditors and designed to identify all internal checks present in each department's systems. The example below assesses the purchasing system of a client company.

INTERNAL CONTROL QUESTIONNAIRE

Client name Bobupandown Ltd   **prepared by**   JT   **date** 28/09/-1

period to   31 March 20-1   **reviewed by**   DB   **date** 12/10/-1

Purchases System _Purchase Ordering_

Process	Yes	No	Comments
1 Are all purchases made as a result of written orders?	✔		
2 Are all orders sequentially numbered?	✔		
3 Are all numbers accounted for?		✔	Spoiled orders destroyed
4 Do all orders have to be authorised by a senior manager?	✔		MD, Purchasing Manager
5 Are orders only sent to approved suppliers?	✔		
6 If there is no approved supplier, Is the procedure for approving a new supplier carried out before the order is placed?	✔		Only recognised suppliers used
7 Do all purchase orders show: quantities prices terms initials of authoriser date	 ✔ ✔ ✔ ✔ ✔		
8 Is there a limit to individual order values?	✔		MD- no limit, Purchasing Manager £50,000
9 Are copies of the purchase order sent to Purchase ledger Stores	 ✔ ✔		
10 Are purchase orders matched to invoices?	✔		
11 Are all orders retained in the Purchasing Department?	✔		

standardised questionnaires and checklists

As we have seen, the use of Internal Control Questionnaires can assist the auditor to document the client's system and help produce the program of audit work to test identified controls.

Most audit firms have developed their own standardised ICQ. Additionally, audit firms will have other standard checklists which auditors will use to:

- document their audit work

- ensure all audit tests are documented and reviewed

- carry out final checks to ensure they comply with the necessary disclosures

The use of standardised questionnaires and checklists has advantages and disadvantages as shown by the table below:

USE OF STANDARDISED CHECKLISTS	
Advantages	**Disadvantages**
Well designed checklists can ensure all relevant points are considered by the audit team.	There is no 'one size fits all' so checklists may have to be amended to suit different audit clients. If this is not done properly key points can be missed.
Checklists can document the work carried out and be used as an aid to the audit supervision.	Checklists inhibit creative thinking by staff on an audit. This can lead to a 'tick the box' mentality where it becomes important to tick off the checklist rather than follow up any unusual answers that are given.
Checklists help improve the quality of audit work by eliminating doubt about whether audit work has been completed.	Checklists must be part of good quality control procedures. On their own they simply record audit work done but do not guarantee the quality of that audit work.
Checklists save time and money by eliminating unnecessary work.	

Most audit firms use checklists to document some of their audit work. Checklists are a useful and worthwhile part of an audit firm's quality control process and do provide valuable evidence that audit work has been carried out. However, the auditors must not rely too heavily on these checklists so that they miss odd or unusual transactions which might indicate a material error or misstatement.

LIMITATIONS ON INTERNAL CONTROLS

No system within a business, however well designed, is foolproof. Internal controls can fail through a combination of factors such as:

- **poor judgement** – decisions can be made by individuals, possibly under pressure, which result in a control being bypassed or ignored to ensure work gets done

- **breakdown** – where humans are involved they will make mistakes, computer systems will sometimes crash or fail or can be too complex to be easily understood, employees may misunderstand instructions or procedures, so controls do not operate as they should

Controls may also be bypassed deliberately which is much more serious and may even involve fraud:

- **management override** – senior managers may override procedures and protocols to benefit themselves

- **collusion** – the internal controls of a business may include segregation of duties. However, if members of staff collude they may still be able to circumvent these controls and commit fraud

Management may look for other reasons to limit the operation of internal controls such as:

- there are insufficient staff for proper segregation of duties – in this case there should be a higher level of supervision by senior management

- it is too expensive – however management must consider the cost of the fraud which could take place if the controls are not in place

- employees are trustworthy so controls are not needed – this may be true in the case of most employees but there must be objectivity to ensure that employees are behaving honestly and with integrity. There have been many cases where employees who are considered trustworthy have been involved in fraud.

Internal controls are a vital part of any accounting and processing system. They must be set up properly and monitored and supervised – this is a key part of the role of management of the business.

Chapter Summary

- Auditors must obtain sufficient knowledge of the client to be able to understand the nature of the business and its transactions and should make themselves aware of the general environment in which the client operates.

- The auditors are required to assess and document significant areas of audit risk, both at the level of the financial statements and also at the individual item disclosure level.

- Auditors have to evaluate the risks involved in undertaking the audit. These consist of the risk of a material misstatement which is divided into:
  - inherent risk, which is based on the client's activities, operations, and management
  - control risk, based on the ability of the internal controls of the financial system to detect and correct errors or misstatements, and
  - the detection risk, which is the risk that an error or misstatement will not be detected by the audit procedures carried out.

- Audit risk is the risk of a material misstatement x detection risk. Detection risk is the risk that the auditors' own procedures will not detect a material error or misstatement.

- The overall audit risk is the probability of auditors giving an incorrect opinion; if the level of audit risk is high, the amount of detailed testing the auditors will carry out will be greater than it would be if the risk were low.

- Auditors set a level of materiality at the start of the audit. Something is considered material if its misstatement or omission from the financial statements would give the users a misleading view of the company's financial position.

- The auditors document the client's system using a combination of methods including narrative notes, flowcharts and internal control questionnaires. Auditors can confirm their system documentation using walk through tests.

- The auditors must decide on the level of materiality or significance for the financial statements as a whole and at the transaction level. They will then set a level of performance materiality lower than this to take account of both detected and undetected errors.

- General client documentation will be retained on the permanent file and reviewed annually.

■ Auditors must evaluate their clients' internal control by examining the control environment and control procedures including the client's procedures for monitoring their effectiveness.

■ The control environment is the overall attitude of the organisation towards control procedures and activities including the audit.

■ Control procedures are designed to minimise the possibility of errors or misstatements and to safeguard the assets of the business.

■ Control procedures and activities should include the segregation of duties, limiting access to information, authorisation of transactions, checking and reconciliations.

■ Internal controls can fail because of errors, mistakes, or deliberate fraudulent action.

Key Terms

permanent file	ongoing information about the client which will be used for successive audits; it includes a copy of the engagement letter and provides a clear picture of the client company, its ownership, management, activities, and its financial systems
audit risk	the risk that an auditor might give an inappropriate opinion on the financial statements – the higher the risk the greater the investigative work that will have to be carried out
materiality	the level of significance or importance of a matter detected by the auditors in relation to the accounts as a whole
performance materiality	a lower level of materiality set by the auditors for the duration of their audit work which will include errors which have been detected and an allowance for possible undetected errors
risk assessment	a documented process by which auditors assess the likelihood of a material misstatement in the accounts going undetected

inherent risk	the risk that the accounts will contain a material error or misstatement because of the nature of the client's business, activities, operations and management
control risk	the risk that the client's internal controls will fail to detect errors or misstatements
detection risk	the risk that audit procedures will fail to detect errors or misstatements
flowcharts	a system of documenting financial procedures using standardised symbols to create a diagram of the system
walk through test	a test involving a small number of transactions which an auditor follows through the system to confirm that the systems notes and flowcharts are a true representation of what actually happens
internal controls	the policies, procedures, attitudes and internal checks which together combine to ensure that the likelihood of significant error or material misstatement is minimised
control environment	the overall context within which internal controls and internal checks operate, founded on management attitude and awareness of internal controls
control procedures	detailed procedures operating within the control environment which minimise the risk of an error or misstatement going undetected
internal control questionnaire (ICQ)	a series of questions which auditors use to identify the internal checks operating in various parts of the client's financial system
collusion	two or more members of staff act together to circumvent internal controls

Activities

3.1 A trainee auditor has been asked to prepare a briefing for clients as to how an audit assignment is planned. Among other things the briefing contained the following statements:

(a) Performance materiality is set for the actual audit work and is lower than the overall materiality level.

(b) Materiality is measured by size. If errors are not very large the financial statements do not need to be adjusted.

(c) Control procedures are what the auditor relies on. If these exist the auditor can sign the report without worrying about the financial statements being wrong.

(d) Walk through tests are there to support flowcharts. If these tests are satisfactory, the auditor can feel confident that the control procedures are working satisfactorily.

(e) Audit risk is the risk of being sued.

(f) Auditors need to find out all about their clients so they can make a decision about the level of inherent risk.

(g) Segregation of duties is an important part of the control environment.

Which of these statements are incorrect, and why?

3.2 When planning their audit the auditors must consider audit risk and the probability of a material error or misstatement not being detected by the company's procedures.

Select whether the following factors are likely to increase/reduce or have no effect on audit risk.

		Increase	Reduce	No effect
(a)	A new computer system was installed during the accounting period			
(b)	The company has been closing its shops and concentrating on Internet trading			
(c)	A new qualified financial director has been appointed to replace the previously unqualified one			
(d)	The company has yet to respond to the points contained in the letter of weakness (management letter) from the previous year's audit			
(e)	The company has appointed two non-executive directors			

3.3 External auditors use a variety of methods for documenting systems of control, including flowcharts and internal control questionnaires (ICQs).

For each of the following situations decide whether it would be best to use a flowchart or an Internal Control Questionnaire.

	Flowchart	Internal Control Questionnaire
(a) Recording a client's system for the permanent audit file		
(b) Discovering the controls within the purchases system		
(c) Designing audit procedures to test internal controls		

3.4 The management is responsible for maintaining the internal control environment in order to minimise the probability of a material error or misstatement going undetected.

In each of the following circumstances state whether the external auditor is likely to place reliance or no reliance on the internal controls:

	Reliance	No reliance
(a) The organisation is a small company with a domineering owner who is also the managing director.		
(b) The company trades through a network of branches all of which have separate autonomous management. There is no centralised accounting system and accounting is based on returns from branches.		
(c) The company has recently dismissed its financial director following an alleged fraud. An internal review decided that she alone was to blame so promoted the company accountant to finance director and the assistant accountant was also promoted upwards. A new unqualified accounts assistant has been appointed.		

3.5 Accounting systems have both control objectives and control procedures. Procedures are designed to reduce the risk that control objectives are not met.

For each of the items below select whether they are a control objective, a risk or a control procedure.

	Control objective	Risk	Control procedure
(a) Employees are paid for work not done			
(b) All purchase orders in excess of £1000 have to be authorised			
(c) Bank reconciliations are prepared monthly			
(d) Purchase ledger balances are reconciled to supplier statements			
(e) Only goods and services that have been ordered are accepted			

4 Audit testing

this chapter covers...

This chapter explains how auditors plan and carry out detailed testing of the client's financial systems. It describes how auditors record their work in their working papers and how they deal with the client staff on a day-to-day basis.

This chapter covers:

- *substance over form*
- *creating the audit plan*
- *drawing up the audit programme*
- *audit testing*
- *sampling – selecting transactions to test*
- *substantive testing*
- *analytical review procedures*
- *audit working papers – documenting the evidence gathered*
- *working with client staff – maintaining a good relationship*

AUDIT TESTING AS PART OF THE AUDIT PROCESS

We saw, in Chapter 3, how the auditors:

■ document the client's systems

■ identify the internal controls

■ perform walk through tests to ensure those controls really do exist and are working in the way in which they have been documented by the auditors

In this chapter we will examine how this information is used by the auditors to design tests to determine how effectively the client's internal controls are operating.

The identification of controls in the client's systems and the testing of them is a key area of your studies. You may be tested on your knowledge of planning procedures and sampling, which we are now going to cover in more detail.

We will first explain what is known as 'substance over form'.

SUBSTANCE OVER FORM

Before we examine the processes of how auditors plan an audit and carry out tests on the client's financial systems you need to understand one of the fundamental principles of auditors' work.

Auditors are not employed merely to check that the financial statements agree with the books and that everything adds up and is neatly reconciled.

A key part of the auditors' role is to gather enough evidence to satisfy themselves that a transaction or a balance in the client's accounts really is what the financial statements say it is.

This is what is known by auditors as **substance over form**.

For example, the auditors need to gather sufficient evidence to prove that:

■ the assets shown on the statement of financial position exist, are described correctly and are worth what the directors state they are worth

■ all liabilities have been fully quantified, are correctly described and are included in the financial statements

■ any estimates are based on reasonable assumptions and are properly disclosed

■ revenue and costs relate to genuine transactions for the accounting period and relate only to that period

In short, auditors are expected to do more than simply accept what they are told by the client. They must gather sufficient evidence so that they can be confident that in their professional opinion what they have been told is a true reflection of what has actually occurred.

The next step in the process of deciding what audit evidence must be gathered is the formulation of the audit plan.

CREATING THE AUDIT PLAN

It is worth reminding ourselves that the purpose of carrying out audit work is so that the auditors can gather **sufficient** and **appropriate** evidence to support their opinion on the truth and fairness of their client's financial statements.

ISA 500 'Audit Evidence' states:

'The sufficiency and appropriateness of audit evidence are interrelated.

'Sufficiency is the measure of the quantity of audit evidence. The quantity of the audit evidence needed is affected by the auditor's assessment of the risks of misstatement (the higher the assessed risks, the more audit evidence is likely to be needed) and also by the quality of such audit evidence (the higher the quality, the less may be required). Obtaining more audit evidence, however, may not compensate for its poor quality.

'Appropriateness is the measure of the quality of audit evidence; that is, its relevance and reliability in providing support for the conclusions on which the auditor's opinion is based. The reliability of evidence is influenced by its source and by its nature and is dependent on the individual circumstances under which it was obtained.'

The two key points that are made by ISA 500 about audit evidence are therefore that it should be:

- sufficient
- appropriate

Put simply:

Sufficient relates to the quantity of evidence – is there enough?

Appropriate relates to the quality of the audit evidence – is it the right type of evidence?

It is important to understand that whilst quality and quantity of evidence are important factors, auditors cannot make up for a lack of good quality evidence by simply gathering large amounts of poor quality evidence.

The production of the audit plan will allow the auditor to decide what constitutes sufficient and appropriate evidence for the particular audit they are doing. They will use the information that they have gained from evaluating the client and the client's systems using the process summarised below.

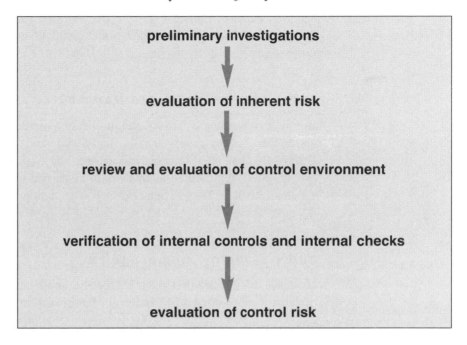

preliminary investigations

evaluation of inherent risk

review and evaluation of control environment

verification of internal controls and internal checks

evaluation of control risk

Auditors must take the information they have gathered and use it to prepare a formal written plan.

AUDIT DOCUMENTATION

ISA 230 'Audit documentation' states:

'The auditor shall prepare audit documentation that is sufficient to enable an experienced auditor, having no previous connection with the audit, to understand:

(a) *The nature, timing and extent of the audit procedures performed to comply with the ISAs and applicable legal and regulatory requirements;*

(b) *The results of the audit procedures performed, and the audit evidence obtained; and*

(c) *Significant matters arising during the audit, the conclusions reached thereon, and significant professional judgments made in reaching those conclusions'*

In Chapter 3 we looked at how auditors gather and document information about the client and its systems and controls. Here we need to look at how the auditors document the actual testing they carry out and the conclusions that they reach about the financial statements as a result of that testing.

The first step in that process is to prepare a written audit plan and then to turn that into a series of specific written instructions, known as an audit programme.

audit plan or audit programme?

Before we go on to describe the audit plan in more detail, you must be clear about the difference between the audit plan and the audit programme. Briefly, the audit plan is the general strategy and scope of the audit. The audit programme is the detailed audit work to be carried out, including details of specific individual tests to be performed. The audit programme is covered in the next section.

audit planning memorandum

Evidence of the detailed planning of the audit is recorded in a written document called the **Audit Planning Memorandum (APM)**.

When the planning has been completed, the Audit Planning Memorandum is usually drafted by the **audit manager**, who is responsible for the day-to-day running of the audit assignment.

The Audit Planning Memorandum is approved by the audit partner who carries overall responsibility for the audit and who will, eventually, sign the auditor's report (covered in Chapter 7).

The Audit Planning Memorandum sets out all the key matters relating to the audit for the year. This will include administrative matters such as staffing and timetable and, more importantly, how the audit will be carried out to ensure it meets its planned audit objectives.

The sample Audit Planning Memorandum shown on the next two pages illustrates the main sections included and what they cover.

In addition to the production and approval of the Audit Planning Memorandum, there will normally be an audit planning meeting where all members of the audit team get together before the audit commences to be briefed about the client, the audit plan and the areas of the audit which they will be working on. This is an opportunity for the audit manager to explain any complicated issues in the Audit Planning Memorandum to the audit team.

AUDIT PLANNING MEMORANDUM

Prepared by ....

Date ....

Reviewed by ....

Date ....

1   Changes since previous audit   **Comments/ref**

-   changes to client's business

-   changes to management structure

-   changes to accounting system /personnel

-   external reporting requirements (IASS/legislation etc)

2   Audit planning focus

-   changes to previous year audit programme

-   changes to sample sizes

-   key areas of internal control considered weak

-   key areas of internal control considered strong

-   indicate areas where material errors have been detected in previous periods

-   systems to be flowcharted

-   update permanent file

-   specialist assistance required

-   schedules to be provided by client

-   other services to be provided to client

3   Evaluation of audit risk

Inherent risk   %

Control risk   %

Audit risk (at 95% confidence level)   %

4   Observations

Attendance at client's premises for:

-   inventory counts

-   wages payout

5 **Visit rota**

- branch visits to be undertaken this year

6 **Audit focus**

- areas for particular attention this year

7 **Systems documentation**

- confirmation that the systems documentation is up-to-date

- arrangements for documenting the system

8 **Internal audit**

- reliance to be placed on internal audit

- liaison arrangements

9 **Specific briefing notes**

- particular matters to be dealt with by the audit team

10 **Staffing**

- Partner

- Reviewing partner (if required)

- Manager

- Senior

- Junior

11 **Timetable and budget**

12 **Analytical review**

- Ratios over three years, to include gross and operating profit %, ROCE, inventory holding period, trade receivables collection period, trade payables payment period, current ratio and gearing.

13 **Conclusion**

- derived from analysis and audit points arising

- leading on to audit planning focus (item 2)

an example of an audit planning memorandum (blank)

THE AUDIT PROGRAMME

When the Audit Planning Memorandum has been completed, the audit manager will review the audit programme or, in the case of a new client, prepare an audit programme containing all the audit tests to be performed.

The audit programme contains the detailed instructions for the audit staff regarding the tests which they must carry out.

It should be based on:

- systems weaknesses identified in last year's audit
- appropriate, relevant tests of internal controls
- key areas identified in the planning process that require close attention
- tests to confirm the figures included in the statement of financial position and statement of profit or loss

The audit programme sets the following for each audit area:

- the objectives which the tests are designed to achieve
- details of actual tests to be performed – including the sample sizes

To show you how this is set out in practice, a sample section from an audit programme for Revenue & Trade receivables is shown below.

AUDIT PROGRAMME

Audit area Revenue & Trade receivables	**Prepared by**
Client	**Date**
Period	**Reviewed by**
	Date

Tests of control

Control objectives

- Sales are made to approved, creditworthy customers in accordance with company objectives.
- Customer orders are authorised, controlled and recorded.
- Uncompleted orders are controlled and recorded so as to be fulfilled at the earliest opportunity.
- Goods delivered are controlled and recorded to ensure that invoices are issued for all sales.
- Goods returned and claims by customers are controlled to ensure that claims are valid and credit notes are approved and issued as appropriate.
- Invoices and credit notes are authorised and checked before being entered in the sales ledger.
- Procedures are in place to ensure that overdue debts are pursued and appropriate provisions made in respect of debts where recovery is doubtful.

Tests of control	**Initial & date**
Test new customer procedure to ensure credit checks and references completed	
Test allocation of credit limits	
Check sample of customer orders to ensure they are approved by sales department	
Check sample of delivery notes to ensure goods signed for by customer on receipt	

	Initial & date
Check sample of sales invoices for authorisation by sales department	
Check sample of sales invoices for matching against sales order and delivery note	
Check sample of sales invoices for evidence of arithmetic checks	
Check batching procedure for posting sales invoices to sales ledger	
Confirm all order forms, sales invoices and credit notes are numerically sequenced	
Review selection of customer claims and check authorisation of credit note or refund	
Check selection of credit notes with copy goods returned note	
Check credit notes authorised by sales manager or equivalent	
Check statements are sent to customers monthly	
Confirm aged trade receivables printout produced monthly and confirm evidence of review by sales manager	
Substantive procedures	
Check sample of sales invoices for:	
– arithmetical check	
– match to sales order	
– match to delivery note	
Vouch sample of sales invoices to customer account in sales ledger	
Check numerical sequence of:	
– customer order forms	
– sales invoices	
– credit notes	
Ensure all sequence numbers accounted for and cancelled documents retained on file	
Test batch processing procedures and ensure batch totals agree	
Check sample of authorised credit notes against customer claims	
Review period-end aged trade receivables analysis for possible doubtful debts	
Review subsequent payment or clearance	
Check client's allowance for doubtful debts	

Note:
Each of the tests of control and the substantive tests will be evidenced by working papers in the current audit file.

As you will see in this example of an audit programme, the person who carries out the test will initial and date the audit programme as evidence that every test included in the audit programme has been completed.

In this sample audit programme there are a number of individual sections covering classes of items included in the financial statements. In this chapter we will be concentrating on the types of testing that are carried out on the client's financial systems, covering control (or compliance) testing and substantive testing. In Chapter 5 we will focus on the way in which the auditors test the three main areas of revenue, purchases and payroll transactions. Finally, in Chapter 6, we describe how the auditors test specific items on the statement of financial position.

AUDIT TESTING

In this chapter so far we have covered the planning of the audit and the formalising of the audit plan. We will now examine in detail the various types of testing that are included in the audit programme, starting with the testing of internal controls.

internal controls

In Chapter 3 we examined the function of internal controls within the client's financial systems and established that their role is to ensure that the risk of a material error or omission in the financial statements is minimised.

The auditors will take the effectiveness of these controls into account when assessing the risk of a serious misstatement in the accounts not being picked up by the client.

Part of the audit process is to test and evaluate these controls in order to ensure that:

- they have been **designed** to pick up material misstatements
- they **operate** effectively for the whole accounting period

The type of testing carried out on the controls will depend on how effective the auditors consider the controls in the system to be.

Chapter 3 explained that the auditors use walk through tests and internal control questionnaires (ICQs) to find out how strong the internal controls are. The auditors' assessment of the strength of the internal controls will determine the type of audit approach that they take.

There are two main approaches that the auditor can take when testing internal controls:

■ a **risk based approach** where they rely heavily on the fact that internal controls function effectively

■ a **systems based** approach where controls are tested but are generally not found to be effective, so the auditors consider that they need to carry out a substantial amount of detailed testing

The diagram below shows the process the auditors will go through to decide which of the two approaches to adopt.

The table that follows the diagram summarises this decision making process. Note that where **compliance testing** is referred to, it means testing of the effectiveness of the client's own internal controls. **Substantive testing** is additional testing carried out by the auditors, eg by examining transactions, balances and ratios, to ensure that the accounts are free from errors or misstatements. These types of testing are explained in more detail on the pages that follow.

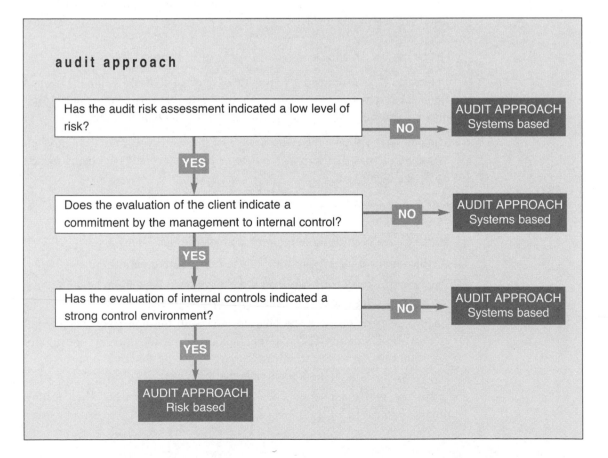

a comparison of the risk based and systems based approaches

Description	Audit approach	Features
Risk based audit approach	Evidencing of controls	Audit tests show that strong controls exist
	Compliance testing	Compliance testing indicates controls functioning effectively
	Substantive testing	Low levels required – substantive testing should be confined to areas where audit risk is considered to be high
Systems-based audit approach	Evidencing of controls	Tests show control weaknesses in the systems
	Compliance testing	Tests indicate a strong possibility of material error or misstatement
	Substantive testing	Medium/High levels required – substantive testing should be used to quantify the size of possible errors and also for areas where audit risk is considered to be high

We referred on the last two pages to compliance testing and substantive testing. We will now describe in detail what we mean by these two terms.

Auditors will use a mixture of compliance testing of controls and substantive testing of transactions and balances in order to provide sufficient reliable evidence to support their conclusions.

COMPLIANCE TESTING

ISA 330 'The auditor's responses to assessed risk' states:

'In designing and performing tests of controls, the auditor shall obtain more persuasive audit evidence the greater the reliance the auditor places on the effectiveness of a control.'

Compliance testing, or testing of controls, will test to assess whether the internal controls have been operating effectively throughout the period. The way in which the auditors do this is through:

- **inspection** – eg looking at sales invoices to ensure that they are authorised for payment
- **re-performance** – 'doing something again', eg preparing a bank reconciliation to ensure that the client has done it properly

■ **observation** – eg watching the client operate the system
■ **sample tests** – eg select a sample of transactions covering the whole accounting period and check whether the controls on this sample have been applied effectively

The Case Study that follows gives an example of how compliance testing operates in practice.

Case Study

SIMPLE SALES LTD: COMPLIANCE TESTING – REVENUE SYSTEM

situation

Simple Sales Ltd is a wholesaler of imported Russian dolls and wooden toys.

The revenue system is as follows:

Sales orders are received from customers by telephone, email or fax. When an order is received the sales department transfer it to a multi-part, pre-numbered order form, which is signed by the member of staff taking the order.

One copy of the order goes to the customer as confirmation, one copy goes to the warehouse for packing/despatch, one copy goes to the accounts office and one copy is retained in the sales office.

Goods are despatched from the warehouse which raises a despatch note; these are also multi-part and pre-numbered. One copy of the despatch note goes with the goods when they are sent to the customer, one copy goes to the sales office, one copy to the accounts office and one copy is retained in the stores.

The sales office invoices the client and sends a copy of the invoice to the accounts office.

Staff in the accounts office:
- check the calculations on the invoice
- match the invoice to the order and the despatch note
- enter the details into the sales day book and from there to the sales ledger
- annotate each invoice to ensure that these checks have been carried out

If the order is only partly completed due to goods being available in inventory, the stores department pin the original order onto a board in the stores with the missing items highlighted. When these are received into inventory they raise a despatch note in the usual way.

required

What compliance tests would the auditors need to carry out in order to establish that internal controls were effective?

solution

The auditors will check the client's internal control systems by performing the following compliance tests:

- Select a sample of sales invoices from throughout the year and agree with the sales order and despatch notes to ensure:
  - quantities and details of goods on the sales invoice agree to what was originally ordered and to what was despatched
  - the sales order has been authorised by a member of the sales staff
  - prices on the order and on the invoice match and agree to the client's official price lists
  - the invoices are arithmetically correct
  - VAT has been calculated and applied correctly
- In addition the auditors should:
  - match the sample of sales invoices to the Sales Day Book and to the customer accounts in the Sales Ledger
  - review the sales invoices either side of each of the sample selected to ensure that there are no gaps in the sequence of numbers

Provided that all these controls are found to be functioning satisfactorily, the auditors will conclude that the revenue system for Simply Sales has operated effectively for the accounting period.

SAMPLING

In the section on compliance testing (see page 97) we referred to the auditors selecting a **sample** of transactions to test. The question is how do the auditors select which items to include in this sample?

ISA 530 'Audit sampling' states:

'The objective of the auditor, when using audit sampling, is to provide a reasonable basis for the auditor to draw conclusions about the population from which the sample is selected.'

It is impossible for the auditors to test all the transactions a company makes, and they are not required to do so. The term used to describe all the items that could be sampled is the population. When considering audit testing, an example of a population is all the sales invoices for the accounting period.

Audit sampling is the application of specific audit procedures to less than 100% of a population of transactions in such a way that each item in the population has an equal chance of being selected. By testing a sample the auditors can draw conclusions about the **population** as a whole.

Sampling is not appropriate when:

- the population is too small for a valid conclusion to be drawn. In this case, it is usually quicker to test the entire population
- the auditors cannot rely on the system or suspect a possible fraud
- all the transactions or balances are material, eg a company that manufactures aeroplanes may only sell 250 per year but each one is sold for several million pounds. In this case all the transactions should be tested

- data has to be fully disclosed in the accounts, eg directors emoluments must be disclosed at the exact figure in the accounts regardless of size. In this case all disclosures must be checked in full
- the population is not homogeneous (all the same), eg all the sales invoices produced by the company are an homogenous population, whereas a mixture of sales invoices and credit notes is not

The next decision facing the auditors is how many items from the 'population' to include in the sample. If a client issues 3,000 sales invoices in the year does the auditor test a sample of ten, 25, 50 or even 100?

Before they can make this decision a number of factors need to be taken into account:

- the number of items in the population from which the sample is selected
- sampling risk – the risk of choosing a misleading sample and reaching the wrong conclusion
- tolerable misstatement – this directly relates to the level of performance materiality set by the auditors (Chapter 3). The level of tolerable misstatement will be the same or lower than the level of performance materiality and is the maximum acceptable misstatement in the sample (in £)
- tolerable rate of deviation – the maximum acceptable level of deviation from the agreed control procedures. For example if the control procedures require purchase orders to be signed (authorised), the auditors will decide what proportion of the sample they would accept without signatures (the tolerable rate of deviation), before the control was deemed to have failed. They would then extrapolate this across the whole population to see what the potential total deviation could be

Another factor is the expected level of risk. We have covered risk in some detail already (see pages 52-58). However, it is worth pointing out that if inherent risk and control risk are considered to be high, the auditors will increase their sample sizes in order to reduce detection risk as much as possible.

We will now look at the factors, other than risk, that affect sample sizes.

factors affecting sample sizes

There are several factors which can affect the size of samples in addition to any statistical calculation of optimum sample size.

Auditors must be aware of the effects of factors such as the outcome of audit risk assessments, the outcome of audit procedures carried out in other areas of the business and significant events such as changes in client personnel or changes to the accounting systems. The table on the next page gives an indication of the main factors influencing sample sizes together with the effect each will have on the size of the sample.

Factor	Effect on sample size (increase/decrease)	Explanation
Improvement in the efficiency of internal controls	Increase	The lower the expected level of errors the larger the required sample size to find any and establish an accurate error rate
An increase in the number of errors the auditor is prepared to accept from the original audit plan	Decrease	The higher the level of errors in the population that the auditor is prepared to accept the smaller the sample size needs to be
An increase in the level of errors found compared with the expected level in the population	Increase	If the number of actual errors detected is more than the number expected in a given population, then the sample size must increase in order to find the actual rate of error in the population
The auditor requires an increased level of assurance that the risk of sampling error is minimised	Increase	If there is an increase in the assurance that the auditor requires that the error rate in the sample is equivalent to the error rate in the population then sample size must increase
An increase in the auditors' estimate of a risk of a material misstatement	Increase	If the risk of material (significant) misstatement increases the audit testing that must be done to quantify the risk or identify the misstatement must increase
An increase in the use of substantive testing elsewhere which has been carried out to validate the same financial statement assertion (Chapter 5)	Decrease	The greater the amount of substantive testing carried out, the smaller the sampling size needs to be
A decrease in the risk that the auditor will wrongly conclude that a material error does not exist when it does	Increase	The greater the level of assurance that the auditors require the larger the sample size needs to be
An increase in the tolerable misstatement the auditor will accept	Decrease	The lower the actual amount of error in the population that the auditor is prepared to accept, the smaller the sample size needs to be
Stratification of the population to focus testing on material items	Decrease	The focus of the audit work is on the higher value items which are more likely to lead to a material error in the financial statements

population

As noted earlier, the **population** in relation to audit is the total number of transactions of a particular type which the client has carried out. For example:

- the total number of purchase invoices processed
- the total number of inventory issues made
- the total number of sales credit notes issued

The sample to be tested should be selected from the population and should be a representative sample of the population as a whole. There are two important points to remember here:

- all the transactions in the population must be of the same type to ensure that the sample chosen has the same characteristics as the rest of the items in the population
- if there has been a major change in the nature of the population during the period – for example, a change during the year from manual invoicing to computerised invoicing – the auditors might be dealing with different populations

This point is illustrated in the Case Study that follows.

Case Study

HILO LTD: SAMPLING METHOD

situation

The auditors of HiLo Ltd are planning the audit testing that they will perform on the revenue system. As part of their testing they need to select a sample of sales invoices.

The year end is 31 December.

HiLo Ltd has always processed the sales invoices manually rather than using a computer accounting package. Each invoice is allocated a sequential number.

However, in August this year, the company installed a new computer system with an integrated accounting package. This has meant that from the end of August all sales invoices have been printed by the computer from information entered on to the sales ledger by sales staff, and invoice numbers have been allocated automatically.

required

What factors will the auditors need to consider when defining the population from which they will select the sample of sales invoices to be tested?

solution

Step 1

The auditors should obtain the first and last invoice numbers for the sales invoices issued during the financial year. This will show the range of the total population of sales invoices. They should also confirm that the number of the first computer generated invoice followed on sequentially from the number of the last manual invoice to be issued.

Step 2

The auditors should ensure that the population consists solely of sales invoices and does not include credit notes, as these should be tested separately.

Step 3

There are two separate populations of sales invoices with different characteristics which will need to be tested differently:

- The first population consists of sales invoices prepared manually by sales staff on a word processor. For these invoices there may be typing and calculation errors as the preparation of the invoices is a separate process from entering the sales information into the customers' accounts in the sales ledger.

- The second population consists of sales invoices produced automatically from information entered into the computerised sales ledger. In this case, entering the sales information onto the system and updating the customers' accounts are automatically linked, so the risk of error is reduced.

Step 4

Separate samples should be taken from each population. The size of the sample to be selected from each population is likely to be different because the risk of errors being found in each sample will vary.

confidence level

When testing a sample the **confidence level** refers to the reliability the auditor places on the sample results being a true reflection of the population as a whole. The greater the confidence level required the larger the sample has to be. A 95% confidence level, is the level generally considered as reasonable. This means the auditor accepts the risk that five out of 100 transactions will not reflect the true characteristics of the population as a whole. This is known as **sampling risk**.

sampling risk

The reason for testing a sample is so that the auditor can draw a conclusion about the population as a whole. **Sampling risk** is the risk that the auditors' conclusion about the whole population, based on the sample, is different from the conclusion they would have reached if they had performed the same test on the whole population.

One possible reason for this happening is if the auditors select a sample which is not truly representative of the population as a whole, even though it has been selected from transactions which are all of the same type.

For example, suppose the auditors decide that they wish to test sales invoices issued in the year by selecting a sample of ten invoices. They then choose five invoices issued in June and five in July because the files containing these invoices are the most convenient to find. Clearly, this will not be a representative sample of sales invoices issued during the year as it does not include any invoices from the other ten months of the year.

The auditors must be sure that a representative sample is selected which reflects, as closely as possible, the entire population from which it has been chosen.

This means that the use of one of the statistical sampling methods detailed below is preferable to methods such as a random selection chosen by the auditor. Statistical sampling eliminates bias, whether conscious or unconscious, and if used properly, forms a sound basis for gathering sufficient, reliable evidence on which to base audit conclusions.

choosing a sample

There are a number of methods which auditors use to select a representative sample and so minimise sampling risk. The main methods are shown in the table below.

Basis of selection	Methodology
random number selection	the auditors select the sample to be tested on a random but organised basis, for example by using random number tables or by computer generated random numbers; if the auditors use this method, each item has an equal chance of being selected
interval sampling	using this method, the auditors select items with a constant interval between each one, for example if there are 200 items in the population and the sample size is to be ten then the auditors would select every twentieth invoice (note also that the first item to be included in the series should be randomly generated). One method of interval sampling commonly used is called value weighted selection (see below)
haphazard selection	this is similar to random selection but may not be based on tables or any other mathematical tool used for selecting the items to test – care has to be taken that the sample is truly haphazard and that the sample is not biased towards the items most easily located

stratified sampling	this is based on dividing the population into strata or layers by size. For example a list of trade receivables balances may be sub-divided into smaller sub-populations by size so that larger balances are separated out from smaller, less material amounts. The layers can represent a range of sizes eg, balances over £100,000, balances between £99,000 – £80,000 and so on. Frequently very large balances form only a small part of the population and are 100 per cent checked. The remaining balances are then sampled

value weighted selection

Value weighted selection (sometimes known as monetary unit sampling) is a form of interval sampling. This is illustrated in the following worked example.

Example

The auditors of a business plan to test a sample of trade receivables balances which they will select using value weighted selection. They must calculate a sampling interval and then apply this to the cumulative total of the balances.

Here is a list of balances:

	Total	Cumulative total	Selected
	£000	*£000*	*£000*
Todd	647	647	
Snodd	286	933	
Bodd	1,749	**2,682**	Yes
Lodd	843	3525	
Codd	3,368	**6,893**	Yes
Hodd	124	7,017	
Fodd	96	**7,113**	Yes
		7,113	

Suppose the auditors wish to select a sample of three balances for testing. The sampling interval will be 7,113/3 = 2,371. The first amount of 2,371 falls within the third balance, that of Bodd. The second (2,371 + 2,371 = 4,742) falls within the second balance, that of Codd and the final item (2,371 + 2,371 + 2,371 = 7,113) falls within the final balance, that of Fodd.

This means that the sample to be tested will be Bodd, Codd and Fodd.

One advantage of this form of interval sampling is that it tends to select higher value items. However, one significant disadvantage is that because of this it fails to identify understatement as it tends towards higher values.

tolerable misstatement

When testing a sample of transactions the auditors will often find misstatements which need to be recorded because they are material or significant. The **tolerable misstatement and tolerable rate of deviation**, as the name suggests, are the maximum errors (in £) in the population as a whole that the auditors are willing to 'tolerate' and still be able to conclude that the objective of the audit test has been met. Because the auditors are testing a sample and not the whole population, they must consider the errors that they have found as being representative for the population as a whole. This process is known as extrapolation. Provided that this error level is below the tolerable error limit that has been set (see above), the auditors can conclude that the test has successfully achieved its objectives.

This 'tolerable' level of errors is directly related to the level of performance materiality that we looked at in Chapter 3.

There are some errors which should not be included in a calculation of tolerable misstatement which might result in an alteration to the accounts.

For example, if the auditors discover that in a test of twenty invoices one invoice has been posted to the wrong purchase ledger account, this will not affect the overall payables figure on the statement of financial position and so does not affect the accuracy of the financial statements.

In this situation, the auditors should still find out why this error has occurred to ensure that it is not a weakness in the system rather than human error.

If the extrapolated error level for the whole population, based on the sample, exceeds the level of performance materiality that has been set for the audit, the auditors will then have to consider the effect of these errors or misstatements on the financial statements as a whole, and whether they are so material to require the financial statements to be adjusted.

Case Study

SAM PULL LTD: INVOICE SAMPLING

The auditors of Sam Pull Ltd are testing a sample of sales invoices.

They select and test a sample of 50 invoices out of a total population of 6,000 and discover calculation errors on those invoices amounting in total to £180.

The objectives of the audit test are to assess the reliability of the controls in the sales ledger processing system and also ensure the accuracy of the sales figure in the financial statements.

required

How should the auditors deal with their findings?

solution

Extrapolating the error from the sample for the population as a whole (ie all the invoices) would be calculated as follows:

Total number of sales invoices

÷   the number of sales invoices in the sample

x   the errors found in the sample

ie   6,000 ÷ 50 x £180 = £21,600

This means if the rate of errors occurring in the population is the same as that for the sample, the total errors would be £21,600.

The auditors must then decide whether this total error is within the tolerable error for the audit, given the level of turnover of the company. A significant error is one which would affect the auditors' opinion as to the truth and fairness of the accounts.

If the error is considered to be significant, the auditors will have to take a view as to whether to extend the sample and test further items to see if this level of error is maintained in the remainder of the population.

As with any error found by the auditors, they may still wish to comment to the client's management about weaknesses in their systems that have allowed these errors to go undetected.

SUBSTANTIVE TESTING

ISA 330 'The auditors' responses to assessed risk' states:

'If the auditor has determined that an assessed risk of material misstatement at the assertion level is a significant risk, the auditor shall perform substantive procedures that are specifically responsive to that risk. When the approach to a significant risk consists only of substantive procedures, those procedures shall include tests of details.'

As we have seen, it is the auditors' role to gather sufficient, reliable evidence to confirm the truth and fairness of the financial situation of the company as shown by the set of financial statements prepared by its management.

One of the ways the auditors do this is by identifying internal controls and carrying out compliance testing of these controls. Here what is being tested is the control not the individual transaction.

The other type of testing that auditors carry out is **substantive testing.**

Substantive testing procedures are designed to support test of controls and to provide sufficient appropriate audit evidence to ensure the accounts are free from material misstatements.

There are two main types of substantive testing:

■ **detailed testing** of transactions and balances

■ **analytical procedures** to test the reasonableness of account balances

ISA 330 requires the auditors to carry out substantive tests on all material account balances, classes of transactions and disclosures in the accounts.

What this means in practice is that:

■ most of the audit work of the statement of financial position will be substantive testing

■ material disclosures in the financial statements eg directors remuneration will have to be tested in detail

■ substantive testing will have to be carried out on any significant, or material, transactions

This may seem strange if the client has an efficient system of internal controls operating within the company. However, balances and transactions must still be tested because:

■ the auditors' assessment of the risks of a material misstatement is based on their judgement and so may not identify all risks

■ there will always be inherent limitations in internal control systems including the risk that management may ignore or override them

detailed testing

Detailed tests take several forms which are summarised in the table opposite.

The auditor will apply a combination of tests to different aspects of the system under review.

They will also ensure that, where necessary, they test transactions in both directions, ie:

■ **forwards** – from the original document to the final entry in the accounting records, eg from the sales invoice to the sales ledger

■ **backwards** – from the entries in the accounting records to the original documents, eg from the wages control account to the timesheet

TYPE OF TEST	DEFINITION	EXAMPLE
Inspection	Physically examining records, documents or assets	Examining non current assets to verify existence (but not necessarily ownership or value) Inspecting documents relating to arrangements with providers of loan finance
Vouching	Checking an entry in the accounting records back to the original document	Vouching an entry in the sales day book with a copy sales invoice Vouching the hours worked recorded on the payroll system back to the original clock cards
Posting	Checking amounts entered in the books of prime entry with the ledger accounts or checking between ledger accounts, to ensure entries are made in the correct account	Sales Day Book entries to Sales Ledger Cash book payments to Nominal Ledger accounts
Inquiry	An independent verification of balances Requests for information from client staff	Independent circularisation of trade receivables Questions such as 'Why is invoice number 32187 not here?'
Computation	Checking the arithmetical accuracy of accounting records	Testing calculations on inventory sheets Testing VAT calculations on invoices
Reconciliation	Reconciling balances in the accounting records with independent evidence	Bank reconciliation Reconciliations between suppliers statements and purchase ledger balances

SIMPLE SALES LTD:
SUBSTANTIVE TESTING – PURCHASES

situation

You are a member of the audit team that is auditing Simply Sales Ltd. You have been allocated responsibility for testing the purchases system.

The objective of the audit testing is to ensure that the procedures for processing purchase invoices are being operated correctly.

required

Following compliance testing of the internal controls of the purchases system, your team has identified a need for substantive testing. What forms of substantive testing might the auditors carry out on the purchases system?

solution

The auditors' tests will take a variety of forms and will use various types of substantive testing in order to gather the evidence needed. These are summarised below.

PURCHASE LEDGER INVOICE PROCESSING	
Test	**Type of test**
For a sample of purchase orders: • Check that the supplier is on the approved supplier list	Inspection
For a sample of Goods Received Notes (GRN's): • Check that details agree with the original order	Inspection
For a sample of purchase invoices: • Check the details agree with the GRN • Check details agree with Purchase Order • Check all calculations • Check VAT computation	Inspection Inspection Arithmetical Arithmetical
For a sample of entries in the purchases day book: • Check with purchase invoice	Vouching
For a sample of entries in the purchases ledger: • Check back to the purchase day book entry	Posting

ANALYTICAL PROCEDURES

The other type of substantive testing involves **analytical procedures**, which analyse and compare financial and other information over time periods in order to detect any inconsistencies in the accounts.

ISA 520 'Analytical procedures' defines them as:

> '...evaluations of financial information through analysis of plausible relationships among both financial and non-financial data. Analytical procedures also encompass such investigation as is necessary of identified fluctuations or relationships that are inconsistent with other relevant information or that differ from expected values by a significant amount.'

The nature and purpose of analytical procedures are then described as follows:

> 'Analytical procedures include the consideration of comparisons of the entity's financial information with, for example:
>
> ■ Comparable information for prior periods.
>
> ■ Anticipated results of the entity, such as budgets or forecasts, or expectations of the auditor, such as an estimation of depreciation.
>
> ■ Similar industry information, such as a comparison of the ratio of sales to accounts receivable with industry averages or with other entities of comparable size in the same industry.
>
> Analytical procedures also include consideration of relationships, for example:
>
> ■ Among elements of financial information that would be expected to conform to a predictable pattern based on the entity's experience, such as gross margin percentages.
>
> ■ Between financial information and relevant non-financial information, such as payroll costs to a number of employees.'

Auditors must also consider the reliability of the data used for analytical procedures. This is affected by the source and nature of the data and is dependent on the circumstances under which it is obtained.

Therefore, the following points are relevant when determining whether data is reliable to use for substantive analytical procedures:

■ the source of the information available; information is generally more reliable when it is obtained from independent sources outside the client company

- the comparability of the information available; general information about the client's industry may need to be adjusted to make it comparable with the client

- the nature and relevance of the information available, ie are comparisons being made to relevant information

- the quality of internal controls and the controls over the preparation of information that are designed to ensure its completeness, accuracy and validity

- the auditors' experience from prior years. If information has, in past years, turned out to be unreliable then this may indicate that similar analysis of the current year may not be reliable

comparison of financial information

The simplest method of performing analytical review is to compare the financial information for the current period to the same information for previous periods. Provided that the client's business has not changed significantly, the auditors would expect the financial information to be consistent from year to year.

In the case of the company below, for example, the financial period being audited is 2010 and the auditors have summarised the following information for further analysis:

Year	20-1 £	20-2 £	20-3 £	20-4 £
Revenue	702,000	744,000	748,000	776,000
Cost of Sales	428,000	447,000	452,000	476,000
Gross Profit	274,000	297,000	296,000	340,000
Closing Inventory	60,100	63,800	65,600	81,200
Trade receivables	86,500	88,100	88,700	93,600
Trade payables	58,500	59,700	56,900	64,200

A study of this table suggests that there is a steady upward trend in the results of the client. However, in order to test the information fully the auditors will perform additional detailed analytical procedures.

You will have come across accounting ratios at various stages in your AAT studies to date. A number of the ratios that you are familiar with can be calculated as part of analytical procedures, including:

Gross profit %   (Gross profit/Revenue x 100)

Operating profit %   (Profit from operations/Revenue x 100)

Trade receivables collection period   (Trade receivables/Revenue x 365)

Trade payables payment period   (Trade payables/Cost of sales x 365)

Inventory holding period   (Inventories/Cost of sales x 365)

In this example the auditors would calculate the following:

	20-1	20-2	20-3	20-4
Gross Profit %	39%	39.9%	39.6%	43.8%
Inventory holding period	51 days	52 days	53 days	62 days
Trade receivables collection period	45 days	43 days	43 days	44 days
Trade payables payment period	50 days	49 days	46 days	49 days

Having performed these more detailed calculations it can be seen that both the gross profit % and the inventory holding period have risen significantly in 2010 whilst all the other ratios have remained reasonably constant.

As part of their analytical procedures the auditors would now investigate the reasons for these increases in the current financial period. From the original data it can be seen that closing inventory has also risen significantly. If for any reason the closing inventory was incorrectly stated and should be lower, this could be the explanation for the increase in gross profit margin and inventory holding period. An overstatement of closing inventory would mean that cost of sales would be lower than it should be, and hence gross profit margin would be higher than it should be.

The same sort of analysis could also be used to compare the results of different branches of a business or to compare information to budgeted figures for the year. However, in all cases, the auditors must investigate any inconsistencies that are discovered.

Analytical procedures can also use other ratios where there are direct relationships – between figures, for example:

■ selling expenses as a percentage of sales revenue

■ direct wages as a percentage of direct costs

The auditors can also calculate expected relationships such as applying the average pay rise for the year to the previous year's total wages and salaries and comparing the result to the current wages and salaries figure.

comparison of non-financial information

Non-financial data can also be used as part of analytical procedures. This analysis can often identify inconsistencies that simple financial calculations will not reveal.

An example of this is the comparison of payroll costs to the number of employees (the non-financial information). A significant increase or decrease in payroll costs over the year could indicate an error or misstatement of the payroll costs. Other examples of the analysis on non-financial data include:

- monthly wastage as a percentage of raw materials quantities for a manufacturing company; a large increase could highlight problems in production or could be as a result of theft

- weekly bed nights in a hotel to establish levels of occupancy from period to period

- miles per gallon for individual vehicles in a transport fleet

analytical procedures – a summary

The analytical procedures that the auditors use will vary from client to client and not all the ratios are appropriate in all situations. However, in all cases the auditors will be looking to:

- investigate any unusual or inconsistent variations in ratios

- obtain explanations and substantiate the variations

- evaluate the results of analytical procedures in relation to other audit evidence

We will examine analytical procedures again in Chapter 7 'Audit completion and audit reporting' when the auditors will use them to assess the overall reasonableness of the financial statements.

AUDIT WORKING PAPERS

It is very important that the auditors are able to demonstrate that sufficient work has been carried out to justify their audit opinion; consequently every step of the audit, from planning to completion, must be thoroughly documented on appropriate **audit working papers.**

ISA 230 'Audit documentation' states:

'Audit documentation that meets the requirements of this ISA and the specific documentation requirements of other relevant ISAs provides:

(a)   Evidence of the auditor's basis for a conclusion about the achievement of the overall objectives of the auditor; and

(b)   Evidence that the audit was planned and performed in accordance with ISAs and applicable legal and regulatory requirements.'

It is important that the auditor documents not only the actual audit work they do but also their objectives and whether or not those objectives have been achieved. This documentation may be hand written or computerised but must include sufficient detail so that an independent third party could:

■ understand the client, its business and the nature of the industry in which it operates

■ understand the audit approach that has been taken

■ understand the audit testing carried out and whether or not the evidence gathered was valid and supported any conclusions the auditors have come to about the achievement of the audit objectives

■ decide if sufficient, reliable evidence has been gathered to support the auditors' opinion.

audit files

There are two main types of audit files that the auditor will produce for each client audit:

■ the permanent file

■ the current year file

You are not expected to remember which information goes in each file.

The permanent file was covered in detail in Chapter 3, so we will now focus on the current year file.

current year audit file

The current year audit file will contain the results of all the audit testing, including the tests of control, substantive tests and analytical procedures carried out as part of the audit. These will normally be filed in separate sections for each of the main audit areas, with a schedule at the front of each section summarising the figures that have been audited.

The current year audit file will also include:

■ copies of the draft financial statements

■ letters of representation from management (see Chapter 7)

■ management letters (see Chapter 7)

■ the audit planning memorandum

■ the audit programme

■ schedules and supporting documentation for each item in the statement of financial position

■ checklists for accounts presentation and audit work completion

■ queries raised and explanations received

- extracts from minutes
- statistical and analytical review information

A sample current file index is included in the Appendix (page 282).

recording audit tests

Every procedure carried out by the auditors must be evidenced by working papers, whether the procedures are:

- compliance tests of controls
- substantive testing of transactions
- specific tests to confirm balances

If the results of audit testing are not recorded, or details of work carried out on the client's systems are not documented, the auditors cannot prove that the work has been carried out.

By convention, audit working papers are prepared in a certain way. This can be illustrated by the example shown on the next page.

Firms of auditors generally have pre-printed paper for use on audits. You will notice from the example that the sheet is pre-printed with space for:

- the name of the client
- the financial period end
- the initials of the person who carried out the test and the date on which it was carried out
- the initials of the person(s) who reviewed the work and the date that they did so

All of these details must be completed on each working paper that is prepared during the audit. The working paper should also include clear evidence of:

- the test being performed
- the objective of the test, for example:

  'To ensure that purchase invoices are matched with approved orders'

- details of the test carried out in order to demonstrate that the objective has, or has not been achieved
- a conclusion as to whether or not the objective has been achieved

Note that there is a pre-printed space on audit working papers for the reviewer to initial and date. This is because every piece of work prepared by any member of the audit team must be reviewed by a more senior member of the team. The audit senior, for example, may review work performed by the audit junior, the audit manager may review work performed by the audit senior and so on.

continued on page 118

Client: Heather Walker plc   **Prepared by:**   JT

                                                 Date: 22.1.10

Period: Year ended 31 December 2009   **Reviewed by:**

                                                 Date:

Objective:

Test of control to confirm that sales invoices are matched against order and delivery note.

To ensure goods ordered and delivered have been invoiced.

Customer name	Delivery note no	Date	Sales order no	Date	Sales invoice no	Date	Agreed
Willco plc	D11021	27.1.09	1002	16.1.09	00684	30.1.09	✔
Harris Bros	D20413	22.9.09	1704	10.9.09	08482	23.9.09	✔
Morton	D19875	16.6.09	1506	10.6.09	06281	17.6.09	✔
PGW Ltd	D13743	2.2.09	1104	28.1.09	01723	4.2.09	✔
Simple Bys	D41026	11.12.09	1911	2.12.09	10416	13.12.09	✔
Ross Dryer	D16424	13.4.09	1251	9.4.09	04783	14.4.09	✔
Ample Charm	D15817	27.3.09	1209	20.3.09	02961	30.3.09	✔
Montaigne	D31041	31.10.09	1802	17.10.09	09281	2.11.09	✔

Conclusion:

All deliveries are matched to sales orders and sales invoices, so goods ordered are delivered and invoiced. The objective is achieved.

sample audit working paper

The reviewer will use his/her experience of the client and of auditing in general to assess the audit test that has been performed. In particular he/she will need to ensure that the conclusion that has been reached is supported by the work carried out. The reviewer will also produce a schedule of audit review points to pass back to the auditor who carried out the test indicating areas where the work performed is unsatisfactory, where further work is required or where the work performed does not support the conclusion that has been reached.

It is important that errors or items of an unusual nature that are encountered during audit testing are documented fully and reported to the audit manager or audit supervisor. Staff engaged in audit testing should not be afraid to question transactions and raise any concerns they have about the possibility of an error, fraud or serious misstatement. These issues should be raised during the audit rather than being ignored. Such issues may reappear later in the audit if a material error is identified in the financial statements or if a fraud is found.

retention of audit working papers

Audit working papers should be retained for six years. Previous year's papers can be used for audit planning and form a frame of reference for the current year's audit.

WORKING WITH THE CLIENT'S STAFF

The final section of this chapter discusses the way in which the auditors approach client staff to obtain information and audit evidence. Throughout the planning and testing stages, the auditors will come into contact with the client's staff at all levels in the organisation.

Audit staff need to maintain good working relationships with the staff operating the systems they are testing. It is important that the audit staff conduct themselves professionally at all times. Particular points that audit staff should remember are:

- client members of staff may feel defensive and protective about their work as they may see the auditors as there 'to check up' on them
- staff are usually busy and the auditors may place additional demands on their time
- client staff may not have a precise idea of what the auditors are there to do – they may believe that the auditors are working for senior management and there to find out if they are doing their jobs properly

Audit staff should bear these points in mind in their general approach to the organisation's employees. Consequently, they should:

- be polite, courteous and professional at all times

- when asking for information, explain why it is needed

- take account of the staff's workload when asking for information to be produced

- keep a list of queries and arrange a meeting with the relevant member of the client staff to deal with in one go rather than continually interrupting them as each query arises

- remember their duty of confidentiality regarding everything to do with the client's affairs – this means that confidential information should not be shared with other members of the client's staff

- do not get involved in office politics or disputes – the auditors must remain independent

- although the auditors have power under the Companies Act with regard to obtaining information, audit staff should be reminded that this is a last resort and denial of access should be dealt with at a senior level

If the auditors can build and maintain a good relationship with the client's staff, the audit can be conducted in a spirit of mutual co-operation. This should in no way compromise the auditors' independence, but it will help the audit to progress to a satisfactory conclusion.

Chapter Summary

- Substance over form means that the auditors have to evaluate what a transaction actually is, not just what it appears to be.

- All audits must be planned, and details of the planning are set out in an Audit Planning Memorandum (APM), which includes all key matters relevant to the current year's audit. All members of the audit team should read the Audit Planning Memorandum.

- The auditors need to obtain evidence that is both sufficient and appropriate to support the audit opinion as to whether the financial statements give a true and fair view.

- A detailed list of all the audit tests that are to be carried out is contained in the audit programme.

- Auditors carry out compliance tests to see if internal controls are working effectively. Depending on the results, they will decide on the level of additional testing that is required.

■ Where the audit test requires a sample to be selected, the auditors must ensure that the sample is representative of the population as a whole.

■ Errors may be found when testing a sample of transactions, but if the level is below the tolerable misstatement that has been set, the test may still achieve its objective.

■ Substantive testing of transactions and balances will always be required in order to provide evidence to support the audit opinion.

■ Analytical procedures are a form of substantive testing which analyse the relationships between financial and non-financial information to establish inconsistencies and unexpected patterns which must then be investigated by the auditors.

■ All the audit work for the current year should be filed in a separate current year audit file.

■ Every test undertaken during the audit must be documented on a working paper, and all working papers must be reviewed by a more senior member of the audit team.

■ Auditors should always remember to be polite and professional when dealing with client staff.

Key Terms

substance over form	the principle that requires the auditors to confirm that a transaction is what it appears to be
audit plan	a document setting out the general strategy and scope of the audit
audit planning memorandum	a document detailing all key matters relevant to the current year's audit.
audit programme	a comprehensive list of all the audit tests to be completed, including a detailed set of instructions for the audit staff to follow
compliance testing	testing of internal controls to ensure that they are functioning correctly
sample testing	the testing of a sample of transactions to enable the auditors to come to a conclusion about all transactions of that type
population	the total number of transactions from which a sample is taken

sampling risk

the risk that the auditors will draw the wrong conclusion about the population as a whole based on the sample selected

confidence level

the reliability the auditor places on the sample selected being representative of the population as a whole. Generally set at 95%

tolerable misstatement

the level of errors in a population which the auditors are prepared to accept and conclude that the objective of the test has been met

tolerable rate of deviation

the maximum acceptable level of deviation from agreed control procedures

substantive testing

all tests other than compliance tests, including analytical review

inspection

the examination of assets, records or documents

vouching

matching an entry in the accounting records with an original source document

analytical procedures

analysis of the relationships between financial and non-financial information to establish inconsistencies and unexpected patterns which must then be investigated by the auditors

permanent audit file

ongoing information about the client which will be used for successive audits; it includes a copy of the engagement letter and provides a clear picture of the client's organisation, ownership, management, activities and its financial systems

current audit files

the audit files containing all the work relevant to the current year's audit

audit manager

person responsible for the day-to-day running of the audit

audit partner

person ultimately responsible for the audit and for signing the auditor's report

Activities

4.1 One of your junior staff has prepared some slides for a presentation to a client on the practical procedures involved in auditing. The slides contain the following statements:

(a) Materiality is generally defined as being about 5% of gross profit or 10% of operating profit .

(b) Audit sampling is always based on the level of materiality – the higher the level the less work you need to do

(c) Vouching is a test of transactions between books of original entry

(d) Analytical procedures are a form of substantive testing where you calculate all the financial ratios you can think of

(e) Auditors need to select samples which represent the population as a whole

(f) Providing the financial statements comply with the law, auditors have to accept them

Which of these statements should you remove from the slides before the presentation is given and why?

4.2 Auditors can approach sampling in a variety of ways, including statistical based sampling or random sampling.

Which of the following does not constitute sampling?

(a) Select 50 purchase invoices and look for evidence of authorisation	
(b) Select every 12th balance from a list of trade receivables balances and check to suppliers statements	
(c) Select all individual sales invoices of amounts over £50,000 during the period and ensure that they have supporting documentation	
(d) Attend inventory count and test check a count of inventory items	

4.3 Auditors use a mixture of tests of control and substantive procedures when gathering audit evidence.

For each of the procedures listed below, select whether it is a test of control or a substantive procedure.

	Test of control	Substantive procedure
(a) Analytical review of payroll costs		
(b) Check evidence that human resources department procedure notifies payroll of starters and leavers		
(c) Check for evidence of matching invoices, GRN's and purchase orders		
(d) Circularisation of trade receivables to verify receivables balances		
(e) Check numerical sequence of purchase orders		

4.4 State whether the following are true or false in relation to carrying out audit testing.

	True	False
(a) Vouching is checking that figures in the cash book or the day books have been entered properly in the ledgers		
(b) Auditors must use substantive testing in order to gather evidence as to the truth and fairness of entries shown in the statement of financial position		
(c) Analytical procedures are a form of substantive testing		

4.5 The figures below are a summary of an analytical review of the draft financial statements of Howdo Ltd. The review was carried out at the planning stage and the comparison was made against the original budget for the financial year.

Based on the results of this review indicate whether or not you would **investigate** or **accept** the reason for any differences.

		Actual	Budget	Investigate/Accept
(a)	Gross profit margin	74%	71%	
(b)	Operating profit margin	18%	26%	
(c)	Trade receivables collection period	52 days	49 days	
(d)	Trade payables payment period	36 days	45 days	
(e)	Inventory turnover	18 times	12 times	

5 Auditing accounting systems

this chapter covers...

In this chapter we will explain what constitutes 'good' audit evidence and describe the detailed audit testing that is carried out on the three main accounting systems operated by an organisation – purchases, revenue and payroll. We will also examine the issues involved when auditing in a computerised environment.

This chapter explains:

- *audit evidence*

- *testing system components – the stages in the accounting process*

- *auditing purchases*

- *auditing revenue*

- *auditing payroll*

- *auditing in a computerised environment*

AUDIT EVIDENCE

In Chapters 3 and 4 we looked at how the auditors obtain an understanding of the client's systems and procedures. We also looked at the different audit approaches and the ways that auditors evaluate the client's internal control systems to establish the level of audit work they need to carry out and the approach they are going to take towards gathering audit evidence.

We will now consider in more detail what is meant by audit evidence and what the evidence is being gathered to prove.

ISA 200 'Overall objectives of the independent auditor and the conduct of an audit in accordance with international standards on auditing' gives us a definition:

> *'Audit evidence – Information used by the auditor in arriving at the conclusions on which the auditor's opinion is based. Audit evidence includes both information contained in the accounting records underlying the financial statements and other information.'*

ISA 200 also defines what the auditor needs to do:

> *'To obtain reasonable assurance, the auditor shall obtain sufficient appropriate audit evidence to reduce audit risk to an acceptably low level and thereby enable the auditor to draw reasonable conclusions on which to base the auditor's opinion.'*

The key points here are that evidence has to be 'sufficient' and 'appropriate'. The ISA defines these terms as follows:

(1) **Sufficiency** of audit evidence is the measure of the quantity of audit evidence. The quantity of the audit evidence needed is affected by the auditor's assessment of the risks of material misstatement and also by the quality of such audit evidence.

(2) **Appropriateness** of audit evidence is the measure of the quality of audit evidence; that is, its relevance and its reliability in providing support for the conclusions on which the auditor's opinion is based.

This Chapter will focus on three main accounting systems – purchases, revenue and payroll – and describe the audit evidence that must be gathered to ensure that these systems operate effectively and produce figures for the statement of profit or loss that are free of material errors or misstatements.

So what do auditors have to do to ensure that the evidence they produce is both sufficient and appropriate?

assertions

The audit procedures that are planned and carried out should be designed to validate the financial statement **assertions**. These are basically a set of statements about what the financial statements say about the assets and liabilities and the transactions of the company. Set out below is the full list of assertions included in ISA 315.

It is split into three sections:

(a) **transactions and events** – which will be covered in this chapter

(b) **account balances** – which will be covered in Chapter 6 (which deals with auditing the statement of financial position)

(c) **presentation and disclosure** – which will be covered in Chapter 7

The list of assertions in ISA 315 is shown in the table opposite (note that the text in italics has been inserted here to explain the assertions).

You will probably notice from the table that there is some repetition between categories of assertions. If the auditors wish to do so, they can perform tests that cover the same assertion for both transactions (a) and balances (b). For example, one test can be used to cover completeness of transactions and completeness of balances. Similarly, testing can cover more than one assertion about a class of transactions or account balance.

When the auditors have gathered sufficient and appropriate evidence to validate these assertions they can then form a valid audit opinion on the financial statements.

One factor that the auditors must remember is that the audit evidence which is used to validate one assertion may not be sufficient to validate another. Performing a detailed test on one class of transactions may not cover all the assertions in (a) above.

This point is illustrated in the Case Study on page 128.

(a) Assertions about classes of transactions and events for the period under audit	
Occurrence	transactions and events that have been recorded have occurred and pertain to the entity (ie they relate to the organisation being audited)
Completeness	all transactions and events that should have been recorded have been recorded
Accuracy	amounts and all other data relating to recorded transactions and events have been recorded appropriately
Cut–off	transactions and events have been recorded in the correct accounting period
Classification	transactions and events have been recorded in the proper accounts
(b) Assertions about account balances at the period end	
Existence	assets, liabilities and equity interests (shares held) exist
Rights and obligations	the entity holds or controls the rights to assets, and liabilities are the obligation of the entity (the organisation being audited)
Completeness	all assets, liabilities and equity interests that should have been recorded have been recorded
Valuation and allocation	assets, liabilities and equity interests are included in the financial statements at appropriate amounts and any resulting valuation or allocation adjustments are appropriately recorded
(c) Assertions about presentation and disclosure	
Occurrence and rights and obligations	disclosed events, transactions, and other matters have occurred and pertain to the entity (the organisation being audited)
Completeness	all disclosures that should have been included in the financial statements have been included
Classification and understandability	financial information is appropriately presented and described, and disclosures are clearly expressed
Accuracy and valuation	financial and other information are disclosed fairly and at appropriate amounts

Case Study

BANJO LTD:
SUFFICIENT AND APPROPRIATE EVIDENCE

situation

You are a member of an audit team testing the controls on the revenue system of an audit client, Banjo Ltd.

One of the audit tests to be performed is as follows:

'Select a sample of invoices and vouch them to the sales ledger. Ensure that all details for each item have been entered in the correct customer account and have been recorded at the right amount.'

required

Which of the assertions for classes of transactions (in this case, sales) will be covered by this test?

solution

If this test is carried out with few errors found, it should support the conclusion that:

- Sales invoices are posted to the sales ledger in the correct period and at the correct amounts.

- With regard to the assertions about transactions, this should provide the following evidence:

Occurrence	the auditor will check the invoice to ensure that the transaction has occurred and relates to the client
Accuracy	the amounts on the invoice have been checked and have been vouched to the sales ledger
Cut–off	the test includes checking the details on the invoice to the customer account which should include the date
Classification	part of the test is to ensure that the invoice has been posted to the correct customer account

The assertion that has been omitted from this list is Completeness. This test would not be good evidence of completeness because the sample has been selected from all sales invoices issued by the client, and so would not detect transactions which had not been invoiced.

gathering audit evidence

Compliance testing, or testing of controls, will test to assess whether the internal controls have been operating effectively throughout the period. Substantive tests will test whether individual transactions and balances are supported by audit evidence. We will now look at how auditors gather the evidence they need.

Sample tests – both substantive and compliance testing can be carried out on a sample basis, however it is more usual to use sampling for compliance tests of internal controls. We have looked at sampling in Chapter 4, but to recap it involves testing a sample of transactions covering the accounting period to check whether the internal controls in the system have operated correctly for the sample. From this the auditor can decide whether or not the controls are reliable for the whole population of transactions (ie, all the transactions).

Inspection – inspection involves examining records or documents, whether internal or external, in paper form, electronic form, or other media. It is also the physical examination of an asset. An example of an inspection test might be inspecting purchase orders to ensure they have each been authorised.

Observation – Observation consists of looking at a process or procedure being performed by client staff. An example of this might be the auditor observing the inventory count by the client's staff.

Confirmation – confirmation involves obtaining evidence from third parties such as banks, customers or suppliers. Examples of confirmation procedures include obtaining a letter from the bank to confirm the figures in the bank reconciliation or the use of statements from suppliers as evidence of purchase ledger balances.

Inquiry – this is the simple matter of asking the client staff who have knowledge or information questions. An example of this might be the inquiries carried out when identifying system internal controls (see Chapter 3).

Re-performance – this involves the auditors independently re-performing a task which forms part of the internal control. An example of this might be re-performing a bank reconciliation to see if the client has done it properly.

Re-calculation – similar to re-performance in that the auditor carries out their own calculations independently of the client to see if they arrive at the same answer. An example of this might be the re-calculation of the net wages figure as part of the audit of the payroll system.

Analytical procedures – this is the analysis of relationships between figures, both financial and non financial, in order to identify fluctuations or inconsistencies. This may indicate to the auditors there is a possible misstatement and cause them to investigate further. An example of analytical procedures is the use of ratio analysis such as calculating gross profit percentages or inventory turnover and comparing them with previous accounting periods.

unusual items

Throughout the period of audit testing, whether it be substantive or compliance type testing, the auditor must be aware of the possibility of **items of an unusual nature**. These are items which do not appear to relate to the client's normal operations or are unusual by virtue of their size, timing or nature.

The following list gives examples of items of an unusual nature which may all be grounds for suspicion and should be referred to an audit manager for discussion with company management.

- large payments evidenced by little or no documentation
- large non routing or 'one off' transactions
- transactions which seem to have no real commercial purpose
- transactions with entities based offshore
- transactions above or below market rates
- large transactions immediately prior to the year end – particularly if they are reversed after the year end
- transactions where revenue appears to have been accelerated or where costs have been delayed
- transactions with entities which require complex processing or where details are restricted

Transactions with **related parties** ie, organisations or individuals with which the organisation is connected in some way will also need to be identified and checked. Related parties include:

- subsidiary and related companies
- directors and senior management and their immediate families and
- shareholders

Transactions with related parties are required to be disclosed in the financial statements and the organisation should have procedures to identify them. The auditors should test these procedures.

Audit staff who identify such transactions should document them and report them to the audit manager or supervisor for further consideration.

quality of audit evidence

All methods of gathering audit evidence above will produce information for the auditors. However not all of it will be of a suitable quality to enable the auditors to achieve their objectives.

The key to good audit evidence is:

- written evidence is better than oral evidence
- evidence generated by the auditors or obtained from an independent third party is better than evidence provided by the client or its directors

This means that evidence gathered and documented by the auditors through:

- carrying out sample tests of controls
- inspection or observation of procedures
- recalculation and re-performance

is the best type of audit evidence as the auditors have obtained it independently of the client.

Confirmation evidence is also good evidence provided it comes from an independent source. A letter from the bank or a supplier's statement is classified as good quality audit evidence whereas a certificate of value obtained from a valuer who is related to one of the client's directors is not good evidence as it is not independent.

Inquiry evidence may be good evidence but as it is often oral this devalues its quality.

The following table summarises what constitutes good quality and reliable audit evidence and what does not.

Type of audit evidence	Which is the more reliable?
Tests on the system carried out by the audit team _or_ Confirmation from the directors that the internal controls are working	Auditors own procedures
Evidence from external sources, eg the client's bank _or_ from internal sources, eg client staff?	External sources
Evidence gained directly (eg a letter sent to the bank to confirm the balance at the year end) _or_ gained from the client (eg the balance on the cash book)?	Evidence gained directly from an external source
Documentary evidence (eg a supplier statement) _or_ oral evidence (eg discussions with client staff)?	Documentary evidence
Original documents (eg a letter from a trade receivable confirming their balance with the client) _or_ photocopies?	Original documents

Therefore examples of the **most reliable** evidence gathered by auditors would be:

■ a letter from the client's bank, sent directly to the auditors' office, confirming the balance on the client's bank account at the year end

■ replies from a sample of the client's trade receivables sent directly to the auditors' office stating the outstanding balance they believe they have with the client at the year end

Examples of **less reliable** evidence would be:

■ an emailed confirmation of the bank balance at the year end from a member of the client's staff

■ a photocopy of a supplier statement taken by the client rather than by the auditors

ISA 500 'Audit evidence' summarises the reliability of audit evidence as follows:

■ the auditors' own procedures are the most reliable

■ confirmations from independent third parties obtained directly by the auditors are extremely reliable evidence

- written confirmation from directors is less reliable evidence particularly if there is a lack of corroborative evidence from other sources
- written evidence, which includes any material stored electronically, is more reliable than oral evidence

The decision as to what is good audit evidence will also be a matter of common sense on the part of the auditors. Professional judgement is as much a factor here as the general rules described above.

TESTING SYSTEMS

important note!

The next section of this chapter will provide you with the practical information and instructions you will need to perform detailed audit testing on the three main financial systems that operate in most commercial organisations – purchases, revenue and payroll.

There is necessarily a large amount of detail covering a very wide range of possible tests that can be carried out. This section should be used as a reference point for possible tests. You will be relieved to hear that you will not have to learn it all off by heart!

system components

In order to test a system that operates in an organisation, you must be able to analyse the system into its component parts and understand how they link together.

For example, in the case of purchases, the system can be sub-divided into:

- placing the order
- receiving the goods
- receiving the invoice from the supplier
- recording the transaction in the accounts
- paying the invoice

Auditors will need to identify each of the following:

- the assertions that the audit work must cover
- the objectives that the controls in the system aim to achieve at each stage of the process – for example at the ordering stage, the objective may be to ensure that all orders are properly authorised

- the type of controls that the auditors would expect to be in place at each stage of the system – for example, all orders should be made on standard order forms and should be authorised before being sent to the supplier
- finally – the best way of testing these controls

In their audit work the auditors will need to:

- test every component part of the system
- provide evidence that the assertions which are relevant to the system being tested have been properly covered
- satisfy themselves that there is sufficient and appropriate evidence to justify the audit conclusions

In this section therefore we will cover each of the three main systems – purchases, revenue and payroll – by focusing on four areas:

1   audit objectives

2   the internal control objectives of the system

3   system controls

4   audit testing

directional testing

Before we look at audit testing in detail one more principle of testing to explain relates to the direction of the testing. This type of test is known as a vouching test. Vouching refers to checking a transaction that has been recorded in the books of account with the original (source) document.

If we consider a simple purchases system the source documents could be purchase orders and the ledger is the purchase ledger.

Now, suppose as part of the audit testing the auditors select a sample of transactions from the purchase ledger and vouch them to the original purchase orders (source documents). In this case, the direction of test is this:

direction of test

Source document ⟵―――――――――― Ledger

Here the auditors are only testing transactions that are already recorded in the system. It does not check that **all** transactions evidenced by source documents have been included in the ledger. This type of test will check for overstatement of assets or liabilities, ie for items included in the ledger for which there is no source document.

The auditor must therefore design audit tests in the opposite direction. That is, from the source documents to the ledgers. In this case, the direction of testing is:

direction of test

Source document ➤ Ledger

This type of test will check for understatement of assets and liabilities as it will highlight valid transactions that are not included in the ledger.

By testing in both directions auditors can increase their confidence that they have tested for both over and understatement.

THE PURCHASES SYSTEM

system components

The diagram below shows the components of a basic purchases system. (Note that *internal controls* are shown in italics.)

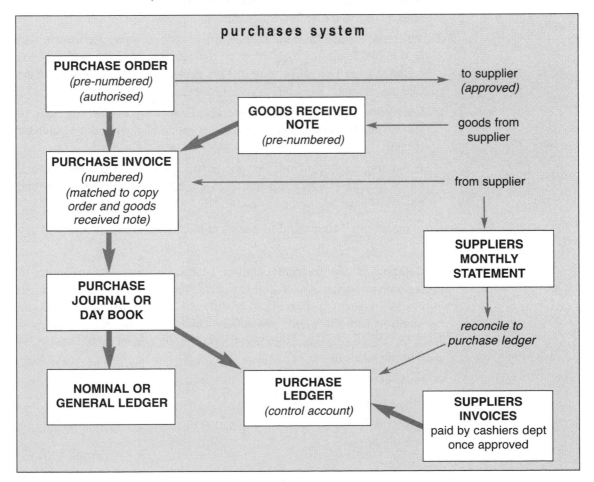

Within this system there are several internal controls. The system will work broadly like this:

- The purchase order will be raised by the buying department. It should be authorised by someone who has the authority to purchase goods or services on behalf of the company and it must be within their authorisation limit.

- Orders should be pre-numbered so the company can control their issue. A copy will be sent to the accounts department and another copy to the department goods inward to tell them to expect a delivery.

- The purchase order will be sent to a supplier who has previously been approved by the company. This approval means the supplier is considered reliable and able to deliver goods or services of the right quality, on time and at the agreed price.

- When the goods are received they will be checked for quality and quantity by the goods inwards or inventory control staff. Details of the items received will be entered into the inventory records.

- Goods inwards staff will issue a pre-numbered goods received note and send a copy to the accounts department.

- When the invoice from the supplier arrives the accounts department will match the details to their copy of the purchase order and the goods received note. This will ensure that the goods were ordered properly and that the company has actually received them.

- Once checked the invoice can be entered into the purchase day book or journal and from there to the nominal or general ledger and the purchase ledger.

- A monthly statement from the supplier will be reconciled to the balance on the purchase ledger account to ensure all invoices, credit notes and payments have been properly recorded.

Once the invoice is approved for payment the accounts department will pay it.

In addition to the internal controls detailed above, the principle of segregation of duties applies in this system. The individuals who carry out each stage of the process should all be different so that no one individual can be involved with the whole transaction. This reduces the risk of errors or fraud on the part of the member of staff. A different person should ideally do each of the following:

- order goods
- deal with the movement of goods
- process invoices
- pay the invoices

audit objectives – purchases system

The audit objective is to carry out audit work to gather sufficient appropriate evidence to validate the assertions about the purchases system. These can be summarised as:

- purchases of goods and services relate only to the company being audited (occurrence)
- all purchases that should have been recorded have been recorded (completeness)
- purchases of goods and services have been recorded at the correct amounts (accuracy)
- all the relevant purchase transactions have been recorded in the correct accounting period (cut-off)
- purchases have been recorded in the correct accounts in the nominal and purchase ledgers and any other related records, eg inventory records (classification)

internal control objectives – purchases system

To re-cap – there are five main sections of the purchase system:

- placing the order
- receiving the goods
- receiving the invoice from the supplier
- recording the transaction in the accounts
- paying the invoice

The control objectives for the system can be identified for each stage of the system as follows:

ordering

- all orders for goods and services are properly authorised
- orders are made only from approved suppliers

receipt of goods

- all goods and services received are for the purposes of the business and not for private use
- only goods and services that have been ordered are accepted
- goods ordered are received in a satisfactory condition
- unsatisfactory goods are returned to suppliers
- all receipts of goods and services are accurately recorded
- receipt of goods or services is evidenced

receipt of invoice

- liabilities are recognised for all goods and services received

- all invoices received are authorised

- any credits due to the business for faulty goods and services have been claimed

- liabilities can not be recorded for goods or services which have not been received

accounting for purchases

- all expenditure is correctly recorded in the books and records of the business

- all credit notes are properly recorded in the books and records of the business

- all entries in the purchase ledger are to the correct suppliers' accounts

- all entries in the nominal ledger are to the correct account

- all purchases are recorded in the correct accounting period (cut-off)

payment

- all payments have been properly authorised

- all payments are for goods and services which have been received (completeness)

risks if internal control objectives are not met

If the client's system of internal control is weak and the internal control objectives are not met this increases the risk of some or all of the following:

- purchasing goods and services the company does not need
- failing to buy goods and services of the appropriate quality and at the lowest cost
- buying from unauthorised suppliers
- loss of discounts or bulk buying opportunities
- orders being placed by staff who are not authorised to do so
- orders being duplicated
- goods received not being checked for quality and quantity
- fraud through the processing of false invoices or fraudulent payments
- invoices not being checked before being paid

- invoices being paid twice or not being paid at all, which may result in loss of supplier confidence
- poor cash flow if invoices are paid without taking advantage of credit terms and discounts
- incorrect inventory records
- incorrect costing records
- purchases and trade payables not being recorded accurately in the financial records
- incorrect cut off procedures

system controls – purchases system

Now that we have identified the internal control objectives of the purchases system, we can examine the controls and procedures that the system should have in place to ensure that these objectives are achieved and also to minimise the risk of fraud and error.

Throughout the whole purchase process there should be formal written procedures for ordering, receiving and paying for goods and services.

Another key control within the system is segregation of duties – there should ideally be separate staff responsible for raising orders, receiving goods, and approving and paying invoices.

ordering

organisational controls	– ordering is only allowed from approved suppliers
physical controls	– blank order forms are kept secure
authorisation	– there are recognised authority levels for orders above defined limits
arithmetic and accounting checks	– standard pre-numbered order forms are always used
	– regular review of orders placed but not received

receipt of goods

physical controls	– quantity and condition of goods received are properly checked
	– pre-numbered goods received notes (GRNs) are always used
authorisation	– GRNs are signed off for all goods received

receipt of invoice and accounting

organisational controls	– stated authority levels should exist for approving invoices
authorisation	– all invoices are approved for payment
arithmetic and accounting checks	– invoices are matched with orders and GRNs
	– prices on invoices are agreed to standard supplier price lists
	– arithmetic accuracy of invoices is checked and evidenced
	– regular reconciliations of suppliers' statements with purchase ledger balances
	– controls exist for processing purchase invoices (eg batch totals)
	– regular reconciliations of purchase ledger control account with purchase ledger balances
	– cut-off checks are performed to ensure goods received but not invoiced are accounted for in the correct period

payment

physical controls	– cheque books are securely located
	– cancelled cheques are retained
authorisation	– recognised list of authorised cheque signatories
	– a minimum of two cheque signatories for all payments
arithmetic and accounting checks	– regular bank reconciliation performed

audit testing – purchases system

The auditors' objective is to test whether the controls listed above are functioning properly within the system being tested.

In Chapter 4 we described the two types of testing that auditors carry out:

- **compliance testing** of the system of internal controls
- **substantive testing** of transactions and balances

Auditors must therefore use both types of tests in order to provide the evidence they need.

Remember – the amount of testing carried out and the emphasis of the tests will be decided by the risk assessment. If the assessment of risk is high, the audit will focus on testing a larger number of transactions and balances and so samples will be large. If the risk assessment is low, the audit approach will be based on testing controls in the system to ensure that they operate effectively.

audit tests – purchases system

Set out below is a detailed list of the audit testing that would be performed to cover each part of the purchases system. Most of these tests would normally be performed on a selected sample of transactions.

ordering

- check that approval has been obtained and is evidenced for purchases
- check sequence of purchase orders to ensure none is missing

receipt of goods

- observe client staff receiving goods into stores to ensure documented procedures are followed
- ensure goods received are checked to the purchase order before they are accepted
- check sequence of GRNs and investigate any missing numbers
- ensure all returns to suppliers are suitably documented and regularly followed up
- ensure correct entry of goods received in the client's inventory records

receipt of invoice and accounting entries

- check all invoices are matched to GRNs and orders
- check details on invoices and ensure invoices are arithmetically correct
- ensure prices agree to the approved supplier price list
- check authorisation of invoices for payment
- check posting of invoice to purchase day book
- check postings to the nominal ledger and the purchase ledger control account
- ensure invoices are posted to the correct supplier account
- check purchase ledger control account reconciliations

- check evidence of reconciliation of purchase ledger balances with suppliers' statements and re-perform a sample of reconciliations

- obtain explanations for items long outstanding, eg unmatched orders or GRNs or unprocessed invoices

- check GRNS issued are matched to credit notes from the supplier

payment

- for a sample of payments in the cash books:
  - check to approved supplier invoice
  - check details and amounts on the invoice to supplier statements

- check payments to suppliers are debited to correct supplier accounts in the purchase ledger

- review bank reconciliations to ensure they are accurately carried out on a regular basis

cut-off

- for the few days immediately before and after the financial year end, review GRNs to check for:

  - goods received for which no invoice has been received

  - goods received for which invoices have been received but which have not been posted in the purchase ledger

  - goods received that relate to the financial year being audited but which have been accounted for in the following year

- for goods returned immediately prior to the year end, ensure that relevant credit notes have been posted correctly

- review credit notes posted immediately after the year end to ensure that they do not relate to the financial year being audited

analytical procedures for purchases

As part of their testing, the auditors may carry out some analytical procedures as follows:

- compare monthly purchases for the year with monthly purchases for previous years and obtain explanations for any unusual variances

- compare revenue with purchases on a monthly basis using the gross profit margin and investigate any unusual results

- compare ratios such as gross profit margin, inventory turnover and trade payables payment period with ratios derived from budgeted figures and prior year figures

- consider the effect of price changes on the value of purchases

a note on the testing process

This comprehensive list of testing for the purchases system may on a first reading appear very long and complicated. However, if you take the information step-by-step, the process is quite logical. The auditors in each case are testing to see whether the control procedures within the client's purchases system are operating satisfactorily.

THE REVENUE SYSTEM

system components

The diagram below shows the components of a basic credit revenue system.

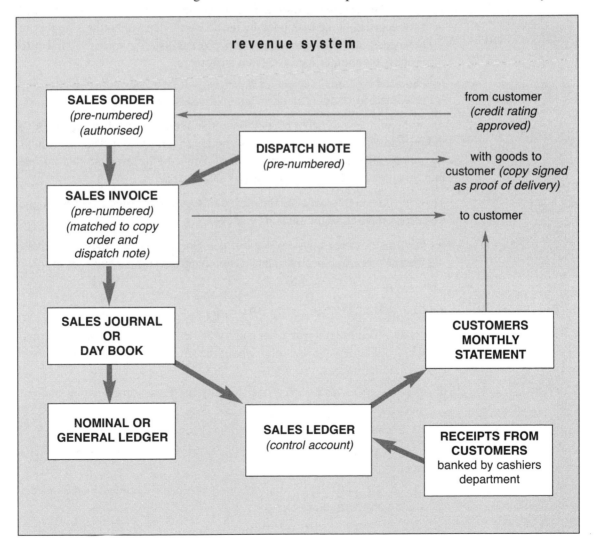

Within this system there are several internal controls. The system will work broadly like this:

■ The sales orders will be taken by a sales department who will check the credit worthiness of the customer.

■ Goods will be despatched to the customer with a delivery note by the staff who deal with inventories and goods outwards. A copy of the delivery note will be signed by the customer and retained by the company as proof the goods were delivered.

■ The sales invoice and the customer statement will be raised by the accounts department.

■ The accounts department will post the sales invoice to the sales day book or to a journal. From there they will post it to the sales ledger and the nominal or general ledger.

■ When the customer pays the invoice the money received will be banked and recorded in the cash book by the accounts department. It is important to ensure that the individuals who process sales invoices do not also process the monies received from customers.

■ Outstanding trade receivables balances will be reviewed to identify any possible bad or doubtful debts and to chase slow payers.

As in the purchases system in addition to the internal controls detailed above the principle of segregation of duties applies to this system. The individuals who carry out each stage of the process should be different so that no one individual can be involved with the whole transaction.

The objectives for auditing the revenue system are again based on the assertions relating to transactions and events.

As with the purchases system we will describe in turn the audit objectives, the internal control objectives, the system controls and the audit testing.

audit objectives – revenue system

The audit objective is to carry out audit work to gather sufficient appropriate evidence to validate the assertions about the revenue system. The objectives can be summarised as:

■ sales of goods and services relate only to the company being audited (occurrence)

■ all revenue that should be recorded has been recorded (completeness)

■ sales of goods and services have been recorded at the correct amounts (accuracy)

■ all the relevant revenue transactions have been recorded in the correct accounting period (cut-off)

- sales of goods and services have been recorded in the correct accounts in the nominal and sales ledgers and any other related records, eg inventory records (classification)

internal control objectives – revenue system

As with purchases there are five main sections of the system:

- receiving the order (and granting credit)
- despatching the goods
- raising the invoice
- recording the transactions in the accounts
- receiving payment

The control objectives can be identified for each stage of the revenue system as follows:

receiving the order (and granting credit)

- goods and services are only supplied to customers on credit if their credit rating is good
- orders are recorded correctly when they are received

despatching the goods

- goods are only despatched on the basis of approved orders
- all despatches of goods and services are accurately recorded
- all returns from customers are recorded and the reasons for rejection are investigated

invoicing

- all invoices raised relate to goods and services supplied by the business
- all despatches of goods or provision of services are invoiced at the correct price and on authorised terms
- credit notes are authorised and only issued for a valid reason

accounting for revenue

- all revenue is properly recorded in the books and records of the organisation
- all credit notes issued are properly recorded in the books and records of the organisation
- all entries in the sales ledger are to the correct customer accounts
- all entries in the nominal ledger are to the correct account
- all revenue has been recorded in the correct accounting period (cut-off)
- procedures exist for identifying bad debts

receiving payment

- all receipts from customers have been properly recorded
- all payments received are for goods and services which have been supplied

risks if internal control objectives are not met

If the internal control objectives are not met then there is an increased risk of the following:

- selling to non creditworthy customers
- failure to record customer orders and therefore supplying incorrect or incomplete orders or not supplying at all and losing a sales opportunity
- goods or services being supplied without being invoiced
- duplication of sales invoices
- sales invoices not being checked before despatch, and issued with incorrect figures
- incorrect VAT calculations
- goods and services sold at the wrong price
- credits notes being issued for something other than goods returned, for example fraudulently writing off debts
- incorrect inventory records, despatches not being recorded correctly or theft of inventory not being detected
- poor credit control resulting in weak cash management
- sales and trade receivables not being recorded accurately and correctly in the financial records
- theft of money received from customers
- incorrect cut-off procedures

system controls – revenue system

Now that we have identified the internal control objectives of the revenue system, we can examine the controls and procedures that the system should have in place to ensure that these objectives are achieved and also to minimise the risk of fraud and error.

In businesses where revenue involves a significant number of cash transactions, there is an increased risk of fraud and auditors have to be very aware of this when they are designing their procedures. For this reason, cash sales will be dealt with separately at the end of this section.

Throughout the revenue process there should be formal written procedures for receiving orders, granting credit, despatching goods and collecting payment for goods and services supplied.

There should also be segregation of duties within the system with different staff responsible for taking orders, granting credit, despatching goods and receiving payment.

receiving orders and granting credit

organisational controls	– there are recognised authority levels for accepting new customers
	– procedures are in place to credit check all new customers
physical controls	– blank sales order forms are kept secure
authorisation	– there are recognised authority levels for changes in customer data (eg increasing discount allowed)
	– all increases to customer credit limits are authorised
arithmetic and accounting checks	– pre-numbered sales order forms are always used
	– prices quoted to customers are checked to standard price list and appropriate discounts applied

despatching goods

organisational controls	– delivery notes are matched with orders and invoices
physical controls	– the quantity and condition of goods supplied are properly checked
	– pre-numbered delivery notes should always be used
	– proof of delivery is obtained for all goods despatched (signed delivery notes)
	– returns from customers are recorded (pre-numbered goods returned notes)

invoicing and accounting for revenue

organisational controls	– invoices and credit notes are pre-numbered and sequentially issued, and spoilt invoices are not destroyed
authorisation	– all credit notes are authorised
	– all non-standard discounts are approved

arithmetic and accounting checks	– invoices are matched with orders and delivery notes
	– credit notes are matched with goods returned notes
	– controls are in place for processing invoices (eg batch totals)
	– invoices and credit notes entered into the accounting records promptly
	– invoices are posted to the correct customer account
	– regular up-to-date statements are sent to customers
	– regular reconciliation of the sales ledger control account with sales ledger balances
	– cut-off checks are performed to ensure goods that have been despatched but not invoiced are accounted for in the correct period

receiving payment

physical controls	– all money received from customers is recorded by two people
	– all money received is banked intact on the same day
arithmetic and accounting checks	– regular bank reconciliations are performed
	– all cash received is posted to the correct customer account

audit testing – revenues system

As when they are dealing with purchases, auditors must use a mixture of compliance tests and substantive procedures in order to obtain the evidence they need. For most of the tests, unless otherwise stated, they would normally be performed on predetermined samples.

receiving orders

- check new accounts to ensure that credit checking has been performed and credit limits properly authorised
- check that orders are only processed for customers who are within their credit limit
- check the sequence of internal sales orders to ensure none is missing
- ensure that unfulfilled orders are regularly reviewed and that either the goods are despatched or the order is cancelled

despatching goods

- observe client staff to ensure documented procedures are followed
- ensure goods being sent out are checked to the order before they are despatched
- check sequence of despatch notes and investigate any missing numbers
- check that proof of delivery is obtained on the despatch note or the GRN from the customer
- ensure all returned goods received from customers are supported by appropriate documentation
- check correct entries are made in client inventory records for goods despatched

invoicing and accounting for revenue

- check sequence of sales invoices and investigate any missing numbers or cancelled invoices
- check all invoices are matched to despatch notes and orders ensuring all details agree
- ensure prices and discounts agree to standard price list and have been approved for the customer
- check arithmetic accuracy of sales invoices, including calculation of discounts and VAT
- check posting of invoice to the sales day book
- check posting to nominal ledger and to sales ledger control account
- ensure invoice has been posted to the correct customer account in the sales ledger
- ensure sales ledger control account reconciliations are performed regularly

- obtain explanations for long outstanding items, eg unfulfilled orders or unmatched goods returned notes

- check goods returned notes are matched to authorised credit notes issued to the customers

- review non-routine revenues, eg scrap items, sales of non-current assets to ensure:
  - appropriate authorisation
  - the asset is removed from the non-current asset register
  - profit/loss on sale is acceptable

- ensure list of aged trade receivables balances is maintained for credit control purposes and long outstanding amounts are regularly followed up

payments received

- observe client staff to ensure procedures for receiving cash are properly followed

- investigate any payments on account or round sum amounts received from customers

- check amounts received from customers are credited in full to the correct account in sales ledger

- review bank reconciliations to ensure they are accurately carried out on a regular basis

cut-off

- for the few days immediately before and after the financial year end, review despatch notes and customer returns to ensure:
  - invoices have not been issued in the current financial year for goods despatched after the year end
  - credit notes have been accounted for in the correct financial year

- review significant invoices raised in the period immediately after the year end to ensure that they are accounted for in the correct accounting period

analytical procedures for revenues

As part of the testing process, the auditors may carry out some analytical procedures as follows:

- compare monthly revenues for the year with monthly revenues for previous years and obtain explanations for any unusual variances

- compare revenue with purchases on a monthly basis using the gross profit margin and investigate any unusual results

- compare selling expenses to revenue to ensure they are appropriately proportional to each other

- compare ratios such as gross profit margin, inventory turnover and trade receivables collection period with budgeted figures and with figures from previous periods

- consider the effect of prices changes on the value of sales

audit of cash sales

There are certain types of business where a significant volume of revenue is received in cash. Examples include supermarkets, bars, restaurants, taxi firms and hairdressers. You will be able to think of others.

When auditing these types of organisations, the auditors have to consider the increased likelihood of fraud. Inadequate controls in the client system over the collection and recording of cash receipts could lead to misappropriation of cash.

Consequently there are additional audit procedures that need to be carried out to ensure the completeness and accuracy of the recording of cash sales.

Audit procedures for cash sales include:

- review procedures for collecting cash sales and observe client staff collecting cash and entering it into the till

- ensure cash is banked intact (cash should not normally be taken from cash sales to pay wages, small bills or petty cash items)

- if the client does allow expenditure to be made out of takings, vouch a sample to supporting documentation (receipts, wages schedules)

- for a sample of cash sales:
    - check record of cash takings (eg daily summary sheet) to an independent record (eg a till roll total) and ensure any differences are investigated
    - check total from the daily takings sheet to the bank statement
    - ensure total on the daily takings sheet is correctly entered in the revenue account

- observe client staff counting cash takings at the end of the day and ensure the correct amount is entered on to the daily takings sheet and matched to the till roll total

- ensure that there is appropriate segregation of duties between staff carrying out the sales and staff counting and banking the cash

- ensure takings are banked daily to reduce risk to cash retained on the client's premises

- if cash is held overnight on client premises, ensure client has set up adequate physical controls to ensure its safekeeping

analytical procedures for cash sales

It is often difficult for the auditors to obtain conclusive proof that all cash sales have been recorded unless the client has very strong controls in place. The auditor will therefore rely on analytical procedures to test the accuracy of the revenue figure by comparing with figures from previous periods. However, the auditor must take into account external factors such as seasonal variations, weather and public holidays, all of which may have a direct effect on the amount of cash takings.

Auditors will often be able to recommend straightforward and practical improvements to the client's systems where cash sales are involved.

THE PAYROLL SYSTEM

The payroll system contains details of the organisation's staff and their wages and salary payments. The organisation's objectives when operating the payroll system are to ensure that it pays the correct rate of pay for the actual amount of work done.

The principal differences between wages and salaries are:

■ wages tend to be paid weekly and salaries monthly

■ wages can vary from week to week, whereas salaries are generally a set payment, and only vary if commission or bonus payments are included

It is becoming increasingly rare for wages to be paid in cash; for security reasons most staff are paid directly into their bank account by BACS. If payments are still made in cash there are a number of issues that are raised which we will look at later in this section.

Key points that relate to both wages and salaries are:

■ all employees must have a contract or written terms of employment

■ rates of pay must be agreed

■ all deductions from gross pay must be statutory (eg PAYE and NI) or authorised by the employee (eg pension contributions)

■ there are defined rules for calculating tax and national insurance contributions, whatever method is used for paying staff

■ staff must be paid regularly and on time

Businesses may have a mixture of staff paid a weekly wage and staff paid a monthly salary. In this case they may operate two payrolls. If this is the case, the auditors will need to carry out separate tests on each payroll to ensure that both are operated correctly.

confidentiality

In Chapter 1 we explained how auditors must treat all the information they obtain during the audit as confidential. This is particularly important when auditing payroll. Matters such as rates of pay and individual's salaries can be a very sensitive area and one that can be of particular interest to other employees!

The payroll system contains much personal information about employees including:

- the hourly rate of pay or annual salary
- additional benefits
- home address
- bank details
- date of birth
- national insurance number

It is the duty of the organisation under the Data Protection Act to ensure that all this information remains confidential.

This duty of confidentiality extends to the auditors which means that it is only the more senior members of the audit team who are allowed access to payroll details. Where possible, the auditors should try to identify client staff by payroll or clock card number rather than by name.

system components

The diagram opposite shows the components of a basic payroll system, whether for wages or salaries. (*Internal controls* are shown in italics.)

In contrast to the purchases and revenue systems we have looked at, there is a limited segregation of duties within a payroll system as, normally, the payroll is prepared by staff in one department who carry out the entire process.

The actual payment of wages or salaries is made by the accounts department but it is the payroll staff who tell them how much to pay to whom.

The key controls in the payroll system are authorisation and management review.

The system works broadly like this:

- Variable data such as overtime or hours worked for casual workers is approved by a manager based on some form of time recording. This could be a clock card or a time sheet. The hours to be paid should be validated and authorised before being input to the payroll system.

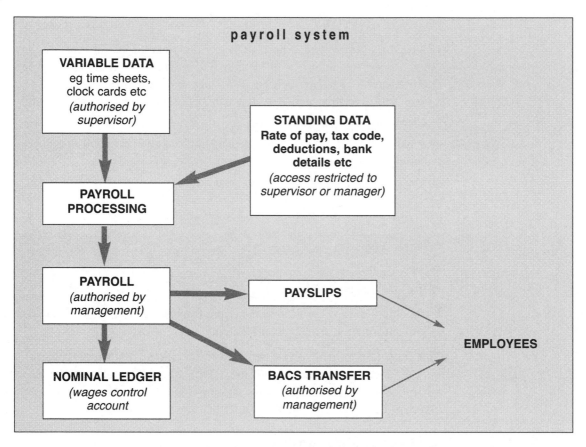

- Salaried staff who are not paid overtime are paid a regular amount each month. However any additional payments such as bonuses or commission should also be authorised.

- The computer will contain a master file which contains fixed data about each employee. Such data includes:
    - staff number
    - rate of pay (hourly, weekly, monthly)
    - tax code
    - National Insurance (NI) number
    - deductions such as pension contributions, subscriptions, court orders etc
    - bank details – sort code and account number

- The payroll software applies the variable data to the standing data and calculates:
    - gross pay
    - deductions (PAYE, NIC, others as notified)
    - net pay
    - gross taxable pay to date
    - tax paid to date

- the software also prepares a payments list; in most cases employees are paid by automatic bank transfers using the Banks Automated Credit System (BACS)
- payslips are prepared to be sent to each employee
- the payroll should be approved by management
- the BACS payment list must be signed ideally by two authorised signatories
- payment is made by direct transfer originated by the accounts department

audit objectives – payroll system

The audit objectives are to carry out audit work to gather sufficient appropriate evidence to validate the assertions about the payroll system. They can be summarised as:

- payment for wages and salaries relate only to work done for the company being audited (occurrence)
- all payments for wages and salaries that should have been recorded have been recorded (completeness)
- wages and salaries and any deductions have been calculated and recorded at the correct amounts (accuracy)
- all the relevant payments and liabilities have been recorded in the correct accounting period (cut-off)
- payments for wages and salaries have been recorded in the correct accounts in the nominal ledger and any other related records (classification)

In addition to the objectives above, the auditors must pay particular attention to businesses where staff are employed on a casual or seasonal basis. This can often mean that there are large numbers of staff coming and joining, often with little documentation of previous employment (P45s). This can then make it difficult for the organisation to comply with tax and NI requirements.

Casual and seasonal staff are often paid in cash, sometimes with little documentation. In situations such as this, there is a risk of fraud which means that the auditors must ensure they cover this risk when designing their procedures.

internal control objectives – payroll system

The main stages of the payroll system are as follows:

- hours are input into the system as required and amendments to staff details are made when necessary
- gross pay, deductions and net pay are calculated and payslips produced
- transactions are recorded in the accounts
- payments are made to staff and HM Revenue & Customs

The control objectives for the system can be identified for each stage of the system as follows:

inputting hours and amending staff details

- all amendments to staff details are properly authorised
- hours worked are approved at an appropriate level
- staff are only paid for hours worked
- only staff who work for the company are included on the payroll
- details of leavers and joiners are authorised and promptly entered onto the payroll system
- staff details remain confidential at all times

calculating payroll and deductions

- payroll is calculated based on approved rates and hours worked
- statutory deductions for PAYE and NI are correctly calculated
- voluntary deductions (eg pension contributions or share save schemes) are correctly calculated

accounting for payroll and payments to staff and HM Revenue & Customs

- net pay is accurately calculated and paid to the correct employee
- payroll figures are correctly recorded in the books and records of the business
- all payments for PAYE and NI are paid on the due date
- wages and salaries are paid on the right date

risks if internal control objectives are not met

The risks to the company if the internal control objectives are not met are:

- paying for work which has not been carried out
- calculating the incorrect gross pay
- paying people who are not employees ie those who have left the company
- failure to pay new employees
- failure to pay wages and salaries on the correct date
- incorrect calculation of net pay
- failing to deduct correct amounts of tax and national insurance
- failure to pay amounts due to HMRC on time
- paying 'ghost' workers ie fictitious employees fraudulently included on payroll
- amounts for wages and salaries incorrectly recorded in financial and costing records

systems controls – payroll

Now that we have identified the internal control objectives of the payroll system, we can examine the controls and procedures that the system should have in place to ensure that these objectives are achieved and the risk of fraud and error minimised.

Throughout the whole payroll process there should be formal written procedures for recording and inputting hours worked, amending staff details, and paying wages and salaries.

There should also be segregation of duties between staff responsible for approving hours worked, making changes to staff details and inputting and calculating payments. Where wages are paid in cash, one person should be responsible for counting the cash and another more senior person should check the amounts paid.

inputting hours and amending staff details

organisational controls	– a written record is kept for each employee containing details of rates of pay and contracted hours; any changes should require appropriate authorisation
	– formal procedures are followed for starters and leavers
	– timesheets and clock cards are approved before hours are entered onto the system
physical controls	– access to the payroll office is restricted to authorised personnel only
	– access to the payroll and staff records is restricted to authorised personnel only
authorisation	– all changes to rates of pay, bonus payments and commission earned should be authorised
	– written approval from employees should be obtained for all voluntary deductions from wages or salaries

calculating payroll and deductions

organisational controls	– up-to-date versions of payroll software should be installed, using the latest tax and national insurance rates
	– staff are fully trained on PAYE and NI issues

	– changes to staff tax codes are promptly and accurately entered on the payroll system
authorisation	– payroll schedules are approved before payment
arithmetic and accounting checks	– wages and salaries control account is regularly reconciled
	– commission and bonuses are reconciled to source documentation (eg sales records)
	– piecework payments (ie payments based on the number of items produced) are regularly reviewed against levels of work completed
	– unusual changes in payments to individuals from month to month are identified

accounting for payroll and payments to staff and HM Revenue & Customs

organisational controls	– a timetable for payment of wages and salaries is maintained and adhered to
physical controls	– staff who count wages in cash are not the same as those who prepare the payroll
	– cash for payment of wages is stored securely at all times
	– payslips are handed to staff members personally or are sent to their home address in sealed envelopes
authorisation	– pay packets can only be signed for by individual staff member
	– BACS payment schedules are authorised by an appropriate person before processing
arithmetic and accounting checks	– the wages control account is regularly reconciled
	– a comparison is made between wages paid and budgeted figures for wages
	– a regular check is made of deductions by accounts staff to ensure consistency with previous periods' deductions

- reconciliations are regularly performed between the total net pay figure and payment shown on the bank statement

- a regular review of national insurance and PAYE accounts to ensure no outstanding balances remain after payment to HM Revenue & Customs

audit testing – payroll

Relatively few organisations now pay their staff in cash. The introduction of reliable payroll software and the use of the inter-bank computer payment system (BACS) has significantly reduced the opportunity for defrauding a business through the payroll.

This does not, however, reduce the auditors' responsibility to ensure that the controls within the systems are operating effectively. As with purchases and revenue the auditors will use a mixture of compliance tests and substantive procedures, including analytical procedures in order to obtain the evidence they need for payroll.

The key areas of audit testing are designed to ensure that:

- all employees exist
- all employees are paid at the correct rate
- all deductions from wages are properly calculated
- net pay and deductions are accounted for correctly in the accounts of the organisation

audit tests

- review a sample of joiners in the year to ensure that they have been correctly recorded in the appropriate month
- review staff files to check that changes in personnel details have been promptly updated on the payroll system
- for a sample of employees:

  - check individual wages or salaries figures from the payroll schedules against individual personnel records to verify rates of pay or salary figures

  - re-perform calculation of gross pay and deductions (eg PAYE, NI, pension) to ensure the calculations are correct

  - ensure voluntary deductions (eg pension contributions) have been authorised by the member of staff

  - confirm existence of staff members by arranging to meet them

- check details of hours worked from payroll records to individual timesheets or clock cards
- ensure clock cards and timesheets have been approved
- ensure all overtime payments have been approved
- re-perform commission and bonus calculations to ensure they are consistent with supporting documentation (eg sales schedules or approved bonus schemes) and ensure that they have been approved for payment
- where staff have been paid piecework, check the production figures on which the payments are based to ensure that the payments have been correctly calculated
- check the calculation of benefits
- confirm payment of net pay to the BACS summary or the cash payments summary

■ review the wages control account and ensure that it is regularly reconciled and all outstanding items are investigated

■ check payroll software to ensure that up-to-date income tax and national insurance rates are being used to calculate payroll figures

■ check figures from the payroll summary to the nominal ledger

■ for a sample of payments to HM Revenue & Customs:
- ensure that the amount paid agrees to the liability shown on the payroll schedule
- ensure that the payment was made to HM Revenue & Customs within the permitted period to clear the income tax and NI liability account

■ for payment of cash wages, observe distribution of pay packets to employees to ensure that:
- each employee receives a pay packet and no more than one pay packet
- procedures are in place to ensure that cash payments are secure
- all wage packets are signed for by members of staff
- a record is kept of unclaimed wages
- explanations are obtained for unclaimed wages

analytical procedures for payroll

As part of their testing, the auditors may carry out some analytical procedures as follows:

■ comparing wages and salaries month-by-month with previous year figures

■ comparing average salary per employee with previous year figures

- review increases in pay rates by comparison with previous year's payroll figures – eg if pay rises were generally 4% during the year, is the current wages and salaries figure approximately 4% greater than last year's figure?

Most payroll systems operate on broadly the same principles, although there are often particular arrangements for calculating items such as overtime, commission or bonuses. Auditors should apply the principles outlined above to their audit testing of both weekly and monthly payrolls, ensuring that they are adapted, where necessary, to suit the particular circumstances of each client.

AUDITING AND COMPUTERS

Nowadays even the smallest organisation is likely to use computers, and many use computerised accounting packages to maintain their accounts. Examples of well known computerised accounting packages include Sage, QuickBooks and Xero.

Computerised systems have the following advantages:

- information can be processed quickly, accurately and efficiently
- up-to-date management information is available at the press of a button
- they have built-in controls over input into the system, including:
  - mandatory fields to ensure that sufficient information is entered for each transaction
  - they do not permit single entry, ie for every debit input there must be a credit, and vice versa

But there are problems associated with automatic accounting systems if they are not properly controlled. In particular, the auditors will be concerned about the loss of a tangible audit trail. Because the system generates transactions electronically the auditor cannot follow the flow of documents which evidence a transaction because there are not any physical documents to follow.

At the planning stage, auditors will have to consider how the computerised aspect of the accounting system affects the tracking of information and the flow of documents, and consequently how this affects audit risk.

audit risk and computers

There are several specific aspects of audit risk which have to be considered in connection with computerised systems, as shown in the table on the next page.

RISK	FEATURES
inherent risk	• computerised systems are more susceptible to fraud if access to information, particularly master file data, is not suitably restricted • management may have little understanding of the detailed operations of the computer system and may leave it in the hands of computer specialists • many of the operations within the system occur automatically and inaccurately input data will continue to generate inaccurate transactions until it is detected – for example a wage rate or a sales price that has been entered incorrectly
control risk	• it is often difficult to detect a case where software has been tampered with or illicit software introduced onto the computer • computerised systems require fewer staff, which can mean there is a lack of segregation of duties • authority for transactions can be difficult to trace where the transaction has been generated by the computer • controls have to be instituted to prevent unauthorised access to systems or tampering with data

One advantage of a computerised accounting system is that managers within an organisation are able to produce a large amount of information at the press of a button. This will allow them to analyse data and may lead to improved control procedures.

the control environment

The principles of good internal control described in Chapter 3 apply equally to computerised and manual accounting systems; therefore the auditor will be looking for many of the same features.

These can be summarised as:

■ organisational controls

■ physical controls, including restricted access to information

■ segregation of duties

■ authorisation

■ arithmetic and accounting checks

These principles are covered by the specific controls detailed below. The auditors should concentrate on these when testing in a computerised environment.

CONTROL OBJECTIVE	CONTROL PROCEDURES
documented procedures	• all staff should be trained to use computer software and should be encouraged to follow documented procedures
systems documentation	• copies of the supplier's handbook should be available to all staff members, together with a telephone helpline number
control of access	• access to modify computer software should be restricted to authorised personnel only • logical access controls should be in place to ensure that staff are only allowed access to parts of the system that they require for their work, eg an accounts assistant would have access to the sales ledger but would not have access to personnel records or to payroll
password controls	• access to the system should be restricted by passwords and authorised log-ons; passwords should be changed regularly and should not be disclosed or shared
application controls	These include: • authorisation of input documentation • batch controls for processing batches of documents, for example agreeing manual batch totals with computer batch totals • sequential numbering systems for entries onto the system • rejection messages for incorrectly entered data (eg inputting four digits for an account number when all accounts have six digit numbers • automatic range checks to ensure data input is within acceptable limits, eg hours worked by a member of staff are not more than 50 per week • automatic records maintained of who has processed each document, and when

audit approach for computerised systems

There are two approaches that the auditors can take when auditing in a computer environment:

■ audit 'around' the computer – ie largely ignoring the computer

■ understand and interrogate the computer system

auditing around the computer

When the use of computers in the workplace was less common, the auditors would take the view that they could carry out their audit procedures by concentrating on the inputs and outputs from the computer system and ignoring 'the bit in the middle', ie procedures that occur within the computer system.

This approach is now limited to the audits of smaller organisations using standard 'off the shelf' accounting software packages. The auditors take the view that the computer simply replaces manual records and there are few, if any, automated routines.

Because it is standard software, it is likely to be well tested and error free and the audit is more likely to be familiar with its inputs and outputs. The audit approach in this situation is to:

■ check the controls for data input to ensure that appropriate authorisation, coding and use of batch totals are used for this data

■ examine standing data which is held on the computer programme to perform calculations – eg standard wage rates, sales price list, rates of VAT – and ensure this standing data is accurate and is currently used by the computer

■ check outputs from the system against relevant input documentation, for example a selection of sales invoices input on to the system could be traced to the customers' accounts in the sales ledger

■ check output from the system against external evidence, for example purchase ledger balances with statements from suppliers

understanding and interrogating the computer system

Where computerised systems are more complex, and the computer program contains predefined routines to generate information automatically, the auditor needs to adopt a different approach.

There are two problems faced by the auditor in this situation:

■ in complex bespoke ('one-off') systems, even the client's own IT staff may not be able to explain all the details of the programme; they may know what the system can do but they may not know how it does it

■ management may consider that because they do not understand the computer system, they have no wish to become involved in its day-to-day operations – this can result in a loss of control on their part, and may lead to a dependence on one or two experts within the company

In cases like this, auditors will adopt an approach where they use the computer's ability to process data to interrogate its operations using **computer assisted audit techniques (CAAT)**. Larger audit firms now have dedicated audit staff who are experts at using CAAT.

There are various types of CAAT, including:

■ **audit interrogation software** – a computer program which examines data in the client's computer files, for example reconstructing the aged trade receivables listing from invoices on the sales ledger and comparing it to the client's version

■ **test data** – this comprises 'dummy data' which is input into the system and for which the company has already predicted the results – the problem with this type of CAAT is that it may corrupt the client's live data or may be difficult to remove from the system after the test has been completed. This problem can be resolved by the auditors using the client's software on their own computers to process dummy data. This will mean that there is no danger of the client's files being corrupted. Care must be taken to obtain the current version of the client's software

■ **integrated test facilities** – also known as system control audit review files (SCARF). These are audit tools set up within the client's systems which can be used by the client and by the auditors to obtain information on demand or on a continuous basis

All of these audit techniques will allow the auditors to carry out equally effectively all the detailed testing that we have considered earlier in this chapter.

audit interrogation software

Current management information systems use methods of data storage which enable the auditors to extract and reformat data in many ways to allow them to interrogate this data as a part of audit testing. There are many versions of this software. Auditors are constrained by the type of data storage available to them rather than the limitations of audit software. Audit interrogation software is designed to accept and analyse data in many formats.

Historically audit interrogation software was expensive however modern programs are now relatively cheap, and if used correctly are economic compared with the costs of employing audit staff.

Audit software can be used for:

- extracting data to define populations for sampling, eg sampling of trade receivables balances

- analysing expenditure or revenue in a number of ways such as by date, size, type, product or location

- calculating aged trade receivables or inventory balances

- sorting and indexing data, eg sorting by value may be used for clusters of transactions around client authority levels, sorting by date may be used to look for high value transactions before a period end

- statistical analysis of data to identify highest/lowest values, average values etc

- analysis of data by time and date processed. This will identify data processed at unusual times such as weekends or out of hours. This could indicate fraudulent activity

- producing trend analysis

- producing exception reports using parameters defined by the auditor

Some of these techniques are particularly useful in fraud investigations but can also be used for routine audit work. In many cases this type of software is now being used in place of CAATs that use parallel simulations or dummy data as more can be gained by interrogating the client's actual data than by running dummy transactions through the system.

Chapter Summary

■ Audit evidence must be sufficient and appropriate. Auditors do not have to examine every transaction, but what they do examine must be representative of all transactions of the same type.

■ ISA 315 sets out assertions which are a set of statements regarding what the accounts state about the transactions of the business and its assets and liabilities.

■ Audit evidence is gathered to validate a series of assertions which relate to occurrence, completeness, accuracy, cut-off and classification of transactions.

■ Good audit evidence is evidence that auditors gather for themselves or which comes from a reliable independent source.

■ Systems can be divided into component stages and internal controls identified for each component. Audit procedures can then be designed to test these internal controls.

■ The three main financial systems operated by most organisations are purchases, revenue and payroll.

■ Audit testing takes the form of a combination of compliance and substantive testing.

■ Some substantive testing is always required when validating transactions and balances.

■ Auditors must take additional steps to ensure revenue is complete and accurate if the sales are made for cash.

■ Confidentiality is a key point to consider when auditing payroll.

■ Auditing in a computerised system environment requires the auditor to specifically evaluate the internal controls which relate to the computer system.

■ Auditors can use two approaches to auditing computerised systems: auditing around the computer or using computer assisted audit techniques (CAATs).

■ CAATs may require specialists to operate them in order to obtain information from client files and to maintain the audit trail.

■ The use of audit interrogation software enables the auditor to carry out a range of tests and to examine client data to produce sufficient reliable evidence concerning transactions and balances.

Key Terms	**internal control environment**	the client's system comprising internal controls and control procedures
	audit evidence	the information used by the auditors in arriving at the conclusions on which the audit opinion is based
	assertions	statements about the validity and recording of transactions, balances and disclosures which form the basis of audit testing work
	compliance tests	tests of internal controls and procedures
	substantive testing	tests to detect material misstatements or errors in the financial statements – this includes detailed tests of transactions and balance and analytical review
	piecework	wages paid based on the amount of work an employee has carried out rather than the time spent at work
	computerised information system	the computer, software and files which make up all or part of the client's financial records
	CAAT	**c**omputer **a**ssisted **a**udit **t**echniques – specialised audit software designed to assist the auditor in evaluating controls within a computerised information system
	exception report	a report produced which lists transactions which exceed pre-set parameters or limits
	audit trail	a series of entries in a set of financial records documenting a transaction through the system

Activities

5.1 You are marking some test papers given to a group of trainee auditors. Among the answers are the following statements:

(a) Substantive testing is always necessary to provide good audit evidence

(b) Documentary evidence is better than oral evidence, but oral evidence is better than nothing at all

(c) Assertions are the statements about the accounts which audit tests are designed to prove

(d) Cut–off means that all the transactions are recorded in the correct accounting period

(e) Completeness can be tested by checking a selection of sales ledger balances to make sure that there is one for every credit customer

(f) You can audit a computer by ignoring it and just testing the output

(g) Computer-assisted audit techniques include special software to tell the auditor what is going on inside the computer

Which of these statements are incorrect, and why?

5.2 Auditors use a range of techniques to provide evidence to substantiate the assertions underlying the financial statements.

For each of the audit procedures set out below select the assertion for which that test will provide assurance.

Test	Assertion
(a) Attendance at the inventory count	Existence/Classification/Accuracy/Occurrence
(b) Review of inventories for condition during attendance at inventory count	Classification/Valuation/Completeness/Accuracy
(c) Obtain details of last despatch note before period end	Existence/Accuracy/Rights and Obligations/Cut-off
(d) Check sales invoices to despatch notes and sales orders	Classification/Occurrence/ Rights and Obligations/Completeness
(e) Examine evidence of preparation and use of batch totals when processing purchases and payroll	Existence/Completeness/ Classification/Valuation

5.3 Auditors use computer assisted audit techniques (CAATs) as part of their audit procedures.

From the list below select **one** statement that is not true about the use of CAATs.

(a) Enables auditors to cope with large volumes of data	
(b) Can organise data to assist audit sampling eg through stratification of balances	
(c) Useful where accounting controls are limited	
(d) Can produce exception reports to highlight potential control weaknesses	

5.4 An entity uses internal control procedures in order to mitigate the risks to which the entity is exposed. Listed below are two internal control procedures which are applicable to an entity's inventory procurement system.

Match each internal control procedure with the risk mitigated from the list below:

1   Ensuring that all goods leaving inventory are for bona fide sales

2   Ensuring inventory records are properly maintained

3   Ensuring that only items required by the organisation are purchased

4   Ensuring all purchase invoices are for goods received

5   Detecting theft of inventory

Internal control procedure	Risk mitigated
Checking despatch records to sales invoices	
Matching purchase invoices to authorised orders	

5.5   The following is a description of a purchases system within Blotto Ltd.

For each part of the system identify whether the procedure is a strength or a weakness.

		Strength	Weakness
(a)	All purchasing is carried out by the purchasing department using pre-printed purchase order forms. The order must detail prices and quantities		
(b)	All orders are authorised by the purchasing manager		
(c)	A copy of the order form is sent to the goods inwards department and a copy to the accounts department		
(d)	When the goods are received they are checked for quantity and quality by the goods inwards staff who raise a Goods Received Note (GRN). A copy of the GRN is sent to the accounts department		
(e)	When the invoice is received the accounts clerk, Stephan, checks it arithmetically, matches it to the GRN and the copy order and, if everything agrees, enters it in the accounting system		
(f)	All items must be purchased from approved suppliers. If an order comes through for a supplier not on the system Stephan creates a new supplier file in the Purchase ledger		
(g)	If the order is signed as approved the accounting procedures mean that the purchase invoice is automatically approved providing it agrees with the approved order		
(h)	At the end of each month Stephan matches the Purchase ledger balances to suppliers statements and instructs the Cashiers department which balances to pay		

6 Verification of assets and liabilities

this chapter covers...

This chapter explains the procedures auditors should follow to verify the existence, valuation and ownership of non-current and current assets and liabilities recorded in the Statement of Financial Position.

This chapter covers the audit of:

- *opening balances*
- *non-current assets*
- *inventory and work in progress*
- *valuation of inventory and work in progress*
- *cut-off procedures at the year end*
- *receivables*
- *bank balances*
- *liabilities*
- *equity (share capital and reserves)*

AUDIT ASSERTIONS

In Chapter 5 we examined the way in which testing the client's financial systems allows the auditors to assess the effectiveness of the internal controls within those systems. The auditors can then form an opinion as to whether all the transactions which have passed through the company's financial systems have been entered in the correct nominal accounts. This testing is carried out using a combination of compliance and transaction testing.

The audit of assets and liabilities focuses on ensuring that the items in the Statement of Financial Position are correctly stated.

In Chapter 5 we introduced the **assertions** which auditors now have to use as the basis for gathering their audit evidence. The assertions about account balances at the period end are:

- **existence**
  assets, liabilities and equity interests (shareholdings) do actually exist
- **rights and obligations**
  the company holds or controls the rights to assets – ie the company owns them – and all liabilities are those of the company
- **completeness**
  all assets, liabilities and equity interests (shareholdings) that should have been recorded, have been recorded
- **valuation and allocation**
  assets, liabilities and equity interests (shareholdings) are included in the financial statements at appropriate amounts and any resulting valuation or allocation adjustments are properly recorded

For simplicity we will refer to the main assertions throughout this chapter as **existence**, **ownership**, **completeness** and **value**.

This chapter will cover the main categories of assets and liabilities in turn, identifying the relevant financial statement assertions and detailing the auditing techniques that are normally used to provide the evidence the auditors need to validate each item.

Remember that the auditors are always considering their evaluation of audit risk when designing audit tests. (See Chapter 3, pages 52-58).

OPENING BALANCES

Before the auditors can test the final balances included in the Statement of Financial Position, they must ensure that the opening balances are correct. Audit testing must therefore be carried out to confirm that the balances at the end of the previous accounting period have been brought forward correctly into the current one.

Where the current auditors were also the auditors last year, this should be relatively straightforward because it will simply be a matter of checking the opening balances to the previous year's audited accounts and audit files.

Where this is the first year that the auditors have been involved, it may require a bit more work. **ISA 510 – 'Initial audit engagements – opening balances'** requires the auditors to obtain sufficient appropriate evidence that the balances brought forward from the previous year are correct and in accordance with the financial statements. In this instance an unqualified ('clean sheet') audit opinion in the previous year is a good starting point, provided that the auditors check that the balances brought forward agree with the previous year's audited accounts.

In both instances the auditors must pay particular attention to provisions, prepayments and accruals which were calculated at the year end to ensure that they have been correctly journalled at the beginning of the current financial period. For example, the auditors will have verified that an accrual for the audit fee has been included in payables at the end of the previous period. However, it may not have been included in the Audit Fee Account in the Nominal Ledger at the last period end. The auditors must ensure that the outstanding amount is correctly included as a brought forward credit balance on this account.

When the auditors have established that the opening position is correct, they can examine the transactions in the period.

NON-CURRENT ASSETS

Non-current assets, because of their size, are often a material balance in the financial statements, although the audit risk may be relatively low. Non current assets in the Statement of Financial Position may be categorised in two principal ways:

- **tangible non-current assets** – land, buildings, plant and machinery, vehicles
- **intangible assets** – patents, trade marks, goodwill, research and development

We will first relate the key financial statement assertions of **existence**, **ownership**, **completeness** and **valuation** to tangible non-current assets.

tangible non-current assets

Tangible non-current assets usually consist of such items as land and buildings, plant and machinery, fixtures and fittings and motor vehicles. Most companies of any size will record their non-current assets in an **asset register**. Typically this will include such information as:

- a description of the asset
- purchase price or valuation
- the rate of depreciation
- depreciation to date
- location
- any serial number (or registration number of vehicles)

The non-current asset register is a useful document for the auditors, providing a significant amount of information to allow them to verify the company's non-current assets. However, auditors should also maintain their own records of opening balances, acquisitions and disposals for each of the main categories of non-current assets.

existence of non-current assets

Common sense would suggest that the most obvious way of ensuring that a non-current asset exists is to go and have a look at it. This is exactly what the auditors will do. The auditors should select a sample of assets from the non-current asset register and perform the following tests:

- physically inspect the assets
- check the identification/serial numbers are correct and that the asset is located where it is stated to be in the non-current asset register
- check that the asset is in use and is in a good condition
- reconcile opening and closing vehicles by registration number and inspect vehicle registration documents

Samples of non-current assets may not necessarily be representative and should include high value items together with a selection of additions made during the financial year.

ownership – non-current assets

The assertion of rights and obligations in relation to non-current assets effectively means asking the simple question: 'Does the client **own** the asset?'

Just because the auditors have verified that an asset included in the company's accounts exists, it does not necessarily mean that the company actually owns it. In order to confirm this the auditors must carry out some further testing:

- **confirm that the organisation owns land and property** by reference to
  - title deeds
  - Land Registry certificates
  - leases

Note that, as with all such tests, auditors should inspect original documents and not copies.

Should any of these documents not be in the company's possession (eg if title deeds are held at the bank), the auditors should obtain a letter or certificate from whoever holds them to confirm their existence. Normally the client's permission will be needed to do this.

The auditors should also find out why a third party is holding these documents. It may be for safekeeping or alternatively it may be because the assets are security for loans. In this case, the auditors must ensure that this is correctly reflected in the financial statements.

- **verify ownership of plant, machinery and motor vehicles** by reference to independent evidence including:

    - vehicle registration documents (log books)

    - invoices for additions

    - maintenance agreements

    - insurance documents

    - last year's audit file

completeness – non-current assets

To ensure that **all non-current assets** are included in the accounts, the audit tests to be carried out should be:

- select a sample of assets that physically exist on the client's premises and check them back to the non-current asset register

- agree the non-current asset register to the nominal ledger and investigate any differences

- if there is no non-current assets register, the auditors will have to work from their own audit files – last year's files should contain details of all non-current assets verified at the end of last year and this can then be linked with schedules of additions and disposals in the current year to provide an analysis of non-current assets at the year end – the totals can then be reconciled to the nominal ledger

valuation – non-current assets

The auditors must also be sure that the tangible non-current assets shown in the Statement of Financial Position are **valued** at the correct amount. One of the characteristics of a non-current asset is that its usefulness to the business extends beyond the financial period in which it was purchased. In most cases, this results in the asset being depreciated over its expected useful life. Hence, unless an asset is revalued, the two components of an asset's value are its original purchase price and the depreciation charged to date.

To test the valuation of non-current assets the following tests should be performed:

- for a sample of tangible non-current assets, agree the purchase price as shown in the non-current asset register to the original purchase invoice or lease agreement
- where assets have been revalued since they were purchased, obtain a valuation certificate from a suitably qualified valuer, and, in the case of property valuations, ensure that they are based on market value
- review depreciation rates for all categories of non-current asset and assess them for reasonableness – for example, substantial profit or loss on disposals would indicate that the rates had not been set correctly
- check that the rates of depreciation have been properly disclosed in the Accounting Policies statement in the accounts
- re-perform depreciation calculations for a sample of assets

non-current asset additions

The area of highest risk in auditing tangible non-current assets is probably in testing **additions** and **disposals**. We will examine each of these in detail.

Most companies will have a policy that requires that only assets over a certain value are capitalised in the accounts. The auditors must ensure that when the company acquires a new asset the capitalisation limit is adhered to and assets valued below that limit are treated as expense items. Similarly, they must ensure that no items that should have been treated as expenses have in fact been treated as non-current assets.

Other areas that the auditors should consider when auditing additions to non-current assets are:

- whether the acquisition has been correctly authorised – for example, whether the purchase invoice was signed off with the appropriate level of authority, or whether substantial purchases have been approved in the board minutes
- whether the assets that have been purchased in the year are valid business expenditure and are not for private use by directors or management – for example, the auditors must ensure that the new office furniture purchased during the year is not actually in the managing director's study at home (a review of the delivery address on the invoice would spot this)

non-current asset disposals

During the year, the company will probably have disposed of some of its non-current assets. The auditors must make sure that their audit testing covers certain points regarding these disposals. They should, for example:

- review the sales invoice or other relevant documentation to establish that a valid sale was made and the correct sale price has been recorded in the accounts
- ensure that the sale of the non-current asset was appropriately authorised
- check the calculation of the profit or loss on disposal and ensure that the sales proceeds have been correctly accounted for and have not been included in revenue
- ensure that a reasonable recovery of any scrap value has been achieved – there is a risk that assets may be sold cheaply to employees or friends

Case Study

BASHIT LIMITED: NON-CURRENT ASSETS VERIFICATION

situation

Bashit Ltd is a company which manufactures hospital beds and chairs from tubular steel. It is an old established company.

The major non-current assets of the company include:

- a freehold factory
- plant and equipment
- two delivery lorries
- three company cars

required

As the auditor of Bashit, how would you verify the existence, completeness, ownership and valuation of the motor vehicles, the property and the plant and equipment.

solution

Existence, completeness, ownership and valuation of motor vehicles

The auditors can test the existence and completeness of the motor vehicles by physically inspecting the five vehicles.

The registration numbers should be noted to ensure that they match with the records in the non-current asset register.

Ownership of the motor vehicles can be tested by inspecting original purchase invoices and also checking details to the vehicle registration documents (log books) and insurance documents.

Invoices will need to be inspected for all additions and sales invoices or other relevant documentation for all disposals. Details of the cost and descriptions of items should be checked to ensure that they agree with the non-current asset register.

If the vehicles were held at the beginning of the year, the auditors will be able to check the opening balances to the details of the vehicles in the previous year's audit file.

To confirm the valuation of motor vehicles is reasonable, the auditors should re-perform the depreciation calculation and check that the rates used are in accordance with the client's accounting policies.

Existence, completeness, ownership and valuation of freehold premises

In order to confirm existence, completeness and ownership of the freehold premises the auditors should inspect the title deeds and also physically inspect the premises.

If, as is often the case, the title deeds are not held on the client's premises, the auditors should obtain written confirmation from the organisation that holds them. This will normally be the client's solicitors or, if the premises are mortgaged as security for borrowing, the client's bank.

Valuation of the premises may require an independent valuation by a specialist valuer such as a chartered surveyor. This may not be necessary every year and will depend on whether the client wishes to disclose a revaluation of the premises in the financial statements.

Existence, completeness, ownership and valuation of plant and equipment

Physically verifying a sample of assets in the non-current assets register and also selecting a sample of physical assets located on the client's premises and checking that they are included in the non-current asset register will ensure that plant and equipment are complete and that they exist.

Ownership of the plant and equipment should be confirmed by reviewing the original purchase invoices. As with the motor vehicles, if the assets were held at the beginning of the year the previous year's audit file should also provide information on the ownership of these assets.

The valuation of the plant and equipment can be checked by agreeing opening balances to the previous year's file, checking any additions to purchase invoices and any disposals to sales invoices, re-performing depreciation calculations to ensure reasonableness, and checking that they are in accordance with the client's accounting policies.

Finally, depreciation policies should be re-assessed to ensure that they continue to be appropriate.

intangible non-current assets

Intangible assets include things such as patents, trade marks, licences, goodwill, and development costs. The main problem auditors have is that these assets cannot be physically inspected, so the auditors are reliant on documentation as the basis for audit evidence. The principles which we applied to the audit of tangible assets also apply to intangible assets.

The auditors will seek as much independent evidence as they can find that these assets exist and are owned by the company. This will mean inspecting legal documents or obtaining written confirmation from people such as solicitors or patent agents.

Valuation is often the main issue with intangible assets. You should be familiar with the principles of IAS 38 (previously covered by SSAP 13), as part of your studies of Financial Statements. Valuation of intangible assets is a very specialised area and frequently auditors will refer to an independent, suitably qualified third party expert to assist them in the valuation.

INVESTMENTS

Investments are another form of asset encountered in the audit, for example:

- properties (held as an investment and not for a trade)
- listed or unlisted stocks and shares
- investments in subsidiary or associated companies

In principle, there is no difference between the audit approach to verify the existence, ownership and value of these types of assets, and that taken to audit tangible and intangible non-current assets, as described above.

In the case of investment properties, the auditors can verify the title deeds and a suitably qualified valuer should be asked to value them.

For investments in stocks and shares and subsidiary companies it will be the share certificates (or electronic equivalents) that the auditor will need to check. Investments in listed companies are relatively easy to value using the Stock Exchange Daily lists or the Financial Times.

Valuing unlisted shares can be complex and expert advice might have to be sought if auditors have any serious doubt as to their value.

As with tangible non-current assets, if title documents are not available the auditors should obtain a letter or certificate from whomever holds them to confirm their existence, and establish on what basis they are holding these documents.

The auditors must ensure that any title deeds and share certificates are held in the client's name.

INVENTORY AND WORK IN PROGRESS

One of the most significant figures in the financial statements is the inventory and work in progress.

The closing inventory figure forms part of the calculation of gross profit and is also shown as a current asset in the Statement of Financial Position.

Material errors or misstatements in the inventory figures can have a significant effect on the truth and fairness of the accounts.

Over-valuation of closing inventory will result in an overstatement of net assets and gross profit and potentially a higher tax liability.

Conversely, under-valuation of closing inventory will result in an understatement of profits and potentially a lower tax liability.

Because of this, auditors will spend a considerable amount of time testing the organisation's inventory.

categories of inventory

Within the overall inventory figure for the organisation, the auditors might be faced with several categories of inventory for which they must assess the existence, ownership, completeness and valuation separately. It is important to appreciate that the results of audit tests on one category of inventory do not extend to another and that all categories must be tested independently. For example, it may be that the inventory recording system records both raw materials and finished goods inventory. In this case, the auditors' tests must ensure that the system works equally well for both categories.

Categories of inventory include:

- goods for resale
- raw materials
- finished goods
- work in progress

Not every client will have every category of inventory. For example, a shop will only have goods for resale, but a manufacturing company is likely to hold all categories except goods for resale.

The audit procedures described below relate to all categories of inventory except for work in progress, which we will examine as a separate category.

If you ask any auditors what the best way of testing inventory is, they will tell you that you must attend the client's year-end inventory count. This will give the most reliable evidence of the existence of the inventory at the year end.

inventory count procedures

ISA 501 'Audit evidence – specific considerations for selected items', states:

> *'If inventory is material to the financial statements, the auditor shall obtain sufficient appropriate audit evidence regarding the existence and condition of inventory by:*

(a) *Attendance at physical inventory counting, unless impracticable, to:*

(i) *Evaluate management's instructions and procedures for recording and controlling the results of the entity's physical inventory counting;*

(ii) *Observe the performance of management's count procedures;*

(iii) *Inspect the inventory; and*

(iv) *Perform test counts; and*

(b) *Performing audit procedures over the entity's final inventory records to determine whether they accurately reflect actual inventory count results.'*

Auditors must, therefore, include, as part of their audit procedures, a physical inspection of inventories. The reason for this is that, however good the company's financial systems and internal control procedures, and however frequently the company carries out its own inventory count, the auditors must always satisfy themselves as to the existence, ownership, valuation and completeness of all inventories held by the company at the financial year end.

There are two types of inventory count that the company can adopt:

■ a **year-end count**, where all items of inventory are counted once at the end of the financial year

■ a **continuous inventory** system, where the management ensures that all inventory is counted at some point during the year on a rotational basis

Even if inventories are maintained on a continuous or rolling inventory system there should be a full inventory count at the year end if possible. However, if this is not possible the auditors should:

■ test count a sample of items at an appropriate time during the audit

■ agree the quantities of items counted to the inventory records and note any differences

■ investigate management's procedures for calculating the value of inventory at the year end

■ review this procedure in the light of the results of the sample testing carried out by the auditors

■ if the auditor's sample testing revealed a significant number of errors between what the inventory records show and the quantities actually counted the auditors would have to consider the materiality of any possible misstatement in the inventory as a whole and whether or not the value of inventories is materially misstated

Whatever system the client uses, the auditors should attend the year-end count and observe the organisation's staff counting the various categories of inventory.

Client's inventory counts are often performed outside normal working hours. This, coupled with the fact that the client may hold inventory at a number of locations, will probably require a considerable level of staffing on the part of the auditing firm. This should have been taken into account during the planning stage of the audit (See Chapter 3).

If the client has a large number of locations where inventory is held, the auditors may decide to attend the inventory count at a sample of locations. This could be based on size, value of inventory on site, results of previous counts, or the results of analytical procedures carried out at the planning stage.

organising the inventory count

During an organisation's inventory count there will be a high level of activity. It is therefore important that the organisation issues detailed written instructions to all staff involved in the count. These instructions should include information covering the following areas:

■ **staff involved in the count**

Ideally, these should be staff who are not normally involved in the process of recording inventory.

This helps enforce the principle of segregation of duties to the count, with staff normally involved in inventory recording only being involved in an advisory role.

■ **locations**

The instructions should identify all locations where inventory is held and list the staff nominated to attend and the time at which counting will start.

■ **timing**

All inventory counts should begin more or less simultaneously to minimise the risk of inventory being moved between locations and consequently being counted more than once.

Counts should take place at a quiet time, eg a weekend, so that movement is kept to a minimum.

In addition **detailed instructions** should be given covering:

■ division of the count area into manageable sizes

■ individual responsibility for the count in each area

■ specific instructions for counting, weighing and measuring, where appropriate

■ cut-off arrangements – These should include ensuring that the staff involved in the count are aware of the final goods received notes to be included in the inventory figure. It should also be made clear to the staff that, where possible, no movements of inventory should be made while the count is taking place.

- procedures for identifying defective, obsolete and slow moving inventory
- identification of inventory on the premises owned by third parties, eg goods which are being held on behalf of someone else should not be included
- identification of the client's inventory held at other company's premises
- issue and return of pre-numbered count sheets – Pre-numbered inventory sheets are used so that the count can be properly controlled and no 'unofficial' sheets included.

  Auditors should note the numbers of the sheets issued and the areas of the inventory count to which they relate.
- control of inventory movements during the count
- any special problems such as dangerous areas or items, sealed containers or toxic substances (protective clothing might have to be supplied to staff and observers)

auditing the inventory count

The main point that you should be aware of is that the auditors are there to observe the count. They are not responsible for counting the inventory or for arriving at a valuation – that is the responsibility of the client's management.

The testing performed at the inventory count will be partly **control testing** and partly **substantive testing**:

- the auditors must **test** that the **controls** that the client has put in place covering the inventory count are effective and are carried out correctly during the count
- the auditors will also perform **substantive testing** to ensure that the year-end value of inventory is accurate; this will involve the auditors re-performing some of the counting as part of their testing together with other audit work detailed later in this section

Before they attend the client's inventory take the auditors should:

- review the details in the audit files of what happened in previous years and note any particular problems encountered
- review the client's inventory count instructions (see above) and highlight any specific areas for concern
- plan specific audit procedures to be carried out
- devise procedures to deal with any potential problem areas
- include any special arrangements, for example measuring equipment to be available where necessary or transport of staff between locations

It is important that specific areas of difficulty are discussed with the client's management before the count takes place.

The audit manager should also brief the audit staff who will be attending about the nature and extent of the inventories to be counted, and ensure that they are fully aware of any potential difficulties that they may encounter. For example, if they have to enter a special area such as a cold store, or carry out a physical procedure such as climbing storage tanks to observe the client staff checking the levels, this should be discussed with the staff concerned to ensure that there will not be any problems and to reassure them they will be safe and protected.

During the inventory count the auditors should carry out all the procedures that have been planned. These will include:

- observe the client's staff carrying out the count in accordance with their instructions
- note any deviation from inventory count instructions for later discussion with the client's management
- select a sample of items and count them independently for comparison with the client's count
- ensure that all items checked are detailed on audit working papers, together with any observed problems with the count
- if any tests prove unsatisfactory, request a recount be performed by the auditors and client staff
- where boxed goods are stored in stacks, ensure the stacks are complete and not hollow
- ask the client's staff to open a sample number of boxes to ensure the contents are as stated on the label – this may disconcert the client's staff, but is an important part of the audit testing
- note any damaged, obsolete or slow-moving inventory to ensure that these are separately identified and can be appropriately valued
- make a note of the count sheet numbers to ensure that all sheets are accounted for
- select a sample of the client's completed inventory count sheets and take a copy for comparison with the final versions used for inventory valuation
- note details of the last delivery of items into inventory and the last issue from inventory – details of the last delivery note or goods received note number should be recorded as this is to assist with cut-off procedures which we will look at in more detail below

after the inventory count

Attending the count is the first element of the auditors' work relating to inventory. However, they must then check that a comparison is made between the result of the actual inventory count and the numbers recorded in the client's inventory records. The auditors must ensure that the client's management have appropriate procedures in place to carry out this important check and to ensure that all differences are investigated and the necessary adjustments made to the records.

The auditors will also need to follow up on the audit work that they themselves carried out during the count. Specifically they should:

■ check the final count sheets with copies they have taken of the actual sheets used in the count

■ check details of any counts performed by audit staff to the final inventory sheets

■ check the final inventory sheets for arithmetical accuracy

■ ensure that certificates have been received for any inventory held by a third party

When the auditors have satisfied themselves that the quantities of inventory are materially correct, they will then have to consider the inventory's value.

Now read the Case Study which follows and summarise the inventory count process.

<table>
<tr><td>**Case Study**</td><td># FRUITYCO LTD: ATTENDING THE INVENTORY COUNT</td></tr>
</table>

situation

Fruityco Ltd is a wholesaler of fruit and vegetables. The company buys in bulk directly from fruit and vegetable growers in the UK and also imports from overseas. Its main customers are fruit and vegetable retailers, small supermarkets and market traders.

Fruityco's year end is 30 June and you are the audit manager planning the audit of inventory. As part of the audit procedures, members of your team will be attending the year-end inventory count.

You have discovered the following key issues from last year's audit file:

• During the previous year's count there were still deliveries being made and goods being collected by customers. It was noted on last year's file that the client's attitude was that a few boxes of fruit was not material to the overall inventory figure.

• There were no written counting instructions because inventory was counted by the warehouse staff who knew exactly where the inventory was, what it was, and how it should be counted.

• During the audit it was discovered that the company had included in inventory a delivery which was still in a ship moored in the docks and hadn't been unloaded.

The inventory count was carried out very quickly and the audit staff attending were only able to independently count a few items themselves. The results of these counts were in accordance with the client's count.

- There did not appear to be any consideration by the client as to the age and condition of some of the inventory or to its saleability.

required

What key points will you raise with the client's management following on from last year's inventory take?

solution

Last year's inventory count was unsatisfactory from an audit point of view because:

- There were continuous inventory movements during the count; this meant that cut-off procedures could not be applied properly.

- There was no proper management control of the count – no instructions were issued and no independent staff appear to have been used. Management seem to have treated the inventory count as a nuisance rather than as a key procedure.

- The inventory count was carried out by people who were normally involved in maintaining inventory records and handling the movement of goods in and out.

- The audit staff did not appear to have had time to carry out sufficient independent testing.

- Consideration had not been given to the true valuation of damaged inventory, particularly with highly perishable items like fruit and vegetables.

- After the count had taken place, it was found that inventory held at another location was included in the inventory figures – and the auditors knew nothing about this.

As audit manager for this year's audit, you should make the following suggestions to improve the year-end inventory count:

- Audit staff should be informed of all locations where inventory might be located – including any in transit.

- Formal counting instructions should be issued to staff involved in the count. Ideally these should be members of staff who are not normally involved in warehouse activities.

- The count should be recorded on pre-numbered count sheets and carried out in a systematic manner, with test counts and checks being made of the contents of individual sacks and boxes.

- All inventory movement should be suspended while the count is carried out. Details of the last goods inwards note and goods outwards note should be recorded so that the cut-off can be properly carried out.

- A note should be made by company staff giving details of inventory in poor condition.

- When opening boxes and sacks to confirm the quantities, audit staff should examine the condition of the contents. They should make a note of any inventory which does not appear to be fit for resale.

VALUATION OF INVENTORY AND WORK IN PROGRESS

From your accounting studies you will know that inventory and work in progress should be valued at the lower of cost and net realisable value.

You should also be aware that the principles of valuing inventory are set out in Financial Reporting Standard, FRS 102.

We will now examine briefly the key aspects of inventory valuation.

cost

The cost of inventory is taken as being:

- purchase price where items have been bought in either as raw materials or goods for resale, or
- production cost, including an allocation of overheads as appropriate

The individual items of inventory should normally be valued on a First In First Out (FIFO) basis, which broadly means that the oldest inventory is used up first.

Case Study

MAKEIT LTD: INVENTORY VALUATION

Makeit Limited has bought the following quantities of blottit, an ingredient of one of their products which has recently increased substantially in price.

11 August	200 kg @ £4.00 per kg
4 September	200 kg @ £4.10 per kg
12 September	150 kg @ £5.50 per kg
Total	550 kg

There was no opening inventory of blottit.

At the year end (30 September) there were 235 kg of blottit in inventory with the other 315 kg having been used in production.

The management have valued the inventory at latest invoice price of £5.50 per kg and have arrived at a value of £1,292.50.

The total value of all inventory held by Makeit at the year end is £54,000.

required

You are required as auditor to confirm the valuation of closing inventory.

solution

Inventory should be valued on a FIFO basis. This means that the earliest inventory is issued to production first. What remains in inventory are the latest purchases made.

The inventory of 200 kg purchased on 11 August is used first so does not form part of the closing inventory.

115 kg of the material purchased on 4 September has been used for production leaving 85 kg of this purchase remaining.

None of the inventory purchased on 12 September has been used.

The correct closing inventory valuation is therefore:

85 kg @ £4.10	=	£348.50
150 kg @ £5.50	=	£825.00
		£1,173.50

The original valuation of closing inventory of blottit is £1,292.50 and therefore overstates inventory by £119. This is not material in the context of the total inventory value of £54,000, but it does represent over 10% of the inventory value for blottit.

If this policy of valuing inventory at the latest invoice price has been used to value all individual inventory categories, this could result in a material overstatement of inventory in the financial statements.

analytical review

In addition to arithmetical tests such as those detailed above, auditors should also use analytical review to test the valuation of inventory.

Analytical review used by auditors compares financial information from different periods to establish trends and to highlight consistencies and inconsistencies in the financial data of individual clients.

You will be familiar with ratios and performance indicators from your other studies. Several of these ratios and percentages relate to inventory and can be calculated to substantiate the inventory value at the year end.

Key ratios that can be calculated in relation to inventory include:

$$\textbf{Gross profit \%} \quad = \quad \frac{\text{Gross profit} \times 100}{\text{Revenue}}$$

If the gross profit percentage varies significantly from previous years, this could indicate that cost of sales is higher or lower than expected. An incorrect valuation of closing inventory could be the cause of this.

$$\textbf{Inventory turnover} \quad = \quad \frac{\text{Cost of sales}}{\text{Average inventory* or closing inventory}}$$

$$\textbf{Inventory holding period} \quad \frac{\text{Average inventory* or closing inventory} \times 365}{\text{Cost of sales}}$$

* Average inventory calculated as (opening inventory plus closing inventory) ÷ 2

An increase in inventory turnover or inventory holding period could indicate slower moving inventory. If all other factors in the business remain unchanged it could also indicate that the year-end inventory has been overstated, as in the Case Study above.

Analytical procedures on their own will not satisfy the auditors of the accuracy of the inventory valuation. However, they will indicate areas of inconsistency which should prompt further investigation.

net realisable value basis of valuation

Net realisable value means the price that the client would be able to sell the inventory for in its present condition – which could be a lower price than cost price. Inventory might have to be valued on this basis because:

- it is damaged, or its condition has deteriorated, or it is obsolete
- a decision has been made by the company to discontinue the product and sell off remaining inventories at a loss
- the business is in difficulties and needs to raise cash urgently

In these cases the auditors have to base the inventory valuation on what the inventory would realise if sold. This may be simply scrap value or it may have no value at all. If it has been valued by the management at a nil value, auditors should still inspect the items to ensure that this value is appropriate.

The main way of checking the scrap value of unsaleable inventory is to review the price obtained by previous sales of scrap or damaged inventory, either during the year or after the year end.

If there is no available evidence to verify the valuation of inventory at net realisable value, the auditors will have to use their professional judgement together with their knowledge of the client in order to judge whether or not the inventory valuation is reasonable.

WORK IN PROGRESS

The audit approach to work in progress (WIP) will differ slightly from the approach to auditing inventory. Physical inspection is a good way to establish that the work in progress exists, but inspecting something which is only part finished will not allow the auditor to assess the valuation with any accuracy.

The approach that the auditors take will be based on:

- performing compliance testing on the accounting system to confirm that costs, particularly for materials and labour, are being correctly coded in the costing system

- the use of analytical review techniques to look at the proportions of materials and labour used in production
- the use of analytical procedures to compare this years's value of work in progress for different inventory lines with last year's figure
- checking the labour costs included in work in progress to wages records, material costs to inventory records, and overhead costs to invoices

CUT-OFF PROCEDURES

The auditors must satisfy themselves that the client company has sufficient controls within its systems to ensure that inventory movements are accounted for in the correct accounting period, ie

- if goods are included in inventory, the costs relevant to those items have also been included in purchases and, if appropriate, in the year-end trade payables figure
- if goods are included in revenue and trade receivables they have been taken out of inventory

This is known as **cut-off.**

The activities of the business continue from day-to-day and do not stop just because it is a period end. Therefore, cut-off must be considered at four separate points in the manufacturing process for the purpose of inventory valuation:

- receipt of raw materials from suppliers
- issue of raw material into production
- transfer of work in progress to finished goods
- delivery of goods to customers

The key point is that inventory should not be counted more than once and that trade payables must be recorded for all inventory received.

Specific points to consider here are:

- goods might have been received and included in inventory, but the invoice may not have been posted to the purchase ledger
- goods might be received and included in inventory, but the invoice may not have been received from the supplier
- goods could have been returned to a supplier before the year end and correctly excluded from inventory, but the suppliers invoice could still be included in the purchase ledger awaiting a credit note
- inventory could have been delivered to a customer close to the year end but not recorded as taken out of inventory

Auditors must carry out procedures to make sure that trade payables have been included for all the items included in inventory, unless of course the goods have been paid for before the year end. Similarly they must carry out procedures to ensure that goods despatched to customers are invoiced and included in revenue and trade receivables.

Looking back to the procedures that the auditors carried out during the inventory count, they should have noted the number of the last goods received note (GRN) issued and the final despatch note raised before the count. This will enable them to audit the cut-off for inventory, trade payables and trade receivables.

The key procedures that the auditors will carry out are:

- review purchase invoices entered in to the company records shortly before and after the year and match them to the GRN to ensure that they are recorded in the correct accounting period

- review GRNs after the year end and ensure that none of these have been included in inventory or trade payables for the current financial period

- check records of goods returned to suppliers before the year end to ensure that any credit notes due have either been received or accrued

- check sales invoices before and after the year end to ensure that goods despatched to customers have been invoiced in the correct accounting period

The following Case Study will help you to understand the key points relating to cut-off procedures.

Case Study

BRIGHTLY PLC: CUT-OFF

situation

Brightly plc is a manufacturer of lighting equipment. Its year end is 31 March and an inventory count has taken place on this date.

The auditors have recorded the last Goods Received Note as no. 3487.

Inspection of invoices received shortly after the year end and posted to the purchase ledger includes the following:

Invoice	Supplier	Invoice date	GRN number	Amount
98984	Kings Ltd	30 March	3485	1200.50
12180	Bulbs & Co.	31 March	3486	750.00
38742	Lights Ltd	1 April	3487	150.00
23726	Phil Amment Ltd	31 March	3488	598.70
52832	Gleam Supplies	30 March	3489	740.00

required

Which invoices have been incorrectly recorded in purchases for the year and should be excluded from the list of trade payables at the year end?

solution

The auditors recorded the last GRN number as 3487, so goods which were recorded on GRN numbers 3488 and 3489 were not delivered in time to be included in the inventory count.

This means that the invoice from Phil Amment Ltd for £598.70 and the invoice from Gleam Supplies for £740 should not be in the list of trade payables at the year end, despite the fact that the invoices are dated prior to the year end.

RECEIVABLES

The Statement of Financial Position heading of 'Receivables' generally includes two categories:

- trade receivables

- prepayments

We will examine each of these in turn from the point of view of verifying existence, ownership and value.

In the case of receivables, the auditors will rely much more heavily on compliance tests of the company's revenue system for evidence of completeness than might be the case with non-current assets and inventories. The reason for this is that the sales ledger where the year-end trade receivables figure is taken from is the final part of the revenue system.

trade receivables

These consist of sales ledger balances. The main objective of the auditors is to gather evidence to prove that these balances are either:

- fully recoverable, or

- an allowance has been made against any doubtful debts

The compliance testing work that has been carried out on the internal controls in the revenue system should provide sufficient evidence as to whether:

- sales have been made to approved customers

- all sales have been recorded

- all amounts received from customers have been posted to the correct sales ledger accounts

In doing this, the auditors confirm that the sales ledger balances exist and that they belong to the client. The next step is to perform substantive tests to confirm the value of trade receivables.

The client will want its Statement of Financial Position to look as healthy as possible and so is more likely to overstate an asset than to understate it. Consequently, the audit objective when testing receivables is to ensure that they are not materially overstated.

The specific audit work that will be carried out on the list of sales ledger balances comprises:

- check that the balance on the sales ledger control account equals the total of the list of balances on the ledger
- test a sample of sales ledger balances to the ledger and vice versa
- review the cash book for receipts from customers after the year end to test if sales ledger balances have subsequently been paid – this is good evidence that the individual customer's balance is correctly stated and recoverable at the year end
- review all credit balances and ascertain the reason for them: they may have been caused by an invoice being paid twice, or a credit note having being issued to the customer; it could also be that an invoice has been sent to the customer and payment received but the invoice has not been entered in the sales ledger

trade receivables' circularisation

One of the best ways for the auditors to establish the existence, ownership and value of trade receivables is to ask the customer what they owe the company. This is usually done by selecting a sample of the year-end trade receivables and performing a **trade receivables' circularisation**. This involves sending each of the customers a letter asking them to confirm their balance with the client.

In addition to confirming existence, ownership and value of the trade receivables balance a circularisation will also:

- provide evidence of the effectiveness of the system of internal control
- assist in the auditors' review of cut-off procedures
- identify items in dispute

The auditors carry out a positive circulation of trade receivables. This means the customer is asked to confirm whether they agree with the balance or not. If they do not agree they are asked to provide the audit with the balance they believe they owe to the client.

The process for performing a trade receivables' circularisation is as follows:

- select a **sample of balances** from the list of customer accounts in the sales ledger

  There are no rules as to what constitutes an appropriate number of accounts to be sampled, but the auditors have to be able to justify the size of the sample in the context of the total value of trade receivables and the total number of accounts.

  If you are not sure about this then look again at the section on sampling in Chapter 4.

- the sample should include not only active accounts but also:
  - nil balances
  - credit balances
  - accounts in dispute or where amounts have been written off in the period

- send letters to the sample of customers (see example on the next page).

  The letter must be signed and sent from the client as the client's permission is needed before customers can be approached.

- the reply is requested to be sent to the auditors and a prepaid envelope is provided

- all the letters should be posted by the auditors to ensure that they have been sent

- replies are received and evaluated by the auditors and any queries fully investigated

- if replies are not received, these customers should be followed up with a second reminder letter – this is often a problem in practice as there may be insufficient time to do this before the completion of the audit

The objective of the trade receivables circularisation is to ensure that trade receivables are correctly stated. Consequently the auditors are keen to achieve as high a response rate as possible to make the test as valid as possible. If the auditors feel that they have not received sufficient response to the trade receivables circularisation letters they will have to test the balances in other ways including a review of after date cash received, as detailed above.

When the replies have been received, the auditors should compare the value certified by the customer with the sales ledger balance. Any differences should be reconciled and the reasons for these differences investigated.

These may be simply timing differences but may also be as a result of errors or mistakes which should be followed up.

To: Sample Ltd
Address

Dear Sirs

Our auditors, Tickett & Wrunne, have requested that as part of their audit you kindly confirm whether you agree or disagree with our records of the balance you owe to us at close of business on 31 March 20-1.

According to our records this amounted to £2,466.50 as shown on the enclosed statement.

If this amount agrees with your records, please complete and sign the slip below and return it to our auditors in the enclosed prepaid envelope.

If this amount does not agree with your records, please notify our auditors directly either by amending the enclosed statement or by providing a reconciliation of the difference.

This request is for audit purposes only and has no other significance.

Thank you for your co-operation.

Yours faithfully

John Brown

John Brown
Financial Controller

- -

Customer ..Sample Ltd..........

The amount shown ~~does~~/does not* agree with our records as at 31 March 20-1

Account number ..DE1098............... Signed ....I M Cross............

Date..10 April 20-1........... Position...Accounts Manager...............

* The balance shown in our records is £..2,266.50... A reconciliation is attached.

a trade receivables circularisation letter, completed by the customer

allowance for doubtful debts

Clients that are concerned about being able to recover debts should make an allowance in the accounts for doubtful debts. Ideally all allowances made by the management should be in respect of specific amounts due. However, companies sometimes make a general allowance based on the value of total trade receivables – this general type of allowance should be reviewed carefully as it may undervalue total receivables (the allowance is deducted from trade receivables).

In assessing the reasonableness of the allowance for doubtful debts the auditors should review the following:

- the adequacy of the credit control system – how effectively does the client chase debts?
- any disputes that are ongoing between the client and the customer
- a comparison of the period of credit allowed and length of time the debt has been outstanding
- reports obtained from credit reference agencies regarding the solvency of the customer
- the way the debt is made up – for example, is the customer paying off specific invoices or are they simply making small payments on account which could indicate cash flow problems
- whether there have been any payments received since the Statement of Financial Position date
- the calculation of any general allowance for doubtful debts – to ensure that it has been accurately calculated and that it is consistent with previous years' provisions

prepayments

Prepayments are amounts that the client has paid before the year end but which relate to the following financial period. Often they will be items such as rent where the amount is paid quarterly but the quarter ends after the client's year end. These can be audited relatively easily using the following audit procedures:

- check the calculation of the prepayments has been correctly done
- check the payment to the cash book and the invoice
- compare the calculations with previous financial periods to ensure that they are consistent with previous years and are prepared on a similar basis

BANK BALANCES

The auditors will rely on compliance testing of the client's accounting systems to provide evidence of completeness of the bank figure in the financial statements – this should confirm that the cash book is being properly maintained. In addition to this they must confirm the balance at the period end.

year-end bank reconciliation

In a system with strong internal controls the auditors would expect to see the client performing regular (usually monthly) reconciliations between the bank account balance in the cash book and the balance on the bank statement received from the bank. The auditors will check the year-end reconciliation in detail by:

- agreeing the balance to the cash book
- agreeing the balance to the bank statement
- checking the arithmetic accuracy of the reconciliation
- tracing unpresented cheques and uncredited lodgements to the client's bank statement after the year end
- investigating any items in the reconciliation at the year end that have not appeared on the bank statement by the time of the audit

The auditors will normally take a copy of the client's bank reconciliation and mark it with appropriate audit ticks to demonstrate that they have checked each item.

bank confirmation letter

The strongest evidence of the accuracy of the year-end bank balance is independent confirmation from the bank itself. This is done by sending a standard request, known as a **bank confirmation letter**, to the bank.

The bank letter should always be in the standard form that has been agreed with the banking authorities and should be sent to all banks and branches where the auditor believes or knows the client has accounts.

The letter is sent directly to the bank by the auditors requesting confirmation of balances on all the client's bank accounts at the period end. It will also include permission from the client for the bank to disclose the information requested. Additional information can be requested by attaching a supplementary request.

Note that some of the terminology applies to specialist areas of bank services which are unlikely to be used by the client, for example 'derivative and commodity trading'.

An example of the standard bank confirmation letter is illustrated on the page opposite.

The bank will reply with details relevant to the client, providing details, for example, of:

- account balances
- loans
- overdraft facilities
- charges and mortgages held over the client's assets
- items held in safe custody, eg title deeds of client property (referred to in the letter as 'custodian arrangements')

The bank is likely to have instructions on its own files of what information needs to be provided to the auditors.

Date

The Manager
NE Bank PLC
High Street
Newtown
NE1 6HH

Dear Sirs

In accordance with the agreed practice for provision of information to auditors, please forward information on our mutual client(s) as detailed below on behalf of the bank, its branches and subsidiaries. This request and your response will not create any contractual or other duty with us.

Companies or other business entities

....Limited

.... Limited

Audit Confirmation Date: ....

Information required	Tick
Standard	
Trade finance	
Derivative and commodity trading	
Custodian arrangements	
Other information (see attached)	

The Authority to disclose information signed by your customer is already held by you. Please advise us if this Authority is insufficient for you to provide full disclosure of the information requested.

The contact name is: ....   Telephone: ....

Yours faithfully

Tickett & Wrunne, Registered Auditors

bank confirmation letter

When the auditors have received a reply from the bank they must ensure that all the information in the letter agrees to the financial statements and has been appropriately disclosed. The bank balance(s) shown on the bank letter should be agreed by the auditors to the balance(s) on the bank statement. Any discrepancies between the financial records and the bank letter must be followed up and the letter should be filed on the audit file in the bank and cash section.

CASH BALANCES

Clients do not normally hold significant amounts of cash, with most only holding small petty cash balances for day-to-day expenses. As the balance is unlikely to be material, the auditors will normally carry out only limited audit testing in this area to ensure that the amount shown in the financial statements agrees to the amount held in the petty cash tin.

For clients where cash plays a major part in the operation of the business – for example cafés, bars, shops and taxi firms – auditors may have to make arrangements to count it at the period end.

If a year-end count is not possible, auditors should make 'surprise' visits to the client's premises to count cash balances and reconcile them with the accounting records.

In all cases when the auditors are handling the client's cash, they must ensure that a member of the client's staff is present as the last thing they want is to be accused of misappropriating cash, particularly if testing shows that the balance of cash counted is less than the records show should be there!

In businesses where large amounts of cash are involved there is a higher level of inherent risk. The auditors will rely on their testing of the controls within the accounting systems to ensure that cash recording is being carried out properly. With the increased risk that comes with large amounts of cash the auditors must be alert to the possibility of fraud and must ensure that their audit procedures take account of this.

In order to gain assurance that cash takings are properly recorded and that cash is not being stolen or lost, the auditors must perform the following testing:

- review reconciliations between cash takings and till rolls or cash sheets
- carry out surprise cash counts
- perform analytical procedures, such as comparing gross profit margin to previous periods, to see whether the level of cash sales appears to be consistent
- review the client's procedures for the safe custody of cash, eg that cash is locked away in a safe or lockable cabinets

■ review banking procedures – ideally cash should be banked daily and 'intact' (ie cash takings should not be used to pay for cash purchases)

■ check the adequacy of insurance arrangements for cash retained on the premises

LIABILITIES

In this section we will look at the methods that the auditors use to confirm the existence, ownership, valuation and completeness of liabilities.

The Statement of Financial Position heading of 'liabilities' includes:

■ purchase ledger balances (trade payables)

■ accruals

■ provisions

■ non-current (long-term) liabilities

When auditing liabilities, the auditors must consider the possibility of understatement. The client will be keen for the Statement of Financial Position to look as good as possible and understating liabilities will help to do this. This factor should be taken into account when the auditors are testing liabilities, particularly trade payables, for completeness.

In the following pages we will look at particular aspects of each type of liability and the way in which the auditor should test them.

purchase ledger balances

In the same way that the audit of trade receivables can be linked to the audit of the revenue system, auditing trade payables balances is linked with the work performed on the purchases system.

The audit work that has been carried out to assess the strength of the controls in the client's purchases system should test whether controls are in place to ensure that:

■ all purchases are authorised and made from approved suppliers

■ all liabilities owed to suppliers are correctly recorded in the purchase ledger

■ liabilities to suppliers are regularly settled

■ payments are made within the suppliers' terms of trade

To audit the year-end trade payables, the auditor will carry out the following substantive tests:

■ check the purchase ledger control account reconciliation with the list of individual ledger account balances

- select a sample from the list of purchase ledger balances and reconcile them with statements from suppliers (we examine how this is done in more detail below)

- where supplier statements are not available for a number of suppliers the balance should be checked to the total of individual invoices and credit notes outstanding – this will verify that the balance exists but it does not provide evidence of completeness, ie that all invoices due to the supplier have been included in the balance

- review payments to suppliers after the year end – payment of the balance by the client is good evidence that the amount due to the supplier at the year end is correctly stated

- investigate all debit balances on the purchase ledger – the debit balance may have arisen because an invoice has not been posted to the account (in which case purchases and trade payables may be understated) or an invoice may have been paid twice which could indicate a systems weakness

- perform cut-off procedures to ensure liabilities are included in the correct accounting period

In certain circumstances, the auditors may decide to perform a trade payables' circularisation by sending out letters. As with trade receivables, this should be a positive circularisation (ie 'please reply anyway') and may sometimes be used when the auditors have assessed the controls in the client's systems as being weak. It may also be used as a method of confirming the trade payables' balances if the client does not receive statements from many of its suppliers.

trade payables (supplier) statement reconciliations

The most conclusive way of testing trade payables balances for existence, ownership, valuation and completeness is by performing supplier statement reconciliations on a sample, as this provides confirmation of the balance by a third party.

There are no rules as to what constitutes an appropriate number of trade payables balances to be sampled, but the auditors must be able to justify the size of the sample in the context of the total value of the purchase ledger and the total number of accounts.

One point that must be remembered is that the auditors are seeking to ensure that trade payables are not understated. Therefore the sample should be selected on the basis of the accounts with the greatest activity in the year rather than those with the highest balance at the year end.

If you need reminding about sampling, look at Chapter 4 (pages 99 - 107).

When the auditors have obtained copies of the supplier statements, they should reconcile the balance shown by the statement with the balance shown in the client's purchase ledger.

Differences are likely to relate to:

- invoices or credit notes in transit between the supplier and the client which will appear on the supplier statement but may not have been posted to the client's ledger

- payments in transit which have been sent by the client but have not been received by the supplier in time to be included on the statement

Case Study

FANCY DANCER LTD:
SUPPLIERS STATEMENT RECONCILIATION

situation

You are a member of the audit team currently auditing Fancy Dancer Ltd, a manufacturer of theatrical makeup and clothing which has a year end of 30 June 20-1. As part of the process of verifying liabilities you have been asked to carry out a reconciliation of a sample of purchase ledger balances with statements from suppliers.

The following accounts have been extracted from the purchases ledger:

BADGERS PLC

Date	Invoice no.	Dr	Cr	Balance
B/Fwd			1,872.89	
2.6.-1	2389		9,653.09	
5.6.-1	2345		6,785.02	
23.6.-1	2453		5,457.98	
				23,768.98

SoSo Ltd

Date	Invoice no.	Dr	Cr	Balance
B/Fwd			5,439.67	
1.6.-1	2563		1,028.00	
6.6.-1	2564		4,398.08	
7.6.-1 Cash	52	5,439.67		
12.6.-1	2578		7,449.90	12,875.98

BLUEBEARD LTD

Date		Invoice no.	Dr	Cr	Balance
B/Fwd				2,341.65	
2.6.-1	CB	54	2,341.65		
19.6.-1		2345		8,759.00	
22.6.-1		2453		1,265.98	
					10,024.98

TRADERS

Date		Invoice no.	Dr	Cr	Balance
B/Fwd				2,341.65	
1.6.-1		2689		1,564.65	
5.6.-1	CB	61	3,906.30		
12.6.-1		2703		6,784.09	
18.6.-1		2734		2,567.78	
22.3.-1		2745		7,649.67	
26.6.-1		2786		9,864.45	
30.6.-1	CB	62	6,784.09		20,081.90

SECONDSOUT

Date		Invoice no.	Dr	Cr	Balance
B/Fwd				3,576.98	
12.6.-1		2854		12,765.89	
12.6.-1	CB	63	3,576.98		
16.6.-1		2874		19,564.34	
16.6.-1		2984		12,675.42	
					45,005.65

SIMPLES

Date		Invoice no.	Dr	Cr	Balance
B/Fwd				543.98	
3.6.-1	CB	63	543.98		
12.6.-1	Credit	398	543.98		
15.6.-1	Journal 2			543.98	
22.6.-1	CB	65	543.98		−543.98

You have obtained the relevant statements for these suppliers:

BADGERS PLC
43 DOWNEER INDUSTRIAL ESTATE
FARTOWN
FX2 3ES

FANCY DANCER LTD

STATEMENT

DATE	INVOICE	DR £	CR £
Forward		1,872.89	
2.6.-1	77456	9,653.09	
5.6.-1	77891	6,785.02	
12.6.-1	Credit 247		1,872.89
23.6.-1	78012	5,457.98	

| **Amount due** | | **21,896.09** | |

SoSo Limited
Unit 2
Narrowly Street
Neartown
NE1 3RL

STATEMENT TO:
Fancy Dancer Ltd
Twinkle Street
Bigtown
BG2 4AU

Date	Invoice no.	Dr £	Cr £
May		5,439.67	
2.6.-1	796	1,028.00	
5.6.-1	801	4,398.08	
7.6.-1	Cash paid		5,439.67
23.6.-1	823	7,449.90	

| **Balance due** | | **£12,875.98** | |

---

bluebeard
downside works
Newtown
NE2 5LE

Fancy Dancer Ltd
Twinkle Street
Bigtown
BG2 4AU

STATEMENT

1.6.-1	Fwd	2,341.65
2.6.-1	CB56	−2,341.65
19.6.-1	34567	7,859.00
22.6.-1	34786	1,265.98

| **Total** | | **9,124.98** |

TRADERS LTD
Roper Street
Bigtown
BG3 4LT

Fancy Dancer Ltd
Twinkle Street
Bigtown
BG2 4AU

	Ref	Dr £	Cr £
B/fwd		2,341.65	
1.6.-1	984	1,564.65	
5.6.-1	35		3,906.30
12.6.-1	991	6,784.09	
18.6.-1	1045	2,567.78	
22.3.-1	1056	7,649.67	
26.6.-1	1083	9,864.45	

| **Due** | | **£26,865.99** | |

SECONDS OUT LIMITED
Second House
Biggar Lane
Neartown
NE3 2TL

STATEMENT TO:
Fancy Dancer Ltd
Twinkle Street
Bigtown
BG2 4AU

		Dr £	Cr £
Fwd		3,576.98	
12.6.-1	878	12,765.89	
16.6.-1	891	19,564.34	
18.6.-1	901	12,675.42	
19.6.-1	2		3,576.98
23.6.-1	942	14,202.83	
Balance		**£59,208.48**	

SIMPLES LTD
14 New Road
Neartown
NE1 4TH

Fancy Dancer Ltd
Twinkle Street
Bigtown
BG2 4AU

STATEMENT

1.6.-1 B/FWD		543.98
8.6.-1 Received	-543.98	
BALANCE		0.00

required

(a) Using the information given to you on the last three pages, complete the table below.

Trade payable	Balance as per client	Balance as per statement	Agrees to statement	Reconciled
Badgers plc	23,768.98	21,896.09		
SoSo Ltd	12,875.98	12,875.98		
Bluebeard ltd	10,024.98	9,124.98		
Traders	20,081.90	26,865.99		
Seconds out	455,005.65	59,208.48		
Simples	−543.98	0		

(b) State what the objective of this test is.

(c) Write notes about the tasks undertaken by the auditing team, mentioning any reconciliations performed and any further work needed in order to reach a conclusion.

solution

(a)

Trade payable	Balance as per client	Balance as per statement	Agrees to statement	Reconciled
Badgers plc	23,768.98	21,896.09		✔
SoSo Ltd	12,875.98	12,875.98	✔	
Bluebeard ltd	10,024.98	9,124.98		✔
Traders	20,081.90	26,865.99		✔
Seconds out	455,005.65	59,208.48		✔
Simples	−543.98	0		✔

(b) The objective of the test is to ensure that trade payables are correctly stated.

(c) It will be necessary for the auditors to follow up all the reconciling items on each of the reconciliations to ensure that they are valid. The invoices and credit note should be agreed to the original document and the cash in transit should be agreed to the bank statement.

The client has not picked up the transposition error in posting to the Bluebeard account and consequently this should be followed up.

The account with Simples Limited seems to have had several adjustments made to it, culminating in an invoice being paid twice. This has created a debit balance on the account which should be investigated to discover whether it is a simple mistake or if it results from a weakness in the systems, or even if it could be a possible fraud.

The workings are as shown below. Note that the comments column on the right sets out the client's explanation for the discrepancies.

Client:	Fancy Dancers Ltd	**Prepared by:**	JSO
Year end:	30-Jun-20-1	**Date:**	03-Aug-20-1
		Reviewed by:	
		Date:	

Purchase Ledger Balance Reconciliation with suppliers statements

Objective of test: To ensure that trade payables are correctly stated.

Badgers plc	£	**Client's explanation**
Balance per purchase ledger	23,768.98	
Credit note not included	−1,872.89	Account posted in July
Balance per Badgers Ltd	21,896.09	

	Client's explanation

SoSo Ltd	£	
Balance per purchase ledger	12,875.98	
Balance per SoSo Ltd	12,875.98	

Bluebeard Ltd		
Balance per purchase ledger	10,024.98	
Transposition error in posting: Invoice 2598 s/be £7,859.00 not £8,759.00	–900.00	Not amended by client
Balance per Bluebeard	9,124.98	

Traders Ltd		
Balance per purchase ledger	20,081.90	
Payment not received by supplier	6,784.09	
	26,865.99	

Secondsout		
Balance per purchase ledger	45,005.65	
Invoice not posted	14,202.83	Included in accrued invoice list
Balance per Secondsout	59,208.48	

Simples Ltd		
Balance per purchase ledger	–543.98	
Invoice paid twice CB 63 & CB 65	543.98	Duplicate invoice paid in error. Client will deduct from next payment.
Balance per Simples Ltd	0.00	

accruals

You will know from your accounting studies that accruals are amounts which are quantified and included in the accounts for the current year being audited, but for which payment is not yet due.

Examples include:

■ VAT liability

■ PAYE and NI

■ interest on borrowings

■ purchase invoices received but not entered in the ledger

In most cases, accruals can be checked by a combination of analytical procedures and professional judgement to assess reasonableness, ie the schedule of accruals for the current year end can be compared to the previous year for consistency. The auditors can also use their experience of the client to assess what accruals would be likely in such a business.

In addition to this, the auditors can specifically check the amounts accrued to supporting documentation. For example:

■ the VAT accrual can be agreed to the VAT control account

■ PAYE & NI deducted from wages but not yet paid to HM Customs & Revenue can be checked against payroll schedules

■ interest calculations can be re-calculated using the loan amount and interest rate verified by the bank letter

■ invoices received but not posted can be checked by examining the actual document

As the audit visit is made after the year end, in most cases accruals can be verified with payments made after the year end, or in the case of VAT to the VAT return submitted after the year end.

provisions

The client will make provision in the accounts for costs which may be incurred but which cannot be precisely quantified. One example of this might be a provision to cover the outcome of a legal claim that has been made against the client which has not yet been settled, or another could be a provision for a possible loss on a contract which has yet to be completed.

In other words, provisions are estimates based on the directors' judgement. This then presents a problem for the auditors, as there is often little reliable evidence to support the estimate. Consequently, the auditors may find it very difficult to find independent evidence to support the existence, ownership and value of these provisions.

You need to be familiar with the accounting rules set out in **IAS 37 'Provisions, Contingent Liabilities and Contingent Assets'** (and previously in FRS 12). This basically requires that a provision be made if it is likely that the client will have an obligation to pay something, as the result of a past event, even if the amount cannot be precisely calculated.

The important point here is that there must be an obligation. A provision should not be simply an amount of money set aside 'for a rainy day' or to reduce profit. It must represent a genuine attempt by the management to quantify a liability that actually exists but for which the exact amount, or when the liability will have to be settled, is not yet known.

When the auditors are testing the provisions in the accounts they need to ask themselves:

- is the provision in respect of a liability which is likely to be incurred?
- what is the probability of it being incurred?
- on what basis has the provision been calculated and is there evidence to support it?

ISA 540 'Auditing accounting estimates, including fair value accounting estimates, and related disclosures' states:

> 'ISA 330 (The auditor's responses to assessed risks) requires the auditor to design and perform audit procedures whose nature, timing and extent are responsive to the assessed risks of material misstatement in relation to accounting estimates at both the financial statement and assertion (transaction) levels.'

If we look at this in more detail, the audit approach to provisions and other accounting estimates states that the auditors should:

- understand how management decide whether an estimate or provision is required
- understand the process by which management arrived at the figure for the estimate
- decide (where management has used an expert to calculate the provision) how qualified and independent the expert is
- review the accuracy of estimates made in previous periods when measured against what actually happened
- consider whether the assumptions used by management when calculating the provision or estimate are reasonable
- confirm if management considered possible alternative bases of calculation
- perform their own calculations and compare their result against the figure arrived at by the management; significant differences should be explored and explained

- consider whether the estimate has been calculated in accordance with IAS 37 (FRS 12)
- ask the management to include details of the provision in the Letter of Representation (see Chapter 7) if it is material

If the provision is to cover a legal claim made against the client, the auditors must contact the company's legal representatives to obtain sufficient independent evidence to support the provision.

If the auditors cannot find sufficient evidence to support the provision calculation, they may request formal written confirmation from the management of the business and will obtain representations from the management to support this. This will be covered in detail in Chapter 7.

non-current (long-term) liabilities

Non-current (long-term) liabilities are amounts that are due for payment in more than one year's time and are, generally, bank loans or other similar forms of long-term finance. Confirmation of loan balances will be included in the bank confirmation letter.

The auditor will also ensure that:

- bank loans and overdrafts have been disclosed correctly in the financial statements in accordance with the provisions of the Companies Act
- that the company has not breached the terms and conditions of the loans
- that the loan facilities will continue for the foreseeable future

If the auditors believe that the client's long-term finance might be withdrawn they must consider whether this will have an impact on the client's ability to continue to operate as a going concern. If the auditors decide that this is an issue, it will have to be disclosed to the shareholders in the audit report. This situation will be discussed again when we examine reporting in Chapter 7.

SHARE CAPITAL AND RESERVES

The verification of the client's share capital and reserves should be relatively straightforward. Most matters relating to this area are recorded in the company's statutory books which are maintained by the Company Secretary.

The statutory books comprise several registers, including the register of shareholders and the register of directors. They also set out the details of share capital issued and contain the minutes of the board of directors and of the annual general meetings.

The procedures that the auditors should carry out in relation to share capital and reserves can be summarised as follows:

- check the opening balances with the previous year's financial statements
- review the statutory books for new shares issued in the relevant period
- ensure that the details have been properly disclosed in the financial statements
- review minutes of board meetings and the annual general meeting – this will provide information about dividend payments and share issues which the auditor can follow through to the final financial statements

The balances on reserves accounts can be audited by checking the opening balances to the previous year's audit file. Movements on reserves during the year, such as a movement on a share premium account, can be verified by reference to the statutory records and minute books. Movements on retained profits will relate to the profit earned in the year which can be checked to the audited Statement of Profit or Loss.

Chapter Summary

- The auditors' task is to gather sufficient audit evidence to validate assertions about the existence, ownership (known as rights and obligations), valuation and correct recording (known as completeness) of all assets and liabilities shown on the Statement of Financial Position.

- Auditors will primarily use substantive testing procedures to verify Statement of Financial Position items, although when verifying current assets and liabilities, the results of compliance testing of system controls is also relevant.

- Non current assets can be verified largely by substantive procedures where evidence is obtained through physical inspection and tests on original documents. In some cases it may be necessary to use independent experts where property or investments are being valued.

- Inventory is a key figure in the financial statement because it affects profits and net asset values. Audit tests on inventory are therefore particularly important.

- The client will normally perform an inventory count at the period end. The auditors must ensure that they always attend this.

- The auditors' role is to observe the inventory count and perform test counts on a sample of items.

- Cut-off procedures must be audited to ensure that both assets and liabilities are included in the correct accounting period.

- The auditor must ensure that inventory and work in progress are valued in accordance with the principles laid down in IAS 2 (and in SSAP 9).

■ Trade receivables can be tested by sending a circularisation letter to a sample of customers who are asked to confirm the balance directly to the auditors.

■ A confirmation letter should be sent to the client's bank(s) to request confirmation of bank balances, loans and securities held.

■ Trade payables can be verified by reconciling suppliers' statements to the purchase ledger balances.

■ Share capital and reserves can be checked with the previous year's accounts and the statutory records.

Key Terms		
assets register	a list of tangible non-current assets recording all relevant details relating to the assets
audit risk	the risk of the auditors signing an incorrect audit report on the financial statements
compliance testing	testing of internal controls to ensure they are functioning correctly
substantive testing	all tests other than compliance tests, including analytical review
tangible non-current assets	assets which have a useful life of greater than one year and which physically exist, eg buildings
intangible assets	assets which have a useful life of greater than one year but which do not physically exist, eg patents
inventory count	a physical count of all inventories of raw materials, goods for resale, or finished goods which belong to the company
cut-off	a procedure to ensure that all aspects of a transaction are dealt with in the correct accounting period
third parties	in relation to the audit – parties other than the auditors and the client
net realisable value	the amount an item could be sold for on the open market

trade receivables circularisation

a form of audit testing where the auditors request a confirmation directly from the customer of the amount outstanding at the year end

bank confirmation letter

a letter sent by the auditors to the client's bank(s) requesting confirmation of the client's bank balances and other details, including loans and overdraft facilities

bank reconciliation

a reconciliation of the balance of the bank account in the cash book with the balance on the bank statement

supplier statement reconciliation

a reconciliation between the amount shown in the purchase ledger and the balances on supplier statements

going concern

the assumption that the company will be able to continue to trade for the foreseeable future

statutory books

the records which have by law to be kept, and which record details of the ownership and management of the business

company secretary

the company official required to maintain the statutory books of the company

Activities

6.1 The following statements have been found in a presentation to be given to some trainee auditors. Which of the statements are incorrect, and why?

(a) Only substantive testing techniques are used for checking the statement of financial position

(b) Suppliers' statement reconciliations are good audit evidence to verify the trade payables figure in the statement of financial position

(c) If the compliance testing goes well there is no real need to test receivables and payables

(d) You do not need your client's permission to write to their bank

(e) Auditors should ideally always attend the inventory count

(f) Do not bother with cash, it's usually not important

(g) One way of verifying trade receivables is by circularising them

(h) Cut-off means ensuring that transactions around the year end have been accounted for in the correct accounting period

6.2 As part of their audit procedures auditors will read the minutes of directors meetings and record any key decisions which might affect the financial accounts.

The auditors have recently carried out a review of the minutes of directors' meetings for Jollybot Ltd , a company which sells plumbing supplies and certain matters were recorded by the audit staff as being relevant to the audit.

Based on the list of points below decide whether or not these might affect the audit , and thus result in specific audit procedures being used to investigate them or whether they can be safely ignored.

		Investigate	Ignore
(a)	A marketing campaign to increase the profile of the company is to be launched in the new financial year		
(b)	One of the firm's major customers as gone into liquidation		
(c)	Revenue had increased by 8% in the year and Receivables were up 10%		
(d)	The company had sold its factory in Todmorden to a finance company		
(e)	New standard measurements for plumbing fittings were introduced by the EC one month after the year end		

6.3 Your firm's client Blotblot Ltd has recently expanded its factory and purchased additional machinery to go in it in order to cope with an expected significant increase in trade. Some of the factory construction work and all of the installation of the new machinery was carried out by Blotblot's own workforce.

The new equipment comprised some new manufacturing machinery as well as new dust extraction and filtration systems which were built into the fabric of the factory building.

You have been asked to set out in a manner appropriate to the audit plan:

(1) The audit risks relating to the inclusion of these non-current assets on the statement of financial position and

(2) The procedures to be undertaken in order to ensure that the non-current assets are properly classified and disclosed in the financial statements.

6.4 You are working on the audit of McBottle Ltd, a bottle manufacturer. During the course of the audit you have uncovered a series of errors and misstatements.

Pre-tax profit shown by the draft accounts is £250,000 and performance materiality has been set at 5% of pre-tax profits.

The errors you have found are:

- A short-term loan of £25,000 has been shown on the statement of financial position as a long term loan. The total value of loans and overdrafts in the statement of financial position is £824,000

- Raw Material inventory (Glass) has been understated by £8,000. The total value of Raw Material inventory is £126,500

- A provision is required against a trade receivables balance of £7,500. The total value of trade receivables is £211,000

- Accruals for costs have been omitted amounting to £9,000. The total value of Payables is £326,000

- Depreciation has been wrongly calculated understating it by £9,000. The carrying value of non-current assets is £1.2m

The Directors have already stated that they are very reluctant to amend the financial statements unless the adjustments are material.

You are asked to consider which is the right course of action for you to take when discussing these issues with the audit manager.

(a) None of the errors are material so no alterations are required	
(b) They must be corrected because they are errors	
(c) The loan is incorrectly described so this must be amended in the financial statements but no other amendment need be made as the individual errors or misstatements are not material as far as the statement of financial position is concerned	
(d) The loan is incorrectly stated so must be amended. The cumulative effect of the other errors or misstatements exceeds the level of Performance Materiality set so it is likely that all the errors or misstatements will have to be amended	

6.5 Weavitere Ltd hires out industrial vehicles to the construction and transport industries nationally from five depots. Their assets comprise:

- five depots situated throughout the UK, which they own as freehold

- a mixture of commercial vehicles including large tipper lorries, flatbed lorries, mobile cranes and large and small vans

- mechanical diggers, dumpers and similar construction machinery

- mobile generators and compressors

- company cars for directors and senior staff

Set out in a manner suitable for inclusion in the audit plan the audit procedures to be undertaken in order to ensure that non-current assets are fairly stated in the financial statements.

7 Audit completion and audit reporting

this chapter covers...

This chapter examines the contents of the audit report and how it is affected when the auditors do not think that the financial statements of the organisation are true and fair. It also describes the report that the auditors produce for the management outlining the weaknesses in the client's internal control systems.

This chapter covers:

- *dealing with 'subsequent events' – events after the year end*

- *'going concern' – can the business carry on for the foreseeable future?*

- *unusual and non-routine transactions*

- *'management representations' – a letter from the client's management providing written confirmation of audit evidence they have provided*

- *final analytical procedures – overall review of the financial statements in comparison with previous years' results*

- *compliance review – compliance of the accounts with legislation and ISAs*

- *audit adjustments for errors and omissions*

- *auditors' reports to shareholders*

- *modified auditors' reports – reports with qualifications*

- *emphasis of matter – highlighting an issue in the accounts*

- *reporting to management by the auditors*

BACKGROUND TO THE REPORTING STAGE

We have now reached the last phase of the audit process – the audit report – but, before we examine this stage in detail, it is worth considering what we have covered so far. The audit processes can be summarised as follows:

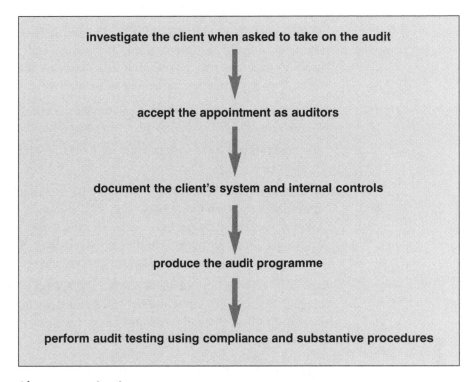

investigate the client when asked to take on the audit

accept the appointment as auditors

document the client's system and internal controls

produce the audit programme

perform audit testing using compliance and substantive procedures

the report stage

The next and final stage – the report stage – has now been reached. By now the audit team have carried out their testing and recorded their findings. Any issues that have been found and any errors that have been identified will have been properly documented and highlighted to the senior members of the audit team.

It is at this point that the senior members of the team start to take a more active role in the audit. Before the auditors can give a final opinion on the financial statements, the **audit manager** and the **audit partner** must carry out the final reviews and procedures.

The last three steps to be carried out are:

■ final audit review

■ final review of financial statements using analytical review techniques

■ final compliance review of the financial statements with the Companies Act 2006 and relevant Accounting Standards

FINAL AUDIT REVIEW

The main audit areas that need to be covered in this final review are:

- subsequent events review (events after the year end)
- going concern (whether the company is able to carry on trading)
- management representations (letters supporting audit evidence)

At this stage of the audit, these issues are often discussed at a senior level by the client's senior management and the partner and manager on the audit team. Discussions may cover issues that have not directly arisen from the audit work that has been carried out and will involve:

- an overview of the company's performance and discussions regarding its future
- a request for written confirmation from the management on difficult audit issues

Auditors must also determine whether any issues raised by management will affect their audit opinion. These may, for example, be issues relevant to whether the organisation can continue as a going concern (page 223), disclosure of significant contingent liabilities or an acceptance by management that some accounting systems are not operating effectively.

Auditors may include these issues in management representation letters (page 227) but they must decide whether the matters raised are serious enough to affect the audit opinion. They should not be influenced by any comments or excuses made by the management.

SUBSEQUENT EVENTS REVIEW

ISA 560 'Subsequent Events' states:

> *'The auditor shall perform audit procedures designed to obtain sufficient appropriate audit evidence that all events occurring between the date of the financial statements and the date of the auditor's report that require adjustment of, or disclosure in, the financial statements have been identified.'*

You will find that some of the points covered here link in with your studies for 'Financial Statements'.

During the course of their checking work, the auditors will have spent most of their time looking at events and transactions that occurred in the financial year being audited. A limited amount of their work will have involved them in looking beyond the year end. For example:

- reviewing payments received from customers after the year end
- tracing uncleared cheques and uncredited lodgements from the bank reconciliation
- carrying out audit work on the client's cut-off procedures

events arising after the date of the financial statements

During the period between the financial year end and the date that the auditor's report is signed, there may be events which shed new light on the financial statements. These are known as **subsequent events**.

There are two types of event which may occur after the date of the financial statements. These are described in International Accounting Standard 10 'Events after the reporting period' which you may cover in your accounting studies. These two types of event are:

- events that provide more information or audit evidence for conditions which existed at the end of the financial period, ie that relate to the financial period being audited. These are known as **adjusting events**
- events that arose after the end of the financial period and do not relate to the period for which the financial statements have been prepared. These are known as **non-adjusting events**

The key difference is that adjusting events provide more information about the items in the financial statements because more time has passed. What this means is that when new information comes to the attention of management or the auditors about something that is included in the financial statements, and the adjustment is material, the financial statements should be altered or amended to take account of the new facts.

Examples of adjusting events are:
- insolvency of a receivable after the year end requiring an adjustment to the bad debt provision
- adjustments to the valuation of inventory or work in progress, for example where inventory has proved unsaleable
- a dispute arising over work carried out on a contract, meaning that the amounts receivable may not be paid to the client
- significant changes to borrowing facilities from banks or other lenders which could affect the financial stability of the business, for example the company's bankers refusing to renew overdraft facilities

However, events which happen after the date of the financial statements and relate to the new financial accounting period are non-adjusting events. Generally, these can be ignored unless they could have some effect on the reader's view of the financial statements.

We can illustrate this point with an example. Suppose the date of the client's financial statements is 31 December and on 1 February the company's factory burned down. This would, ordinarily, not be an adjusting event because it happened after the date of the financial statements. However, it would probably interest the shareholders to know that it had happened so the directors should add a note to the financial statements explaining what has happened. However, the important point is that the figure for non-current assets would not be amended in the Statement of Financial Position as at the date of the financial statement the fire had not occurred and the factory was still a non-current asset of the business.

Other examples of non-adjusting events include:

■ loss or destruction of a major asset after the date of the financial statements

■ an issue of shares after the Statement of Financial Position date

■ a change in the way business is conducted

Note that while these events are informative and add to the general financial picture of the company, they do not relate to something which actually existed at the date of the financial statements or happened within the financial period.

It is primarily the responsibility of the client's management to take these events into account when drafting the financial statements.

In some situations the auditors may disagree with the way in which the directors of a company decide to treat these events. In these cases, the auditors will have to consider how this will affect their audit report. We will discuss this in more detail later in the chapter.

audit tests for a subsequent events review

In order to satisfy themselves that all events after the year end have been appropriately dealt with and disclosed in the financial statements, the auditors should carry out certain audit tests. These will include:

■ reading minutes of board meetings held since the date of the financial statements

■ reviewing management accounts and other information since the date of the financial statements

■ ensuring the adequacy of procedures that the client management has in place to identify such events

■ asking management whether any significant issues have arisen since the year end

In particular ISA 560 suggests that auditors should ask about:

- any new commitments, borrowings or guarantees
- any sales or acquisitions of assets
- any increases in share capital
- whether any agreement to merge with another company or to dispose of the company being audited has been made or is planned
- whether any assets have been lost or destroyed, for example, by fire or flood or nationalised by the government
- whether there have been any developments regarding contingent liabilities
- whether any unusual accounting adjustments have been made or are planned
- whether any events have occurred or are likely to occur that will bring into question the appropriateness of accounting policies used in the financial statements, as would be the case, for example, if such events call into question the validity of the going concern assumption (see below)
- whether any events have occurred that are relevant to the measurement of estimates or provisions made in the financial statements
- whether any events have occurred that are relevant to the recoverability of assets, for example trade receivables or the full value of work in progress

Once auditors have gathered the information and evidence they need they should consult the directors to ensure that any necessary amendments to the financial statements are made. If the Directors refuse to amend the financial statements the auditors will have to consider whether any modification is needed to their Auditors' Report. We will look at modified audit reports later in this chapter.

GOING CONCERN

ISA 570 'Going Concern' states:

'The auditor's responsibility is to obtain sufficient appropriate audit evidence about the appropriateness of management's use of the going concern assumption in the preparation and presentation of the financial statements and to conclude whether there is a material uncertainty about the entity's ability to continue as a going concern.'

One of the fundamental accounting concepts is that the accounts of the company are assumed to be prepared on a **going concern** basis. What does this mean?

The assumption is that the business will carry on its activities in the same way for the 'foreseeable future'. In this case, the term 'forseeable future' generally relates to a period of twelve months after the date of the financial statements. In practice this means that:

- the management will be able to influence the way the business is run
- its products or services will continue to be bought by its customers
- suppliers will continue to supply the company
- it will have sufficient cash to fund its operations
- it will be able to repay loans or other fixed interest borrowing on the due date
- it has not lost any key members of staff
- there have been no uninsured catastrophes

the warning signs

How will the auditors be able to judge whether a business is a going concern? Various events and situations could indicate that a business may no longer be able to carry on for the foreseeable future:

- requested borrowing facilities have been turned down by the bank
- continuing negative cash flows (more cash out than in) from current activities with little prospect of improvement
- inability to pay suppliers on the due dates
- loss of a major customer or key supplier
- fundamental changes in the market or in technology to which the company cannot respond
- changes in legislation which might adversely affect the business
- major legal claims against the company which cannot be met

It is the responsibility of the management to decide whether the company can continue as a going concern and to draft the financial statements accordingly.

The auditors will consider evidence such as budgets and cash flow forecasts prepared by the management. This is particularly important as most businesses fail because they simply run out of funds to meet their liabilities. The key decision the auditors have to make is whether or not they consider the assumptions which the management have used in preparing these financial projections are reasonable in the circumstances.

If the auditors do not accept that this is the case because of over-optimism or a refusal to face reality by the management, the auditors may have to refer to this in their auditor's report. We will explain this later in the chapter.

You should be aware that any mention in the accounts or the auditor's report that the company is not a going concern is extremely serious and is not something that is undertaken lightly. In all probability it will mean that the company will have to cease to trade.

UNUSUAL AND NON-ROUTINE TRANSACTIONS

During the course of their audit work the auditors may become aware of transactions that:

■ are non-routine in nature, ie they are concerned with matters which are outside the normal business activities of the client

■ are exceptionally large and have no obvious commercial purpose

■ are made between the client and other organistaions which the client owns or has control over – these are known as related parties

■ are carried out on a non-commercial basis

■ give reason to believe that there is the possibility of fraud

Some examples that auditors may come across are:

■ loans to or contracts or transactions with third parties that are not dealt with in the normal course of trading and that are outside of the main accounting systems

■ transactions with partnerships or joint ventures that have been set up for no obvious commercial reason

■ management override of controls

■ evidence of collusion between individuals in different departments to bypass internal checks

■ unexplained inventory losses

Misstatements in the accounts may arise through error or fraud. The auditor must be aware of the possibility that fraud exists, however, it is not the auditors' responsibility to actively look for it.

ISA 240 states:

> *'The primary responsibility for the prevention and detection of fraud rests with both those charged with governance of the entity and management'.*

As we have seen, it is the auditors' role to obtain reasonable assurance that the financial statements are free from material misstatements. Consequently, any unusual transactions or any transactions that give rise to a suspicion of fraud must be investigated to ascertain whether they are deliberate or simply errors.

As we saw on page 73, **ISA 315 'Identifying and assessing the risks of material misstatement through understanding the entity and its environment'** requires that audit teams actively discuss the possibility of fraud when evaluating the internal control systems. The audit team should obtain information to assist them in identifying the risk of fraud when performing their audit risk assessments.

To be able to carry out this assessment, auditors must identify and evaluate how management assesses and responds to the risk of fraud. The auditors must also enquire of management if they are aware of any actual or suspected fraudulent activity. However, the audit team must consider the fact that it may actually be the management committing the fraud through deliberate misrepresentation of the financial statements or through using their authority to bypass internal controls and checks.

It is more difficult to detect fraud than to find mistakes. This is simply because the fraudsters will deliberately set out to conceal their activities. We saw on page 38 that auditors are required to adopt an attitude of **'professional scepticism'**; this will assist them in investigating unusual or non-routine transactions.

If unusual or non-routine transactions are discovered during the audit work, these should be discussed by the audit team and all available evidence gathered. The audit manager or audit partner should be informed at the time if these are considered to be serious.

Clearly the auditors will want explanations of such transactions and it is likely that further reassurance would be requested by including them in the **management representation letter**.

MANAGEMENT REPRESENTATIONS

ISA 580 'Written Representations' states:

'The objectives of the auditor are:

(a) *To obtain written representations from management .... that they believe that they have fulfilled their responsibility for the preparation of the financial statements and for the completeness of the information provided to the auditor;*

(b) *To support other audit evidence relevant to the financial statements or specific assertions in the financial statements by means of written representations if determined necessary by the auditor or required by other ISAs.'*

In Chapters 4 to 6 we examined the ways in which the auditors gather evidence to come to a conclusion about the truth and fairness of the financial statements prepared by the directors.

Wherever possible the auditors will:

■ generate their own evidence through compliance and substantive testing, attending inventory takes, physically verifying assets

■ obtain third party evidence, eg trade receivables circularisation, bank confirmation letters

However, during the course of the audit, there may be certain items for which the auditors are unable to find sufficient appropriate evidence and so require written assurance from the management, ie **management representations**. Examples of these items include:

■ a provision has been made for a future loss on a major contract based on the opinion of the directors and for which there is no supporting documentation

■ the directors state that a legal claim against the company has been settled and they anticipate no further claims for the issue involved

In each of these cases, there may be little evidence to substantiate the figures shown in the financial statements, and consequently the auditors are reliant on the word of the directors.

The auditors will request that the management provide them with a **management representation letter** to provide assurance of the information given to the auditors.

It is important to realise that this additional supporting evidence is not a substitute for audit testing.

The management representation letter should also contain an acknowledgment from the directors that it is their responsibility to prepare the financial statements in accordance with the Companies Act 2006 and the appropriate Accounting Standards.

If the management refuse to supply such a letter, or if the auditors consider it to be unreliable because they have doubts about the integrity of the management, the auditors should:

■ consider what other evidence they have concerning the points raised in the management letter

■ consider what effect any lack of evidence may have on their Auditors' Report

A sample management representation letter is shown on the next page.

WIBBLE LIMITED
GRUB STREET, NEWTOWN, NE3 4 TT

Messrs Tickett & Wrunne
Addit Road
Bigtown BG1 5ER

6 June 20-1

Dear Sirs

We confirm to the best of our knowledge and belief, and after having made enquires of other directors and officials of the company, the following representations made to you in connection with your audit of the financial statements for the year ended 31 March 20-1.

We acknowledge, as directors, our responsibilities under the Companies Act 2006 for preparing the financial statements which show a true and fair view and for making accurate representations to you. We confirm that all the accounting records have been made available to you and all transactions made by the company have been recorded in those records. All other information and any related records, including minutes of directors' and management meetings have been made available to you.

The legal claim against us by Hugo Faster plc has been settled out of court by a payment of £250,000. No further claims have been received.

We confirm that the factory premises at Smalltown were properly valued by Messrs G Estimate & Co., Chartered Surveyors and Valuers, who are qualified to undertake this work. Their valuation of those premises on an open market existing use basis was £1.75 million, which has been properly reflected in the accounts.

The loan and overdraft facilities were renewed by the bank on 2 May 20-1 with no adjustments to the terms and conditions of the loans.

The fire at the offices in Grub Street is not expected to cause any detriment to the trading capability of the business.

There have been no events since the Statement of Financial Position date which would require any amendment to the financial statements or any notes.

Signed on behalf of Wibble Ltd

A Balir   *G Bowen*

Managing Director   Financial Director

Minuted by the board at their meeting on 6 June 20-1

T Ricky
Company Secretary

a management representation letter

FINAL ANALYTICAL REVIEW

When the financial statements have been completed, the auditors should carry out final analytical review procedures on the accounts as a whole.

This will involve comparing the figures in the financial statements to the figures in the accounts for the previous year to assess their reasonableness. It will involve calculating selected ratios such as gross profit margin, operating profit margin, return on capital employed, trade receivables collection period, trade payables payment period and inventory turnover. These ratios will be compared to the same ratios from previous years and also to appropriate industry averages if available.

The purpose of these procedures is to ensure that the financial statements as a whole make sense. Up until now, the auditors have been concerned with their detailed testing of the balances and systems and may have lost sight of the overall picture. Final analytical review will allow the auditors to stand back and take an objective look as to whether the financial statements are a true and fair view of the financial position of the business.

At this point in the audit process the auditors should also ensure that the figures in the financial statements agree to the figures that they have been auditing throughout the audit.

COMPLIANCE REVIEW

The auditors in their report are certifying that the accounts comply with the Companies Act 2006 and United Kingdom Generally Accepted Accounting Practice (GAAP). They will normally use a pre-prepared checklist to ensure that the accounts comply in all necessary respects.

AUDIT ADJUSTMENTS

ISA 450 'Evaluation of misstatements identified during the audit' states:

> *'The auditor shall accumulate misstatements identified during the audit, other than those that are clearly trivial.*
>
> *The auditor shall determine whether the overall audit strategy and audit plan need to be revised if:*
>
> *(a) The nature of identified misstatements and the circumstances of their occurrence indicate that other misstatements may exist that, when aggregated with misstatements accumulated during the audit, could be material or*
>
> *(b) The aggregate of misstatements accumulated during the audit approaches materiality determined in accordance with ISA 320.'*

When all the audit work has been completed, including the subsequent events review, the auditors prepare a summary of all the errors and omissions that they have found which would affect the Statement of Profit or Loss and Statement of Financial Position. They will then have a meeting with the client management to discuss which, if any, of these items will be adjusted for in the financial statements.

Materiality is a key issue here. If the errors or omissions the auditors have found are not material (ie the accounts still give a true and fair view even if they are left out) then no further action needs to be taken. What the auditors have to remember is that each item on its own may not be material but they have to consider what happens when all the errors are taken together.

If the auditors consider the errors and misstatements to be material but the directors are not prepared to amend the financial statements the auditors will have to consider the effect this has on their auditors' report. They should also, if possible, obtain a written representation from the directors as to why they were not prepared to correct the misstatements.

This could be because the directors do not consider the suggested adjustments to be misstatements in which case they are entitled to make that clear to the auditors in writing. Regardless of what the directors say, the auditors must still decide whether or not to modify their auditors' report.

The following Case Study shows how audit adjustments might be presented.

<table>
<tr><td>

**Case
Study**

</td><td>

CAPONE LTD: AUDIT ADJUSTMENTS

situation

The auditors have completed their work on the audit of their client Capone Ltd. They have found several errors and omissions which they want to bring to the attention of the directors. These items are:

- an under-provision for a possible bad debt from Bugsy Ltd of £10,350
- £5,260 worth of inventory had been left out of the closing inventory value
- the audit of the bank reconciliation showed that the bank figure shown in the cash book was £1,250 less than it should be
- the client had missed out an accrual for light and heat estimated to be £3,400
- no provision had been made for a legal claim made by a large customer which could potentially cost the company £22,000

required

Prepare a schedule showing all the errors and omissions found and the effect they have on the financial statements.

solution

The auditors prepare a schedule showing all the necessary double-entry adjustments as follows:

</td></tr>
</table>

Capone Ltd – year ended 31 March 20-1
Schedule of unadjusted errors

	P & L Account		Statement of financial position	
	Dr £	Cr £	Dr £	Cr £
Provision required for Bugsy Ltd debt	10,350			10,350
Closing inventory undervalued		5,260	5,260	
Cash balance incorrectly stated		1,250	1,250	
Accrual omitted: light & heat	3,400			3,400
Provision for legal claim	22,000			22,000
	35,750	6,510	6,510	35,750

When they have prepared this schedule the auditors have to decide if these items are material and discuss any adjustments to the financial statements with the directors.

Obviously if the directors agree to amend the accounts then the auditors can issue a 'true and fair' audit report. If the directors decide not to amend the accounts the auditors will have to decide how material the adjustments are and what effect they might have on the readers of the financial statements.

If the auditors consider that without adjustment for the errors and omissions the accounts are misleading, they will have to issue some form of modified report. (**Note:** we will discuss this, in detail, later in the chapter, but first we will examine what is included in an unqualified auditor's report.)

ASSURANCE

As we explained in Chapter 1 auditors are only required to give 'reasonable assurance' to shareholders that the financial statements they have audited present a true and fair view of the state of the company's affairs.

There are three types of assurance which could be given by the auditors. These are:

- **Absolute assurance** – everything is true, correct and accurate and the financial statements are free from any errors or mistakes

- **Reasonable assurance** – the financial statements give a substantially true and fair view and any errors or mistakes the auditors have found are not material – this is the level at which auditors provide assurance to shareholders

- **Limited assurance** – based on a limited amount of work there is no reason to believe that something is not true or correct in accordance with predetermined standards or criteria

Auditors cannot give an absolute assurance about the financial statements because:

- they use selective sample testing and so do not check every transaction
- they use their judgement to gather and evaluate audit evidence and to form conclusions based on this evidence
- the company's internal controls may have weaknesses and be subject to human error
- audit evidence tends to be persuasive rather than conclusive ie the auditors' tests may show that on the 'balance of probabilities' the item being tested is correctly calculated and described

The objective of an audit is to reduce audit risk to an acceptably low level so that the auditor can give a positive opinion based on reasonable assurance that the opinion is correct. We look at forms of audit report later in this chapter.

Providing reasonable assurance means that the auditors are not certifying that the financial statements are true, accurate and correct in every respect, this would be absolute assurance. Their opinion gives reasonable assurance based on audit testing carried out and their enquiries of management.

limited assurance

Some assignments which are not audits require the auditor to give much more limited assurance. These are based on much more limited procedures for gathering audit evidence. These may be confined mostly to analytical review and questioning of management. Examples of these types of assignments are where the auditor is required to provide a report on specific internal control procedures.

These types of assignments will result in a **negative assurance** opinion – in other words the auditors' report is based on the statement that 'there is no reason to believe that something is not reasonable or effective'. A negative assurance report might say:

'Based on our work described in this report, nothing has come to our attention that causes us to believe that internal control is not effective, in all material respects, based on XYZ criteria.'

Contrast this form of wording with the positive statements later in this chapter when reasonable assurance is required.

benefits of assurance

The important benefit of assurance is the fact that an independent professional is giving an opinion on, or drawing a conclusion about, a particular matter. The user of the report can rely on the skill and judgement of the reporting auditor in expressing their opinion. They will be reassured by the fact that the matter has been looked at by an independent third party who then expresses an opinion on it.

Where an audit is carried out this should be giving positive assurance based on the audit evidence and the work performed by the auditor. This gives reassurance to the shareholders that the financial statements do not contain any material issues which could invalidate them.

In the case of other forms of assignment, where negative assurance is given, the users of the report are normally the management or a third party. These users will be assured that an independent financial professional has reviewed the matter and expressed an opinion, despite this being only limited.

There are additional benefits to assurance reporting where a third party uses it as a factor when making a decision. For example, an unmodified audit report may encourage a bank to lend money to a client. Also, the fact that management know that reports or documents are going to be independently reviewed may help reduce management bias when preparing these reports and also discourage fraud or misrepresentation.

AUDITOR'S REPORT TO SHAREHOLDERS

ISA 700 'The Auditor's Report on Financial Statements' states:

'The auditor's report on the financial statements shall contain a clear written expression of opinion on the financial statements taken as a whole based on the auditor evaluating the conclusions drawn from the audit evidence obtained, including evaluating whether:

(a) sufficient appropriate audit evidence as to whether the financial statements as a whole are free from material misstatement, whether due to fraud or error has been obtained;

(b) uncorrected misstatements are material, individually or in aggregate. This evaluation shall include consideration of the qualitative aspects of the entity's accounting practices, including indicators of possible bias in management's judgments

(c) the financial statements, including the related notes, give a true and fair view

In respect of all frameworks the financial statements have been prepared in all material respects in accordance with the framework, including the requirements of applicable law'.

In the final paragraph above, the frameworks referred to the Companies Act 2006 and the relevant financial reporting standards.

As we stated at the beginning of this book, the auditors' primary task is to report to the shareholders on the truth and fairness of the financial statements prepared by the directors.

Having gathered all the necessary audit evidence and reviewed events since the Statement of Financial Position date, the auditors are now in a position to come to an opinion on the financial statements.

The audit opinion can either be:

- an unqualified opinion
- a modified opinion

In contrast to your own efforts to become 'qualified' as AAT technicians, the client is keen to receive an unqualified audit report. This means that, in the auditors' opinion, the accounts do give a true and fair view.

If the auditors' opinion is that the accounts do not give a true and fair view, or that something has prevented them from forming an opinion on all or part of the financial statements, the client will receive a **modified audit report**.

an important note on terminology

The term 'modified audit report' has been introduced by the requirements of international auditing standards, on which this book is based. The traditional term, based on the older UK standards, is **qualified audit report**. You will see this term commonly quoted and used by auditors. Remember:

qualified audit report = modified audit report

Note also that international auditing standards still refer to 'unqualified' audit reports.

unqualified audit reports

There are a number of different types of modified audit report that we will consider later, but first we will examine in detail the contents of an unqualified auditor's report.

For the purposes of your studies you will not be expected to write a full auditor's report but you should be familiar with:

- what is contained in an unqualified report and what it looks like
- when a modified audit report is appropriate and how it should be worded

contents of an auditor's report

The auditor's report to the shareholders is a detailed document which should leave the reader in no doubt as to the way in which the audit has been carried out. It should also give the reasoning behind the opinion that has been given.

The schedule on the next page sets out what an unqualified report contains, together with the type of wording that would be used. This report contains all the key issues you will need for your studies. You do not have to remember the precise form of words of an auditor's report, but you should be familiar with its contents.

Note that the auditors have to confirm that the information in the Directors' Report and any other reports included in the accounts is consistent with the information given in the financial statements. The full annual statements may include some additional statements to the financial statements and the directors' report. These might be:

■ chairman's statement

■ five year summary

■ trading review of the year

In addition to these listed companies complying with the Corporate Governance Code will have many other statements included in their statutory accounts, including, for example:

■ financial review

■ environmental and social review

■ statement of principal risks and uncertainties

■ corporate governance report

■ directors renumeration report

Note that the auditors' report is not required to comment on these. The auditor must simply make sure that these statements are not inconsistent with the audited financial statements.

An example of a full auditor's report is reproduced on pages 238-239.

Contents of the auditor's report	Sample wording
An appropriate title including reference to the 'independent auditor'.	'Independent auditors' report'
It should be addressed to the members.	'to the shareholders of XYZ Limited'
It should identify the financial statements, ie, what has been audited and the period covered by the audit.	'We have audited the financial statements of XYZ Limited........for the year ended........'
It should include a disclaimer known as the Bannerman wording (see page 240).	'This report is made solely to the company's members, as a body, in accordance with Chapter 3 of Part 16 of the Companies Act 2006. Our audit work has been undertaken so that we might state to the company's members those matters we are required to state to them in an auditor's report and for no other purpose. To the fullest extent permitted by law, we do not accept or assume responsibility to anyone other than the company and the company's members as a body, for our audit work, for this report, or for the opinions we have formed'.
It should include a statement setting out the respective responsibilities of the directors. This will refer to a detailed statement of Director's Responsibilities set out elsewhere in the financial statements.	'As more fully explained in the Director's Responsibilities statement [set out on pages.....to.....], the directors are responsible for the preparation of the financial statements and for being satisfied that they give a true and fair view'.
It should include a statement that the auditors' responsibility is to carry out an audit in accordance with applicable legal requirements and also in compliance with the APB's Ethical Code.	'Our responsibility is to audit and express an opinion on the financial statements in accordance with applicable law and International Standards on Auditing (UK and Ireland). Those standards require us to comply with the Auditing Practices Board's (APB's) Ethical Standards for Auditors'.
The report should include a description of the scope of the audit. This can be done by: • referring to a description on the FRC's website • referring to a description set out elsewhere in the financial statements • including a standardised form of wording – this is what we have shown here	'An audit involves obtaining evidence about the amounts and disclosures in the financial statements sufficient to give reasonable assurance that the financial statements are free from material misstatement, whether caused by fraud or error. This includes an assessment of: • whether the accounting policies are appropriate to the company circumstances and have been consistently applied and adequately disclosed; • the reasonableness of significant accounting estimates made by the directors, and • the overall presentation of the financial statements In addition, we read all the financial and non-financial information in the annual report to identify material inconsistencies with the audited financial statements and to identify any information that is apparently materially incorrect based on, or materially inconsistent with, the knowledge acquired by us in the course of performing the audit. If we become aware of any apparent material misstatements or inconsistencies we consider the implications for our report'.

Companies that are listed on the Stock Exchange and have to comply with the UK Corporate Governance Code must incorporate a great deal of additional information and there are specific requirements for the auditors to report on these.	*(we have not suggested any wording here as this is outside the scope of this unit).*
The auditors must express an opinion on the financial statements. The opinion can be modified or unmodified – an unmodified opinion is shown here.	'In our opinion the financial statements: • give a true and fair view of the state of the company's affairs as at 31 March 20-1 and of its [profit] / [loss] for the year then ended; • have been properly prepared in accordance with United Kingdom Generally Accepted Accounting Practice; and • have been prepared in accordance with the requirements of the Companies Act 2006'
The auditors must give an opinion on other aspects of the financial statements required to be produced by the Companies Act 2006. They have to give an opinion as to consistency within the financial statements.	'in our opinion the information given in the Director's Report for the financial year for which the financial statements are prepared is consistent with the financial statements.'
The auditors report by exception on other matters such as the maintenance of proper books and records etc. They state that they have nothing to say (unless of course there is something they need to report on)	'We have nothing to report in respect of the following matters where the Companies Act 2006 requires us to report to you if, in our opinion: • adequate accounting records have not been kept, or returns adequate for our audit have not been received from branches not visited by us; or • the financial statements are not in agreement with the accounting records and returns; or • certain disclosures of directors' remuneration specified by law are not made; or • we have not received all the information and explanations we require for our audit; or • the directors' were not entitled to prepare the financial statements in accordance with the small companies regime and take advantage of the small companies exemption in preparing the director's report
The auditor must sign using their own name and the words 'Senior Statutory Auditor'.	Jane Smith Senior Statutory Auditor
The report must be dated.	1 May 20-6
The location of the office must be stated.	Tickett & Wrunne Manchester

INDEPENDENT AUDITOR'S REPORT TO THE MEMBERS OF XYZ LIMITED

We have audited the financial statements of XYZ Limited for the year ended ..... on pages ..... to ..... The financial reporting framework that has been applied in their preparation is applicable law and United Kingdom Accounting Standards (United Kingdom Generally Accepted Accounting Practice), including FRS 102, *'The Financial Reporting Standard applicable in the UK and Republic of Ireland'.*

This report is made solely to the company's members, as a body, in accordance with Chapter 3 of Part 16 of the Companies Act 2006. Our audit work has been undertaken so that we might state to the company's members those matters we are required to state to them in an auditor's report and for no other purpose. To the fullest extent permitted by law, we do not accept or assume responsibility to anyone other than the company and the company's members as a body, for our audit work, for this report, or for the opinions we have formed.

Respective responsibilities of directors and auditors

As more fully explained in the Directors' Responsibilities Statement (set out on pages.....to .....), the directors are responsible for the preparation of the financial statements and for being satisfied that they give a true and fair view. Our responsibility is to audit and express an opinion on the financial statements in accordance with applicable law and International Standards on Auditing (UK and Ireland). Those standards require us to comply with the Auditing Practices Board (APB's) Ethical Standards for Auditors.

Scope of the audit of the financial statements

An audit involves obtaining evidence about the amounts and disclosures in the financial statements sufficient to give reasonable assurance that the financial statements are free from material misstatement, whether caused by fraud or error.
This includes an assessment of:

- whether the accounting policies are appropriate to the company's circumstances and have been consistently applied and adequately disclosed;

- the reasonableness of significant accounting estimates made by the directors;

- and the overall presentation of the financial statements

In addition, we read all the financial and non-financial information in the annual report to identify material inconsistencies with the audited financial statements and to identify any information that is apparently materially incorrect based on, or materially inconsistent with, the knowledge acquired by us in the course of performing the audit. If we become aware of any apparent material misstatements or inconsistencies we consider the implications for our report'.

continued...

Opinion on financial statements

In our opinion the financial statements:

- give a true and fair view of the state of the company's affairs as at .... and of its [profit] / [loss] for the year then ended;
- have been properly prepared in accordance with United Kingdom Generally Accepted Accounting Practice; and
- have been prepared in accordance with the requirements of the Companies Act 2006.

Opinion on other matters prescribed by the Companies Act 2006

In our opinion the information given in the Directors' Report for the financial year for which the financial statements are prepared is consistent with the financial statements.

Matters on which we are required to report by exception

We have nothing to report in respect of the following matters where the Companies Act 2006 requires us to report to you if, in our opinion:

- adequate accounting records have not been kept, or returns adequate for our audit have not been received from branches not visited by us; or
- the financial statements are not in agreement with the accounting records and returns; or
- certain disclosures of directors' remuneration specified by law are not made; or
- we have not received all the information and explanations we require for our audit; or
- the directors' were not entitled to prepare the financial statements in accordance with the small companies regime and take advantage of the small companies exemption in preparing the director's report

Jane Smith
Senior statutory auditor

For and on behalf of ABC LLP
Chartered Accountants and Statutory Auditors

Address ....

Date ....

Sample unqualified Auditor's Report issued by the Financial Reporting Council

when is an unqualified report used?

As you have seen from the sample wording on the last two pages, an unqualified report states:

'In our opinion the financial statements:

■ *give a true and fair view of the state of the company's affairs as at .... and of its profit (or loss) for the year then ended;*

■ *have been properly prepared in accordance with United Kingdom Generally Accepted Accounting Practice; and*

■ *have been prepared in accordance with the requirements of the Companies Act 2006.*

What this means is that:

■ the auditors agree that proper accounting records have been kept and proper returns have been made from any branches they have not visited

■ the financial statements agree with the underlying accounting records and returns

■ all information and explanations they needed have been received from the staff and the directors and managers

■ the auditors have had unrestricted access to the books and records

■ details of all transactions involving the directors have been correctly disclosed

■ there are no material misstatements in the accounts

In other words, the audit has been completed satisfactorily and the auditors have been able to gather all the evidence they need to support their unqualified opinion.

If, however, there is a difference of opinion between the directors and the auditors about something in the financial statements, or the auditors have had problems gathering the evidence they need, they may have to issue a modified audit report.

Bannerman wording

In Chapter 2 we looked at the auditors' duty of care to readers of the financial statements. This is conventionally taken to be the shareholders but could include potential investors provided the auditors were aware, when they signed their report, that the financial statements might be used by the potential investor in some way.

The scope of this responsibility has potentially widened to include the company's bankers following a legal case in Scotland (*Royal Bank of Scotland v Bannerman, Johnstone Maclay* and others).

In the Bannerman case, the bank maintained that the auditors must have known that the bank would be reviewing the financial statements and relying on the auditors' report to help decide whether or not to continue to lend to the company. In order to avoid widening the scope of auditors' liabilities, it was suggested that a disclaimer be introduced to the audit report. The wording of this disclaimer is:

> *'This report is made solely to the company's members, as a body, in accordance with Chapter 3 of Part 16 of the Companies Act 2006. Our audit work has been undertaken so that we might state to the company's members those matters we are required to state to them in an auditor's report and for no other purpose. To the fullest extent permitted by law, we do not accept or assume responsibility to anyone other than the company and the company's members as a body, for our audit work, for this report, or for the opinions we have formed.'*

This wording should be inserted into the auditors' report as part of the section on the auditors' responsibilities. (See the example on pages 236-237.)

This wording was used successfully in a defence by chartered accounts Grant Thornton against a claim brought against them by Barclays Bank after the collapse of the Van Essen Hotel Group. *(Barclays Bank Plc v Grant Thornton UK LLP[2015] EWHC320 (Comm).)*

MODIFIED AUDIT REPORTS

Remember: 'modified' = 'qualified'.

ISA 705 'Modifications to the opinion in the independent auditor's report' states:

> *'The objective of the auditor is to express clearly an appropriately modified opinion on the financial statements that is necessary when:*
>
> *(a) The auditor concludes, based on the audit evidence obtained, that the financial statements as a whole are not free from material misstatement; or*
>
> *(b) The auditor is unable to obtain sufficient appropriate audit evidence to conclude that the financial statements as a whole are free from material misstatement.'*

It is unlikely that you will be asked to draft an audit report in your assessment. However, you may have to produce an extract from a modified report. We have included some sample wording to illustrate how a modified audit report might be drafted (see pages 245-250).

Firstly, it is important that you understand that auditors do not have the power to insist that the financial statements are amended for any errors or omissions that have been found during the course of the audit. The financial statements are the responsibility of the directors and the auditors have no authority to overrule them when it comes to the content.

What the auditors can do is use their auditor's report to tell the shareholders of the company what they have discovered and to express their opinion as to whether this affects the truth and fairness of the financial statements.

The auditors are required to explain to the shareholders the reasons why they have modified their report. This should be included in an explanatory paragraph, headed 'Reasons for the modified opinion' or 'Reasons for the adverse opinion' as appropriate. It should go immediately before the audit opinion.

effect of a modified audit report

Auditors generally consider that modifying their report is a last resort.

In practice they will discuss the 'problem' issues with the client's management at some length in order to avoid having to issue a modified report. In most cases the directors will be prepared to adjust the financial statements for errors and omissions which the auditors have brought to their attention, as they are keen for the accounts to be accurate.

They will also be aware that a modified report can have serious consequences for the company:

- it could affect the shareholders' confidence in the company and its management
- it could discourage potential investors
- it could affect the willingness of lenders to continue offering a borrowing facility to the company
- it could affect the company's creditworthiness with its suppliers

However, if the auditors consider that a modified opinion is appropriate, they must be able to justify the basis for their decision and explain it fully in the audit report.

issuing modified audit reports

If the auditors have serious doubts about the truth and fairness of the financial statements, or have been prevented from carrying out their work to its full extent they must consider issuing a modified audit report.

The auditors must use their professional judgement to decide how serious the issues involved are. This will then influence precisely which form of modification will be included in the audit report.

The three situations which give rise to the types of qualification above are:

■ **qualified 'except for' opinion**

The issue is material but not to the extent that the financial statements no longer give a true and fair view, ie the auditors agree that the accounts give a true and fair view 'except for' the issue in question.

■ **disclaimer of opinion**

The auditors' work has been limited, either by the management preventing them from performing the work they needed to do, or by other factors preventing them from gathering all the evidence they require – this is known as a 'limitation of scope'.

■ **adverse opinion**

The issue is so material, that it affects the truth and the fairness of the financial statements as a whole – a situation described in ISA 705 as being **'pervasive'**.

It is also possible for the auditors to be faced with a minor limitation of scope. In this case the auditors would also use an 'except for' opinion.

The examples below of situations where each type of report might be issued will make this clearer.

The wording of the modified report depends on how serious the issue is. Clearly the issue has to be material – if it were not then there would be no need to modify the audit report.

However the issue might be so serious that it fundamentally undermines the credibility of the financial statements. It may be that:

■ the auditors could not validate a substantial proportion of the figures in the financial statements, or

■ the auditors disagree with the directors on some of the figures which are large enough that if the financial statements were adjusted as the auditors recommend, they would be fundamentally different from what they presently show.

This level of seriousness is known as 'pervasive'.

The table below summarises which opinion an auditor should give depending on the seriousness.

Seriousness of the issue		
Nature of issue which may cause a modification to the audit report	**Material but not pervasive**	**Material and pervasive**
Disagreement that the financial statements are correct	'Except for'	Adverse opinion
Limitation of scope of audit evidence available	'Except for'	Disclaimer of opinion

As you can see, where there is a limitation of scope or the disagreement is material but not pervasive the auditor should modify their report to say *'except for…(the issue)… the financial statements give a true and fair view etc'*.

Where the issue is more serious the auditor should modify their report as suggested in ISA 705 which we look at in more detail later.

The examples below show some situations where the modified reports might be used.

USE OF DIFFERENT TYPES OF MODIFIED REPORT

'Except for' – issues are material but not pervasive (minor limitation of scope)

Inadequate allowance for doubtful debts.

Disagreement over the value of some part of inventory, eg obsolete inventory that is still valued at cost instead of scrap value.

Non-disclosure in the accounts of going concern problems.

Except for – limitation of scope

Client maintained limited record of cash purchases.

Some cash sales records lost due to accidental flooding at the client's premises.

Statements of cash flows only prepared for nine months after the year end, so full consideration of going concern issues not possible.

Disclaimer of opinion – limitation of scope

Auditors appointed after the year end and so unable to attend inventory count where inventory is a material item.

Directors deny the auditors access to information regarding significant legal claims against the company.

No cash flow forecasts or cash budgets prepared so the going concern situation cannot be considered.

Adverse opinion

Failure to comply with Companies Act 2006, Accounting Standards or UK GAAP without an acceptable reason.

Significant uncertainties regarding the existence, ownership, valuation or recording of material assets and liabilities, eg failure to provide for material probable losses on long-term contracts.

The company's accounts have been prepared on a going concern basis despite significant concerns on the part of the auditors about the company's ability to continue as a going concern.

THE WORDING OF MODIFIED AUDITORS' REPORTS

The wording of modified auditors' reports must be clear and precise, ensuring that the reader is in no doubt as to why a qualification has been necessary. **Note that** the examples shown below are for illustrative and study purposes only; their wording is not definitive.

Whatever the basis of their qualification the auditors should always:

■ explain the facts of the disagreement

■ detail the implications to the financial statements

■ quantify the financial effect where possible

As stated earlier, ISA 705 offers a range of alternative reports, but for simplicity we have only included the most common example of each type of qualification so that you can see how auditors formally word these qualifications in their auditor's report. In each of the reports below we have extracted the wording from some sample auditors' reports to illustrate the different types of qualification. Key words and phrases have been underlined to make them clearer.

'except for' qualifications

If the issue is material but not pervasive the auditors will use an 'except for' qualification. This means that the auditors are saying that the financial statements give a true and fair view, except for the matters in dispute.

1 **example of an 'except for' opinion on financial statements arising from a disagreement about accounting treatment which is material but not pervasive.**

The auditors agree that the accounts still give a true and fair view 'except for' the disagreement in question.

In this example the company has not made a bad debt provision which the auditors consider should be made.

INDEPENDENT AUDITORS REPORT TO THE MEMBERS OF XYZ LTD (extract)

Reasons for the modified opinion

Included in the trade receivables shown on the Statement of Financial Position is an amount of £Y due from a company which has ceased trading. XYZ Limited has no security for this debt. In our opinion the company is unlikely to receive any payment and full provision of £Y should have been made.

Accordingly, trade receivables should be reduced by £Y, the deferred tax liability should be reduced by £X and profit for the year and retained earnings should be reduced by £Z.

Except for the financial effect of not making the provision referred to in the preceding paragraph, in our opinion the financial statements:

- give a true and fair view of the state of the company's affairs as at ... and of its profit [loss] for the year then ended;

- have been properly prepared in accordance with United Kingdom Generally Accepted Accounting Practice; and

- have been prepared in accordance with the requirements of the Companies Act, 2006.

Opinion on other matter prescribed by the Companies Act 2006

In our opinion the information given in the Directors' Report for the financial year for which the financial statements are prepared is consistent with the financial statements.

Matters on which we are required to report by exception

We have nothing to report in respect of the following matters where the Companies Act 2006 requires us to report to you if, in our opinion:

- adequate accounting records have not been kept, or returns adequate for our audit have not been received from branches not visited by us; or

- the financial statements are not in agreement with the accounting records and returns; or

- certain disclosures of directors' remuneration specified by law are not made; or

- we have not received all the information and explanations we require for our audit.

[Signature]   *Address*

John Smith (Senior statutory auditor)   *Date*

for and on behalf of ABC LLP, Statutory Auditor

2 example of an 'except for' opinion caused by a limitation of scope which is material but not pervasive

The auditors agree that the accounts still give a true and fair view 'except for' the area where their investigations were limited by lack of documentation and/or suitable audit evidence.

In this example the auditors were appointed after the inventory count and were thus not able to attend.

INDEPENDENT AUDITORS REPORT TO THE MEMBERS OF XYZ LTD (extract)

Reason for the modified opinion

With respect to inventory having a carrying amount of £X the audit evidence available to us was limited because we did not observe the counting of the physical inventory as at 31 December 20-1, since that date was prior to our appointment as auditor of the company. Owing to the nature of the company's records, we were unable to obtain sufficient appropriate audit evidence regarding the inventory quantities by using other audit procedures.

Except for the financial effects of such adjustments, if any, as might have been determined to be necessary had we been able to satisfy ourselves as to physical inventory quantities, in our opinion the financial statements:

- give a true and fair view of the state of the company's affairs as at 31 December 20-1 and of its profit [loss] for the year then ended;
- have been properly prepared in accordance with United Kingdom Generally Accepted Accounting Practice; and
- have been prepared in accordance with the requirements of the Companies Act 2006.

Opinion on other matters prescribed by the Companies Act 2006

In our opinion the information given in the Directors' Report for the financial year for which the financial statements are prepared is consistent with the financial statements.

Matters on which we are required to report by exception

In respect solely of the limitation on our work relating to inventory, described above:
- we have not obtained all the information and explanations that we considered necessary for the purpose of our audit; and
- we were unable to determine whether adequate accounting records had been kept.

We have nothing to report in respect of the following matters where the Companies Act 2006 requires us to report to you if, in our opinion:
- returns adequate for our audit have not been received from branches not visited by us; or
- the financial statements are not in agreement with the accounting records and returns; or
- certain disclosures of directors' remuneration specified by law are not made.

[Signature]   *Address*

John Smith (Senior statutory auditor)   *Date*
for and on behalf of ABC LLP, Statutory Auditor

3 disclaimer of opinion

If the scope of the auditors work has been so limited that they have not been able to carry out enough audit testing to allow them to form a view on the financial statements they must issue a disclaimer of opinion.

This basically says 'we cannot express an opinion because the scope of our work has been so restricted'.

In this example the auditors were faced with two limitations of scope, firstly the non attendance at the inventory count and secondly a problem with trade receivables.

INDEPENDENT AUDITORS REPORT TO THE MEMBERS OF XYZ LTD (extract)

Reasons for the disclaimer of opinion

The audit evidence available to us was limited because we were unable to observe the counting of physical inventory having a carrying amount of £X and send confirmation letters to trade receivables having a carrying amount of £Y due to limitations placed on the scope of our work by the directors of the company. As a result of this we have been unable to obtain sufficient appropriate audit evidence concerning both inventory and trade receivables.

Because of the possible effect of the limitation in evidence available to us, we are unable to form an opinion as to whether the financial statements:

- give a true and fair view of the state of the company's affairs as at ... and of its profit [loss] for the year then ended;

- have been properly prepared in accordance with United Kingdom Generally Accepted Accounting Practice; and

- have been prepared in accordance with the requirements of the Companies Act 2006.

Opinion on other matters prescribed by the Companies Act 2006

Notwithstanding our disclaimer of an opinion on the view given by the financial statements, in our opinion the information given in the Directors' Report for the financial year for which the financial statements are prepared is consistent with the financial statements.

Matters on which we are required to report by exception

In respect solely of the limitation of our work referred to above:

- we have not obtained all the information and explanations that we considered necessary for the purpose of our audit; and

- we were unable to determine whether adequate accounting records have been kept.

We have nothing to report in respect of the following matters where the Companies Act 2006 requires us to report to you if, in our opinion:

- returns adequate for our audit have not been received from branches not visited by us; or
- the financial statements are not in agreement with the accounting records and returns; or
- certain disclosures of directors' remuneration specified by law are not made.

[Signature]   Address

John Smith (Senior statutory auditor)   Date

for and on behalf of ABC LLP, Statutory Auditor

4   adverse opinion

If the auditors consider that the items they are disputing with the directors are so serious that as a result the financial statements are misleading, they must issue an **adverse opinion**. This basically states that 'the financial statements do **not** give a true and fair view'.

In this example there is a fundamental disagreement concerning a provision for losses on long term work in progress which is considered to be pervasive.

INDEPENDENT AUDITORS REPORT TO THE MEMBERS OF XYZ LTD (extract)

Reasons for the adverse opinion

As more fully explained in note [x] to the financial statements no provision has been made for losses expected to arise on certain long-term contracts currently in progress, as the directors consider that such losses should be off-set against amounts recoverable on other long-term contracts. In our opinion, provision should be made for foreseeable losses on individual contracts as required by International Standard on Accounting 11: *Construction contracts.* If losses had been so recognised the effect would have been to reduce the carrying amount of contract work in progress by £X, the deferred tax liability by £Y and the profit for the year and retained earnings at 31 December 20-1 by £Z.

In view of the effect of the failure to provide for the losses referred to above, in our opinion the financial statements:

- do not give a true and fair view of the state of the company's affairs as at December 20X1 and of its profit [loss] for the year then ended; and
- have not been properly prepared in accordance with International Standards on Accounting.

In all other respects, in our opinion the financial statements have been prepared in accordance with the requirements of the Companies Act 2006.

Opinion on other matters prescribed by the Companies Act 2006

Notwithstanding our adverse opinion on the financial statements, in our opinion the information given in the Directors' Report for the financial year for which the financial statements are prepared is consistent with the financial statements.

Matters on which we are required to report by exception 38

We have nothing to report in respect of the following matters where the Companies Act 2006 requires us to report to you if, in our opinion:

- adequate accounting records have not been kept, or returns adequate for our audit have not   been received from branches not visited by us; or
- the financial statements are not in agreement with the accounting records and returns; or
- certain disclosures of directors' remuneration specified by law are not made; or
- we have not received all the information and explanations we require for our audit.

[Signature]   Address

John Smith (Senior statutory auditor)   Date

for and on behalf of ABC LLP, Statutory Auditor

As you can see from this last example, although the auditors only had an issue with one aspect of the accounts they decided that the effect it had on the financial statements was so significant that not mentioning it would completely mislead anyone reading them.

Now read the following Case Study which illustrates the principles of modified reports and refers back to the examples just given.

Case Study

AUDITOR'S REPORTS:
HATCHES, MATCHES AND DESPATCHES

situation

You are the audit manager of Tickett & Co, registered auditors, and you are reviewing the audit files of three clients, all of whom have 31 December year ends. The three clients are Hatches Ltd, Matches Ltd and Despatches Ltd.

Hatches Ltd

Hatches is an old-established audit client which manufactures pine furniture in a factory in the town. It is a family company, owned by the directors.

The following information has been extracted from the audit file.

Most of Hatches' sales are to credit customers. Unfortunately at the year end their offices were flooded and many of the company's records were damaged. The main problem with respect to the audit was that the sales records for May to August were completely lost. The audit team were able to carry out audit work on the sales records for the other months of the year. At the year end there were no other significant audit points to report.

Matches Ltd

Matches has only been in business for two years and has never made a profit. It operates as a nationwide internet-based dating agency and operates from offices in the city centre. It is owned and run by Mike Match and his brother Roy.

The business is financed by Mike and Roy and members of their family. They also have a start-up loan from Venture Bank plc.

The latest accounts show another loss and a post Statement of Financial Position review has revealed the following points:

- The budget prepared by the company shows that the business is due to make a profit within the next three months and its cash flow projection indicates that it will start to generate enough cash to pay off its loans within the next twelve to eighteen months. The audit senior who reviewed the budget and cash flow forecast thinks they are very optimistic and does not think that they show a realistic picture.

- The auditors have reviewed a letter to Matches from Venture Bank reminding them that the start-up loan must be repaid within the next twelve months. It also says that, unless there is a major improvement in the company's financial performance, they will not continue lending money to the business.

Despatches Ltd

Despatches is a cash and carry warehouse which buys tinned, packaged and frozen food, drinks and tobacco from manufacturers and importers and sells it to shops, cafes and restaurants.

It does not accept credit cards and most of its transactions are by cash or cheque. It does not give credit.

The operating profit for the year is £220,000 and the net asset value of the business is £3 million.

This is the first year your firm has been the auditors for Despatches. The audit file reveals the following:

- Controls over cash sales are very poor. Customers are given a receipt when they pay at the till. The tills are emptied at the end of the day by the directors who also bank the cash. The following weaknesses have been identified by the auditors:
    - The directors do not always reconcile the till takings with the till rolls.
    - The directors often pay wages and other bills out of the cash takings.
    - The directors only record in the cash book what was banked.

- The biggest item on the Statement of Financial Position is the inventory which is valued at over £1 million. The company carries out a rolling inventory check but did not do a year-end one because of pressure of work and the forthcoming public holiday. The audit team carried out some sample tests during the course of the audit which did not reveal any problems.

required

You have been asked to make a recommendation to the audit partner as to the type of audit report that should be prepared for each of these three clients.

solution

Hatches Ltd

The audit work was generally satisfactory and no real problems were revealed. However the auditors could not examine the sales records from May to August because these had been destroyed.

The scope of the audit work has been limited, but only partially, so the report should contain:

an 'except for' opinion arising from a limitation of scope.

Study the example wording on pages 246-247.

Matches Ltd

The company seems to have a major going concern problem. They have produced some optimistic forecasts but these are of very limited value. Also, the bank has indicated that they will not continue to support the business in the future without a major improvement in its fortunes. At the moment this does not look likely.

A realistic prediction might be that the company cannot survive. It might be possible for Matches to find alternative forms of financing, but as it has yet to make a profit and as the future is still uncertain, this is unlikely.

The way in which the accounts have been prepared means that the audit report will include an:

adverse opinion because the accounts have been prepared on a going concern basis which is not appropriate.

The accounts do not show a 'true and fair view' of the company's financial position.

Study the example wording on pages 249-250.

Despatches Ltd

The auditors have been faced by two serious issues.

They have had problems gathering evidence about cash sales as the system is so poor and they were not able to verify inventory by attending the inventory count because it did not take place!

This casts doubt as to whether the auditors have been able to gather any meaningful

evidence about two of the key figures – cash sales and inventory – in the financial statements. The scope of their audit work has been limited to such an extent that they cannot express an opinion.

The audit opinion should, therefore, be a:

disclaimer caused by a limitation of scope.

Study the example wording on pages 248-249.

EMPHASIS OF MATTER

ISA 706 'Emphasis of matter paragraphs and other matter paragraphs in the independent auditor's report' states:

'The objective of the auditor, having formed an opinion on the financial statements, is to draw users' attention, when in the auditor's judgment it is necessary to do so, by way of clear additional communication in the auditor's report, to:

(a) A matter, although appropriately presented or disclosed in the financial statements, that is of such importance that it is fundamental to users' understanding of the financial statements; or

(b) As appropriate, any other matter that is relevant to users' understanding of the audit, the auditor's responsibilities or the auditor's report.'

There is one final situation which the auditors may have to consider when drawing up their auditor's report. This is where they wish to draw the attention of the shareholders to a significant matter in the accounts. In other words, they want to **emphasise** a certain **matter** which they consider important.

Although there is no disagreement between the auditors and the management as to how the matter has been treated in the accounts, the auditors consider that it should be highlighted to the shareholders in the auditor's report. The auditors would expect the client to discuss the issue in more detail in a note to the financial statements.

The auditors are therefore **not** qualifying their report in relation to this matter but **are** drawing attention to its disclosure in the accounts.

An example of this kind of situation is the outcome of legal proceedings between a company and another party where there are claims and counterclaims on both sides and the question of liability cannot easily be settled.

Set out below is an example of the wording of an emphasis of matter based on that type of situation. The wording is placed as a note at the end of the 'opinion' section which appears at the end of each report illustrated earlier in this chapter. It is underlined in this example (although not in practice!).

Opinion on financial statements

In our opinion the financial statements:

- give a true and fair view of the state of the company's affairs as at ... and of its profit [loss] for the year then ended;

- have been properly prepared in accordance with United Kingdom Generally Accepted Accounting Practice; and

- have been prepared in accordance with the requirements of the Companies Act 2006.

Emphasis of matter

In forming our opinion on the financial statements, which is not modified, we have considered the adequacy of the disclosures made in note [x] to the financial statements concerning the possible outcome of a lawsuit, alleging infringement of certain patent rights and claiming royalties and punitive damages, where the company is the defendant. The company has filed a counter action, and preliminary hearings and discovery proceedings on both actions are in progress. The ultimate outcome of the matter cannot presently be determined, and no provision for any liability that may result has been made in the financial statements.

Opinion on other matter prescribed by the Companies Act 2006 etc

REPORTING TO MANAGEMENT

ISA 265 'Communicating deficiencies in internal control to those charged with governance and management' states:

'The auditor shall also communicate to management at an appropriate level of responsibility on a timely basis:

(a) In writing, significant deficiencies in internal control ...

(b) Other deficiencies in internal control identified during the audit that have not been communicated to management by other parties and that, in the auditor's professional judgment, are of sufficient importance to merit management's attention.'

In the course of their audit the auditors have:

- carried out a review of the accounting systems
- reviewed and tested the internal controls
- examined the way the client records assets and liabilities

During this detailed work the auditors will have seen all aspects of the client's business and the systems that it operates. It is likely that this work will highlight possible areas for improvement to the client's systems that would strengthen the internal control procedures and the control environment within which they operate.

significant deficiencies

During their audit work the auditors may encounter various deficiencies in the system of internal control. These may be either:

- a **significant deficiency**, ie the control is so weak that it would be unable to detect a material misstatement or that something is missing altogether, or
- not a significant deficiency but of sufficient seriousness as to warrant bringing it to the management's attention

A significant deficiency may be more than simply the absence of a control or the fact that there is one poorly performing control. It may be a combination of several weaknesses which, together, significantly increase the risk of a material misstatement going undetected, or that increase the risk of fraud.

Significant deficiencies are generally much more than simply a failure to authorise a document or the lack of a physical control, they are usually more fundamental to the whole of the internal control environment. They may include:

- indications that significant transactions in which management are financially interested are not being appropriately scrutinised
- identification of some level of management fraud, whether or not material, that was not prevented by the company's internal control
- management's failure to implement appropriate remedial action for significant deficiencies previously communicated
- absence of a risk assessment process within the client company where this would ordinarily be expected to have been set up
- misstatements detected by the auditor's procedures that were not prevented, or detected and corrected, by the company's own internal control
- evidence of management's inability to oversee the preparation of the financial statements

In other words these are fundamental failings in the internal control of the company and in management's actions.

These significant deficiencies should be reported by the auditors in a management letter, sometimes known as a letter of weakness. If the significant weakness involves failures by executive directors ie those with defined management roles such as the Chief Executive Officer, the Financial Director, or the Sales Director, the auditors may wish to communicate these sorts of deficiencies to independent non executive directors, if there are any, or to an **audit committee**, if one exists.

We will now look at the content of the management letter in more detail.

management letter

The main purpose of this letter is to ensure that the management are aware of these weaknesses and the implications that they could have on the company if action is not taken. The auditors will also make recommendations as to how these controls could be improved.

The auditors must ensure that the points that are included in the management letter are:

- significant deficiencies – as indicated above
- weaknesses that may be material but are not significant. Management will not take reports seriously if they contain minor or trivial weaknesses which are unlikely to have any impact on the financial statements
- 'one-off' events which lead to a systems weakness but which are unlikely to be repeated. Management should be aware of the potential significance of such events
- capable of improvement – if it is not possible to improve the system there is little point raising it as an issue (unless the auditors acknowledge the point and are simply making management aware of the situation)

The auditors should try to ensure that the management see the letter of weakness as being useful to them. The management is responsible for operating the financial systems and so will only be prepared to change the way in which these systems work if they see the suggestions as valid and useful.

Management will be reluctant to make changes if:

- the points made are fine in theory but in practice are too difficult or complicated to operate easily
- the suggestions have been tried before and do not work, despite the auditors believing that they will
- the cost of introducing new controls outweighs any possible losses if the system was to remain as it is

Experienced auditors will always aim to 'add value' with their management letter. Whether the management agree or not, the auditors should ask that they reply to each point individually. The management letter and the management's responses should then be filed on the permanent file.

When the next audit commences the audit team should then check that the management have acted on what they agreed to do to rectify the weaknesses. Study the example below.

contents of a management letter

There is no standard layout for a management letter, but the table below and on the following two pages shows what it can contain.

The management letter would be sent with a covering letter addressed to the directors of the client company.

To the Directors

The following points arose from the audit for the year ended 31 March 20-1.

Please note that this is not a comprehensive statement of all weaknesses which may exist or of all improvements which could be made. We set out below those matters which we consider to be of fundamental importance.

Tickett & Wrunne, Registered Auditors.

WEAKNESS	IMPLICATION	RECOMMENDATION
INTERNAL CONTROL – GENERAL POINTS **Budgeting** At the moment we understand that you prepare an annual budget prior to the commencement of the financial year and submit it to the bank to support the application for the renewal of your overdraft. Budgeting is a useful management tool and it would greatly assist the management of your business if the budget was used to monitor the progress of the business.	As the budget does not appear to be used other than to support the finance application, an opportunity is being lost to improve the management's control of the business. It is preferable for management to respond positively at the time problems or opportunities appear rather than have to rely on historical data which may be several months old by the time they see it.	A budgetary control system should be introduced comprising a monthly budget and management accounts and an explanation of significant variances. This should be produced in a timely manner each month and presented to the board for discussion.

WEAKNESS	IMPLICATION	RECOMMENDATION
Internal control – computer accounting system The computer software currently being used is obsolete. You are using Version 3. The latest issue is Version 8. Whilst it continues to support the basic accounting system, that is the day books and ledger, it has no facility for inventory control nor has it any facility for recording costing information.	Use of outdated software is a missed opportunity to enhance the speed, accuracy and flexibility of financial reporting. The additional features provided by the upgraded software will improve managers control of business activities and provide the information on which they could base business decisions.	The computer software should be upgraded to Version 8. The cost of doing this is likely to be outweighed by increased efficiencies in the system and the reduction in the current paper based systems. For example, improved inventory control might serve to reduce current inventory holding levels and free up cash for use in the business.
INTERNAL CONTROL – DETAILED POINTS **Internal control – payroll** There is no evidence of review of the payroll. There is no independent evidence of authorisation of recruitment of new staff. At present the new employee form is signed by the wages clerk.	The payroll may contain unauthorised or fictitious employees or payments at incorrect or unauthorised rates. Fictitious employees might be introduced to the payroll. Details for new employees may be entered incorrectly on the new employee form as the wages clerk may not be aware of all the information required.	The payroll should be reviewed and signed by the production manager each week. New employee forms should be authorised by the personnel manager and countersigned by the production manager.

WEAKNESS	IMPLICATION	RECOMMENDATION
Internal control – trade receivables An aged trade receivable analysis is only produced quarterly. Slow paying customers are often not identified until well after their terms of trade have expired.	Poor credit control means that slow paying customers are not identified quickly enough so that steps could then be taken to collect money due. This means that the working capital requirement is greater than it otherwise could be. As this is presently financed by overdraft facilities the company is currently incurring excess interest cost because of slow paying trade receivables.	Aged trade receivables reports should be prepared monthly. The acquisition of new computer software should enable this to be done automatically. All customer should be reminded of the terms of trade and credit control procedures introduced to collect overdue debts.

Now read the Case Study which follows. It illustrates the issues that can be raised in a management letter.

Case Study

MANAGEMENT LETTER: MEGASTORES LTD

situation

Megastores Ltd is a small chain of three local supermarkets operating in Hightown, Lowtown and Toptown.

All the stores are roughly the same size and operate from high street premises selling a range of groceries, fresh fruit and vegetables, alcohol, tobacco and newspapers. They open seven days a week from 8am to 10pm (except Sundays when they open at 10 am) and they only close on 25 December.

Together they employ about 40 full time staff in the stores plus another ten part-time staff at weekends.

Each store has its own small warehouse attached which is replenished daily by deliveries from a central depot in Toptown. Store managers re-order by email every day from the central stores.

A significant part of their takings are in cash.

Takings in each store are counted and banked locally by store managers and they are responsible for reconciling the takings from each till every day to the internal till rolls. They submit a weekly cash sheet to the head office, which is in Toptown, recording the cash takings, the till roll totals and noting any discrepancies.

If store managers are away from the store or on holiday each store has a designated assistant manager who will carry out these duties. This is usually an experienced member of staff who does not receive any extra pay for carrying out these duties.

Head office is responsible for ordering goods into the central warehouse, maintaining the accounting records and preparing the payroll.

During the audit the following points were established:

The person who was the designated assistant manager at the Lowtown store had left the company early in the financial year. Since she left, three different people had been involved in dealing with cash takings and re-ordering at weekends. The most recent one has only been with the company two months. The manager takes every weekend off.

Managers were allowed to recruit casual workers for temporary posts and pay them from takings in the store, provided they entered this on the cash sheet. No other information was required by head office and these workers were not included on the payroll. Investigations revealed the manager at Lowtown had employed 27 casual workers during the year paying them approximately £100 each for 'weekend cover'.

The computer system does not have an inventory control facility and it is the warehouse manager at the central warehouse who is responsible for re-ordering.

There was a year-end inventory count at each store and the central warehouse. The inventory records at the central warehouse, which are maintained on a card index file, were found to be completely out-of-date. The stores did not maintain any inventory records so the staff just counted what was on the shelves and did not agree what they had counted back to any inventory records.

The stores and the warehouse were closed when the year-end inventory count was undertaken, as it was done late at night. The auditors were happy with the actual count and the year-end inventory figure.

When the cash sheets from the stores were received in the accounts department the information about sales, bankings and any payments were taken from the sheets by the accounts staff and the sheets filed in the accounts office. No other checking or review of them was carried out.

required

Prepare the necessary points to be included in a management letter to be sent to the management of Megastores Ltd.

solution

The letter should contain the points set out below. **Note** the alternative presentation to the tabular format shown on pages 257-259.

TAKINGS AT LOWTOWN

weaknesses   Cash takings at the weekend at the Lowtown store are currently counted and banked by an inexperienced member of staff. There is no formal review of any reconciliations performed between the till and the cash takings.

implications   Takings might be incorrectly recorded and reconciliations with till rolls might be incorrectly carried out.

It may not be sensible to assume that the new member of staff is trustworthy.

recommendation   Ask the manager to work weekends and have other days off in the week. Cover the manager's days off with staff seconded from another store until a more experienced person can be recruited or transferred from another store permanently.

CASUAL WORKERS

weaknesses   Managers are permitted to recruit temporary staff without them being included on the payroll.

Casual workers are paid out of cash takings.

implications   There is no verification that the casual staff actually worked or to whom the money was paid.

HM Revenue & Customs procedures for employment of casual workers have not been followed – penalties could be incurred.

The practice of making payments out of takings could mean that takings are incorrectly recorded.

recommendation   Employment of all casual staff should be authorised by head office.

HM Revenue & Customs procedures should be followed for all casual staff.

Takings should be recorded and banked intact. A petty cash float on an imprest basis should be introduced into each store so that no money needs to be taken from the till.

INVENTORY CONTROL

weaknesses   There is no inventory control at the central warehouse because the card index system does not work.

The computer system has no inventory recording facility.

There is no inventory control in place at individual stores.

implications   The lack of control over inventory levels has several implications:

1   Lack of control over inventory levels could mean the company is holding excessive inventory which is not efficient use of working capital.

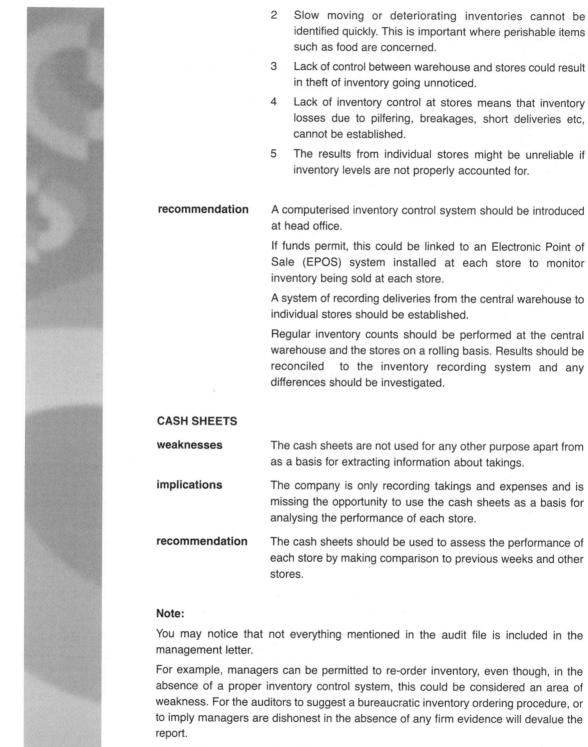

2   Slow moving or deteriorating inventories cannot be identified quickly. This is important where perishable items such as food are concerned.

3   Lack of control between warehouse and stores could result in theft of inventory going unnoticed.

4   Lack of inventory control at stores means that inventory losses due to pilfering, breakages, short deliveries etc, cannot be established.

5   The results from individual stores might be unreliable if inventory levels are not properly accounted for.

recommendation   A computerised inventory control system should be introduced at head office.

If funds permit, this could be linked to an Electronic Point of Sale (EPOS) system installed at each store to monitor inventory being sold at each store.

A system of recording deliveries from the central warehouse to individual stores should be established.

Regular inventory counts should be performed at the central warehouse and the stores on a rolling basis. Results should be reconciled to the inventory recording system and any differences should be investigated.

CASH SHEETS

weaknesses   The cash sheets are not used for any other purpose apart from as a basis for extracting information about takings.

implications   The company is only recording takings and expenses and is missing the opportunity to use the cash sheets as a basis for analysing the performance of each store.

recommendation   The cash sheets should be used to assess the performance of each store by making comparison to previous weeks and other stores.

Note:

You may notice that not everything mentioned in the audit file is included in the management letter.

For example, managers can be permitted to re-order inventory, even though, in the absence of a proper inventory control system, this could be considered an area of weakness. For the auditors to suggest a bureaucratic inventory ordering procedure, or to imply managers are dishonest in the absence of any firm evidence will devalue the report.

The auditors' role is to highlight systems weaknesses, point out the implications and come up with suggested improvements.

Chapter Summary

■ Before the auditors sign their report, they should review 'subsequent' events from the Statement of Financial Position date up to the date of signing their report. They have to consider the effect that events since the date of the financial statements have on the financial statements and decide if they are significant enough to require the financial statements to be amended.

■ If events after the date of the financial statements do not relate to conditions which existed at the year end then the financial statements do not require amendment, but a note to the accounts might be needed to explain the situation to readers.

■ Auditors have to review the viability of the business to ensure that the business can continue as a going concern for the foreseeable future.

■ The auditors should obtain representations from the management in respect of matters for which there is a limited amount of evidence or where knowledge is confined to senior management. Management should also acknowledge responsibility for preparation of the financial statements.

■ Auditors should summarise the errors and omissions that they have found during the audit and discuss them with management to identify any changes needed to be made to the accounts.

■ If the auditors are happy that the accounts give a true and fair view they can sign an unqualified report. Otherwise they will have to sign a modified report.

■ If the scope of the audit has been limited, auditors must either issue an 'except for' opinion or a disclaimer of opinion depending on to what extent their work has been limited, and how material that limitation is to the accounts.

■ If the auditors disagree with the accounting treatment or disclosures they can issue either an 'except for' opinion, or an 'adverse' opinion if the disagreement is material and pervasive, and the auditors consider the financial statements do not give a true and fair view.

■ Auditors may include an emphasis of matter paragraph in their report if they want to draw the shareholders' attention to a particular matter included in the notes to the accounts.

■ A management letter is used to report to management any significant deficiencies that the auditors have found during their audit work on the financial systems. The letter will contain recommendations for improvement of the systems.

■ Management should respond to each of the points in the letter so that over time the internal control environment can be improved.

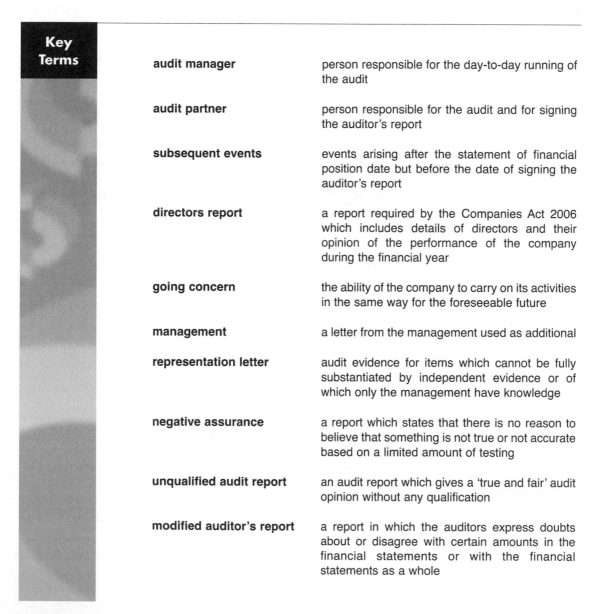

Key Terms		
audit manager	person responsible for the day-to-day running of the audit
audit partner	person responsible for the audit and for signing the auditor's report
subsequent events	events arising after the statement of financial position date but before the date of signing the auditor's report
directors report	a report required by the Companies Act 2006 which includes details of directors and their opinion of the performance of the company during the financial year
going concern	the ability of the company to carry on its activities in the same way for the foreseeable future
management representation letter	a letter from the management used as additional audit evidence for items which cannot be fully substantiated by independent evidence or of which only the management have knowledge
negative assurance	a report which states that there is no reason to believe that something is not true or not accurate based on a limited amount of testing
unqualified audit report	an audit report which gives a 'true and fair' audit opinion without any qualification
modified auditor's report	a report in which the auditors express doubts about or disagree with certain amounts in the financial statements or with the financial statements as a whole

limitation of scope	where the auditors have been prevented from carrying out all the audit work required to gather the evidence they need
annual report	the annual report to the shareholders, prepared within the company, which includes not only the financial statements but various management reports and summaries which do not have to be audited
chairman's statement	a report to the shareholders from the chairman of the board presenting the company's performance in the financial year
pervasive	an event which is fundamental to a full understanding of the financial position of the company
management letter	a report to management which identifies systems and control weaknesses and their implications and which makes recommendations to rectify them
significant deficiencies	individual weaknesses or a combination of weaknesses in the financial systems such that the systems would be unable to detect a material error or misstatement. This includes failures by directors and management
related partners	companies, partnerships or joint-ventures over which the audit client has some measure of control either through ownership or management control

Activities

7.1 You have been asked to mark some student exercises. Set out below is a selection of the comments that have been made. Which of these are incorrect, and why?

(a) Management representation letters place responsibility for providing the audit evidence with the management not the auditors

(b) Disclaiming an opinion means that the auditors' scope of work was so limited that they could not carry out a proper audit

(c) A letter of weakness should highlight management failings in running the business

(d) Modified (also known as 'qualified') audit reports are issued when there is a disagreement between the auditors and the directors or when auditors are unable to gather the audit evidence that they require

(e) 'Except for' reporting means all is well apart from items specifically mentioned

(f) Auditors should only insist on the accounts being adjusted for something that is material

(g) Events that happen after the statement of financial position date can be ignored until the next year's audit

7.2 You are carrying out the audit of the salaries system at Winkle Ltd. Your review of the system has highlighted that information from the time recording system is downloaded directly into the salaries system by Miss Smith who also is able to amend the computer records in respect of starters and leavers, who are notified to the salaries office by the HR department, and for any changes in pay rates or other details. The only other employee in the salaries office is a part time assistant.

Prepare extracts, suitable for inclusion in a report to management of Winkle Ltd, which set out:

1. any weaknesses, their possible consequences and,

2. the recommendations you would make in respect of this situation.

7.3 You are the audit junior on the audit of Basildon Ltd. During your review of the cash book you spot a payment of £2,000 described as 'Overtime' paid to the Factory manager. You ask the cashier about this and she tells you that this was a special bonus paid to the factory manager for all the work he did reorganising the factory after a flood, which involved lots of weekend and night working.

She said it had been paid on the orders of the Chief Executive who had approved it.

The total value of Wages and Salary costs in the statement of profit or loss is £2.6m.

You must decide whether to take no further action in respect of this or refer it to the audit supervisor

No further action	
Refer to supervisor	

7.4 You are reviewing the files following completion of the audit work on three audit clients and find that the audit files contain the following points. For each client indicate which type of audit opinion should be given.

Hong Ltd

The directors refused permission for the auditors to carry out a circulation of trade receivables balances. Audit work on the Revenue system did not reveal any particular issues and approximately 40% of the balances had been paid in full by the time the audit team carried out their review.

(a)	Not modified	
	Modified:	
(b)	'Except for' – limitation of scope	
(c)	'Except for' – material disagreement	
(d)	Disclaimer – pervasive limitation of scope	
(e)	Adverse opinion – pervasive disagreement	

Kong Ltd

The company was currently renegotiating all its bank finance. The bank had written to the company stating that as the company was £100,000 over its overdraft limit the bank required the overdraft to be repaid in full within four weeks. The directors have already indicated that they will be unable to do this without additional funding which does not appear to be forthcoming.

(a)	Not modified	
	Modified:	
(b)	'Except for' limitation of scope	
(c)	'Except for' material disagreement	
(d)	Disclaimer – pervasive limitation of scope	
(e)	Adverse opinion – pervasive disagreement	

Bong Ltd

The company has on its statement of financial position long-term work in progress amounting to £6.4m. The auditors have identified that a provision for a loss on one of the contracts amounting to £100,000 should have been made. This amount is material. The directors disagree and will not amend the financial statements. No other issues are apparent.

(a)	Not modified	
	Modified:	
(b)	'Except for' limitation of scope	
(c)	'Except for' material disagreement	
(d)	Disclaimer – pervasive limitation of scope	
(e)	Adverse opinion – pervasive disagreement	

7.5 You are reviewing the audit files of Monty Ltd with a view to finalising the audit. From your review of the files you identify the following factors. Identify:

(a) Whether or not they can be ignored

(b) Whether the financial statements might have to be amended

(c) Whether or not the financial statements should include a reference by way of a note without any adjustment to the figures

In the table below tick the response you feel is the most appropriate.

	Ignore	Amend financial statements	Refer by way of note
A trade receivable amounting to £15,000 has gone into liquidation after the year end and no amounts will be recovered. Total trade receivables amount to £1.2m and the pre-tax profit for the year is £750,000			
Since the year end the company closed four out of its eight branches			
Audit investigations have indicated that the latest position on one of the long-term contracts in progress is that it is likely to make a loss of £200,000. The value of long-term work in progress is £5.0m and the pre-tax profit for the year is £750,000			
Since the year end the company acquired one of its smaller competitors for £1.25m. They financed this acquisition by means of an issue of shares amounting to £1m			
The bank financing arrangements were revised and renewed shortly after the year end. There were no changes to previous arrangements except an increase in the overdraft limit of £250,000			
The Chief Executive left one month after the year end. The Chairman is currently carrying out her duties whilst a replacement is being sought			
After the year end the Head Office was flooded and the ground floor meeting rooms and staff kitchens were badly damaged. The accounting function and IT facilities were not affected. The costs of repair are covered by insurance			

Answers to chapter activities

CHAPTER 1: INTRODUCTION TO AUDITING

1.1   **(a)** False   Auditors must be alert to the possibility of fraud and should, if they discover a fraud, investigate and report it. They are not expected, however, to hunt for frauds.

   (b) True   The Companies Act 2006 sets out the responsibility of the auditors and the directors.

   (c) False   Auditors are responsible to the shareholders who appoint them

   (d) False   Some small companies and dormant companies do not require an audit (see pages 6-7).

   (e) False   It is the responsibility of the management of the company to prepare the financial statements.

   (f) False   Not all professional accounting qualifications are eligible to carry out a statutory audit (see page 7 for details of recognised supervisory bodies).

   (g) True   Directors manage the business and the auditors are appointed by the shareholders to give an opinion on the financial statements.

1.2   An audit is a process by which an **independent**, qualified third party expresses an **opinion** as to whether a set of **financial statements** of a company represent a **true and fair** view of its financial affairs for a reporting period and comply with the Companies Act 2006 and **International Accounting Standards**.

1.3   The following statements are true:

   •   Auditors should gather sufficient reliable evidence to give them reasonable assurance

   •   AAT members can carry out audit work but cannot sign the Auditor's Report

   •   Auditors should not accept a new appointment without some preliminary investigation into their proposed client

1.4   All companies must have a statutory audit except those that satisfy two of the following three criteria: a turnover less than **£10.2m**; a statement of financial position value less than **£5.1m**; employs fewer than **50** people. **Dormant** companies are exempt.

   The **Expectation** Gap is the difference between what the auditors actually do and what the public think they do.

   Only members of the **ACCA** and the **Institutes of Chartered Accountants** are eligible to be auditors. **AAT** members cannot be registered.

   The role of the auditor is to gather **sufficient** and **reliable** evidence so as to give them **reasonable** assurance that the financial statements represent a true and fair view.

CHAPTER 2: AUDITING – THE LEGAL FRAMEWORK

2.1 Correct: (b), (d), (e).

Incorrect:

(a) The auditor is appointed by, and is responsible to, the shareholders of the company. Consequently the shareholders would be able to sue the auditors, but the company would not.

(c) The Caparo case decided that auditors did not have a duty of care to third parties unless they knew that these accounts were going to be relied upon for the purposes of making an investment.

(f) The guidelines issued by the Recognised Supervisory Bodies do not allow auditors to hold shares in client companies.

(g) The auditors must exercise their professional judgement as to what gifts they can accept from a client. The test is whether the gift is significant enough to influence the independence of the auditor.

2.2 (b) Tickett & Run owe a duty of care to Bloater even though Bloater wasn't their client because of the statements made by the audit partner at the meeting

2.3 (f) The shareholders

2.4 **(a)** False

(b) True

2.5

	True	False
Auditors perform their work objectively and with integrity. Integrity means truthfulness and openness	✔	
The fact that the senior partner of Tickett & Wrunne's brother in law is the sales director of Floggit Ltd would not prevent them being appointed auditors		Firms cannot accept an appointment where a family member has a senior position with the potential client
The audit manager on the audit of Megablast Ltd has been left some shares by his auntie. He must sell them as soon as possible	✔	
Auditors have a duty of confidentiality to their client which can only be breached with the client's permission		The duty of confidentiality can be breached if it is in the public interest, if it is a legal requirement, or if their is a professional duty to disclose

CHAPTER 3: PLANNING THE AUDIT ASSIGNMENT

3.1   (a) and (f) are correct.

The remainder are incorrect:

(b)   Materiality has both quantitative (size) aspects and qualitative aspects. Something may be of relatively small size but is material by nature, eg statutory disclosure of director's emoluments.

(c)   The auditors have to gather sufficient evidence to support their audit opinion and they cannot simply rely on the client's control procedures. They must carry out their own tests as well.

(d)   Walk though tests will confirm that the flow charts (or narrative notes) are a true representation of the way in which the system operates.

(e)   Audit risk is the risk that the auditors might give an incorrect opinion on the truth and fairness of the financial statements.

(g)   Segregation of duties is part of the control procedures.

3.2   **(a)**   Increase

(b)   Increase

(c)   Reduce

(d)   No effect

(e)   Reduce

3.3   **(a)**   Flowchart

(b)   Internal Control Questionnaire

(c)   Flowchart

3.4   **(a)**   No reliance

(b)   No reliance

(c)   No reliance

3.5   **(a)**   Risk

(b)   Control procedure

(c)   Control procedure

(d)   Control procedure

(e)   Control objective

CHAPTER 4: AUDIT TESTING

4.1   The following statements should be removed from the slides before the presentation is given:

(a)   There is no fixed calculation for materiality – the auditors must set materiality on the basis of their assessment of each client.

(b)   Audit sampling is not directly related to the level of materiality. Samples should be selected to be representative of the population as a whole.

(c)   Vouching is a test of transactions recorded in the accounting records to the underlying documentation, eg purchase day book entries are vouched to purchase invoices.

(d)   Analytical procedures is a form of substantive testing which compares financial and/or non-financial information. Relevant financial ratios can be used as part of this testing.

(f)   Auditors have to give an opinion as to whether the accounts give a true and fair view of the financial position of the company. Merely complying with legal requirements is not sufficient.

4.2   (c)   Select all individual sales invoices of amounts over £50,000 during the period and ensure that they have supporting documentation

4.3   **(a)**   Substantive procedure

     (b)   Substantive procedure

     (c)   Test of control

     (d)   Substantive procedure

     (e)   Test of control

4.4   **(a)**   False

     (b)   True

     (c)   True

4.5   **(a)**   Accept

     (b)   Investigate

     (c)   Accept

     (d)   Investigate

     (e)   Investigate

CHAPTER 5: AUDITING ACCOUNTING SYSTEMS

5.1   (a)   Correct   Substantive testing, ie detailed tests of period end balances and transactions will always be required to provide appropriate evidence to support the audit opinion.

       (b)   Correct   Documentary evidence is what auditors generally require to validate the assertions they are testing. They should always try to inspect original documents. If documentary evidence is not available oral evidence may be accepted but will ideally be supported by additional evidence such as a letter from the directors.

       (c)   Correct   Assertions detailed in ISA 315 have to be evidenced by the auditors. (see page 126 for details of these assertions).

       (d)   Correct   Cut-off is one of the assertions referred to in (c) above.

       (e)   Incorrect   Checking that there is a sales ledger balance for every credit customer in a sample will not test the completeness of the sales figures.

       (f)   Incorrect   Auditors must test both the inputs and the outputs if a decision is made to audit 'around the computer'.

       (g)   Correct   CAAT are specialised audit programs which allow the auditor to assess the controls within the computerised information system.

5.2   **(a)**   Existence

       (b)   Valuation

       (c)   Cut-off

       (d)   Occurrence

       (e)   Completeness

5.3   (c)   Useful where accounting controls are limited

5.4

Internal control procedure	Risk mitigated
Checking despatch records to sales invoices	Ensuring that all goods leaving inventory are for bona fide sales
Matching purchase invoices to authorised orders	Ensuring that only items required by the organisation are purchased

5.5   **(a)**   Strength

       (b)   Strength

       (c)   Strength

       (d)   Strength

       (e)   Strength

       (f)   Weakness

       (g)   Strength

       (h)   Weakness

CHAPTER 6: VERIFICATION OF ASSETS AND LIABILITIES

6.1   The following statements are correct: (b), (e), (g), and (h). The following statements are incorrect:

(a)   In addition to substantive testing the auditors will also rely on tests of controls, particularly when gathering evidence regarding current assets.

(c)   Auditors should carry out substantive testing procedures to verify the figures in the statement of financial position, particularly to evidence existence, rights and obligations and valuation.

(d)   Banks are bound by confidentiality rules. The auditors can write to the client's bank but the bank will not disclose any information without the client's written permission.

(f)   Whether or not any asset is subject to audit procedures is determined by the assessment of materiality, so this statement is not true as a general rule. The decision as to how much audit work to carry out on any balance will be made on an individual audit basis.

6.2   **(a)**   Ignore

        (b)   Investigate

        (c)   Investigate

        (d)   Investigate

        (e)   Ignore

6.3   Audit risks:

- The amount of own labour used in construction cannot be verified to wages records
- The 'cost' of new assets includes general overheads

Verification procedures:

- Vouch expenditure on machinery to purchase invoices
- Vouch materials costs to purchase invoices
- Check allocation of labour hours from costing records
- Reconcile costing records to payroll
- Review hourly rate charged into labour cost
- Review calculation of overhead used in cost calculation – ensure only direct overhead included

6.4   (d)   The loan is incorrectly stated so must be amended. The cumulative effect of the other errors or misstatements exceeds the level of Performance Materiality set so it is likely that all the errors or misstatements will have to be amended

6.5   Set out in a manner suitable for inclusion in the audit plan the audit procedures to be undertaken in order to ensure that non–current assets are fairly stated in the financial statements

- Inspect vehicles at main depot and at branch visits

- Inspect title deeds to freehold property

- Check with bank confirmation letter to ascertain if assets subject to any charge or mortgage with the bank

- Check sample of vehicle details to relevant documentation eg insurance schedules/repair invoices/rental or hire documentation etc for evidence of existence

- Reconcile nominal ledger accounts to non-current assets register for additions and disposals in financial year

- Vouch additions with purchase invoices or other relevant documentation eg HP documents etc

- Review bank payments for evidence of payments to leasing or finance companies

- Vouch disposals with sales invoices

- Ensure assets properly recorded in nominal ledger

- Ensure asset disposals properly recorded

- Check depreciation in accordance with accounting policies

- Check calculation of depreciation

- Review disclosure in financial statements

CHAPTER 7: AUDIT COMPLETION AND AUDIT REPORTING

7.1   The following are correct: (b), (d), (e), (f). **Note that** in (e) 'all is well' is not appropriate language for an audit report. Instead the student should state that the financial statements present a true and fair view 'except for' the matters noted in the report.

The following are incorrect:

(a)   Auditors are responsible for gathering audit evidence; the management representation letter will provide additional evidence which is proving difficult to substantiate fully.

(c)   A letter of weakness is designed to highlight weaknesses in internal controls. It is not the role of the auditors to criticise the management's style or business strategy.

(g)   Events after the statement of financial position date should be reviewed to ascertain whether they provide any evidence for items contained in the financial statements being audited.

7.2

Weaknesses	Consequences	Recommendations
Information is downloaded into the salaries system by Miss Smith without any verification	Staff may be paid for hours they have not worked or not paid for hours they have worked	The information from the time records should be reviewed by the office manager before being confirmed into the salaries system
Miss Smith has access to master file data and processes transactions	Miss Smith may be able to manipulate financial standing data without any review	Miss Smith should not be able to access standing data. Amendments should be made by a senior manager

7.3   Refer to supervisor

7.4   **Hong Ltd**

(a)

Kong Ltd

(e) – going concern

Bong Ltd

(c)

7.5

	Ignore	Amend financial statements	Refer by way of note
A trade receivable amounting to £15,000 has gone into liquidation after the year end and no amounts will be recovered. Total trade receivables amount to £1.2m and the pre tax profit for the year is £750,000.	✔ Not material		
Since the year end the company closed four out of its eight branches.			✔ Shareholder interest
Audit investigations have indicated that the latest position on one of the long-term contracts in progress is that it is likely to make a loss of £200,000. The value of long-term work in progress is £5.0m and the pre-tax profit for the year is £750,000.		✔ Adjusting item. ISA 11 compliance. Material to profit for the year.	
Since the year end the company acquired one of its smaller competitors for £1.25m. They financed this acquisition by means of an issue of shares amounting to £1m.			✔ Shareholder interest
The bank financing arrangements were revised and renewed shortly after the year end. There were no changes to previous arrangements except an increase in the overdraft limit of £250,000.	✔ Nothing significant to report		
The Chief Executive left one month after the year end. The Chairman is currently carrying out her duties whilst a replacement is being sought.			✔ Shareholder interest
After the year end the Head Office was flooded and the ground floor meeting rooms and staff kitchens were badly damaged. The accounting function and IT facilities were not affected. The costs of repair are covered by insurance.	✔ Not material		

Appendix

SAMPLE PERMANENT AUDIT FILE INDEX

CONTENTS OF FILE		
Section	**Heading**	**Information provided**
1	**Memorandum & articles of association**	'Objects' clause (where applicable)
		Minimum share capital
		Rights and duties of directors
		Voting rights
2	**Background and history of client**	Nature and history of business
		Ownership
		Registered office
		Nature of business/trade
		Management structure
		Directors
		Key staff other than directors
		Position in industry
		Premises details
		Key products
		Major suppliers
		Customers (details of major customers)
3	**Systems**	Flow charts
		Systems notes
		Location of records
		Computer system details
		Specimen documents
		Code list

4	**Legal documents/minutes**	Contract details
		Finance agreements
		Leases
		Title deeds
		Company books (including minutes)
5	**Group structure**	Subsidiary companies
		Associated undertakings
6	**Taxation**	Tax district and reference
		VAT information
7	**Other advisors**	Bankers
		Solicitors
		Valuers
		Other auditors (if any)
8	**Rotational visits**	Branches to be visited
9	**Reporting**	Copies of previous year management letters
10	**Administration**	Letters of authority
		Letter of engagement
11	**Any other relevant points**	

SAMPLE CURRENT AUDIT FILE INDEX

Section	Heading	Information
1	**Draft and financial statements**	Copies of draft and final signed accounts
2	**Letters and reports**	Letter of representation Management letter Points to carry forward
3	**Checklists**	Directors' Report disclosure Financial accounts disclosure Audit file review checklist

4	**Statement of financial position**	Lead schedules and audit verification details, including verification letters
		Items covered:
		    Tangible non-current assets
		    Intangible assets
		    inventory and work in progress
		    Receivables
		    Bank balances
		    Cash balances
		    Short-term payables
		    Long-term payables
		    Loans
		    Share capital
		    Reserves

5	**Statement of profit or loss**	Lead schedules and audit verification details, including verification letters

6	**Statement of cash flows**	Lead schedules and audit verification details, including verification letters
7	**Systems audit**	Audit programs
		Control tests
		Walk through tests
		Queries and notes
		Weaknesses – letter of weakness
8	**Trial balance**	Copy of extended trial balance
9	**Statutory audit**	Extracts from minutes
		Details of changes
		Rotation of directors
10	**Analytical review and data**	Ratio analysis
		Comparison with Planning Memorandum
		Five year summary
11	**Any other points**	Notes and points relevant to the audit but not leading to material adjustments

SAMPLE ENGAGEMENT LETTER

> **important note**
>
> This letter is not required as part of your assessment, but is included here for reference and interest as it forms an important part of the auditing documentation.

LIMITED COMPANY: AUDIT

This letter deals solely with the audit requirements of a company under the Companies Act 2006 and ISA 210 Agreeing the terms of audit engagements.

Other services such as accounts preparation or completion of tax returns should be dealt with in a separate letter or by adding paragraphs as appropriate from the Limited Company — other services letter.

The addressees and references in the letter would be those that are appropriate in the circumstances of the engagement. It is important to refer to the appropriate persons (eg the directors or to a named individual eg the financial director)

Throughout this letter, references to "you," "we," "us," "management" and "auditor" would be used or amended as appropriate in the circumstances.

Address

To the appropriate representative of management of ABC Company

You have requested that we audit the financial statements of ABC Company, which comprise the Statement of financial position as at December 31, 20-1, and the Statement of profit or loss, statement of changes in equity and statement of cash flows for the year then ended, and a summary of significant accounting policies and other explanatory information. We are pleased to confirm our acceptance and our understanding of this audit engagement by means of this letter. Our audit will be conducted with the objective of our expressing an opinion on the financial statements.

We will conduct our audit in accordance with International Standards on Auditing (ISAs). Those standards require that we comply with ethical requirements and plan and perform the audit to obtain reasonable assurance about whether the financial statements are free from material misstatement. An audit involves performing procedures to obtain audit evidence about the amounts and disclosures in the financial statements. The procedures selected depend on the auditor's judgment, including the assessment of the risks of material misstatement of the financial statements, whether due to fraud or error.

An audit also includes evaluating the appropriateness of accounting policies used and the reasonableness of accounting estimates made by management, as well as evaluating the overall presentation of the financial statements.

Because of the inherent limitations of an audit, together with the inherent limitations of internal control, there is an unavoidable risk that some material misstatements may not be detected, even though the audit is properly planned and performed in accordance with ISAs.

In making our risk assessments, we consider internal control relevant to the entity's preparation of the financial statements in order to design audit procedures that are appropriate in the circumstances, but not for the purpose of expressing an opinion on the effectiveness of the entity's internal control. However, we will communicate to you in writing concerning any significant deficiencies in internal control relevant to the audit of the financial statements that we have identified during the audit.

Our audit will be conducted on the basis that management acknowledge and understand that they have responsibility:

(a)   For the preparation and fair presentation of the financial statements in accordance with International Financial Reporting Standards;

(b)   For such internal control as management determines is necessary to enable the preparation of financial statements that are free from material misstatement, whether due to fraud or error; and

(c)   To provide us with:

    (1)   Access to all information of which management is aware that is relevant to the preparation of the financial statements such as records, documentation and other matters;

    (2)   Additional information that we may request from management for the purpose of the audit; and

    (3)   Unrestricted access to persons within the entity from whom we determine it necessary to obtain audit evidence.

As part of our audit process, we will request from management, written confirmation concerning representations made to us in connection with the audit. In particular, where we bring misstatements in the financial statements to your attention that are not adjusted, we shall require written representation of your reasons. In connection with representations and the supply of information to us generally, we draw your attention to Section 501 of the Companies Act 2006 under which it is an offence for an officer of the company to mislead the auditors.

We look forward to full cooperation from your staff during our audit.

Our legal and professional duty is to make a report to the members stating whether, in our opinion, the financial statements of the company which we have audited give a true and fair view of the state of the company's affairs, and of the profit or loss for the year, and whether they have been properly prepared in accordance with the Companies Act 2006. In arriving at our opinion we are required by law to consider the following matters, and to report on any in respect of which we are not satisfied:

(a)   whether proper accounting records have been kept by the company and proper returns adequate for our audit have been received from branches not visited by us;

(b)   whether the company's statement of financial position and statement of profit or loss are in agreement with the accounting records and returns;

(c)   whether we have obtained all the information and explanations which we think necessary for the purpose of our audit; and

(d)   whether the information in the directors' report is consistent with that in the audited financial statements.

As noted above, our report will be made solely to the company's members, as a body, in accordance with Section 495 of the Companies Act 2006. Our audit work will be undertaken so that we might state to the company's members those matters we are required to state to them in an auditor's report and for no other purpose. In those circumstances, to the fullest extent permitted by law, we will not accept or assume responsibility to anyone other than the company and the company's members as a body, for our audit work, for the audit report, or for the opinions we form.

The form and content of our report may need to be amended in the light of our audit findings.

In addition, we have a professional duty to report if the financial statements do not comply in any material respect with Financial Reporting Standards or Statements of Standard Accounting Practice, unless in our opinion non-compliance is justified in the circumstances. In determining whether or not any departure is justified we will consider:

(a)   whether the departure is required in order for the financial statements to give a true and fair view; and

(b)   whether adequate disclosure has been made concerning the departure.

Our professional duties also include:

(a)   incorporating in our report a description of the directors' responsibilities for the financial statements, where the financial statements or accompanying information do not include such description, and

(b)   considering whether other information in documentation containing the financial statements

is consistent with the audited financial statements. Please sign and return the attached copy of this letter to indicate your acknowledgement of, and agreement with, the arrangements for our audit of the financial statements including our respective responsibilities.

Yours faithfully

Tickett & Wrunne

Acknowledged and agreed on behalf of ABC Company by

(signed) ....

Name and Title and Date

Index

for your notes

for your notes

for your notes

for your notes

for your notes

for your notes

for your notes

for your notes

for your notes

for your notes